Measurements for Cooking

▲▼▲▼▲▼▲▼▲▼▲▼▲▼▲▼▲▼▲

Food ingredients and package sizes in metric, Imperial & American-cup measures, plus quick-reference charts of measurements & food staples . . . and some recipes, to lighten it up

▼▲▼▲▼▲▼▲▼▲▼▲▼▲▼▲▼▲▼

Delora Jones

GLENCOE HOUSE PUBLICATIONS
BURTON UPON TRENT

www.glencoehouse.co.uk

Also by Delora Jones
American Cooking in England
The Pocketbook Guide to American Cooking in Engalnd

First published in Great Britain in 2011 by
Glencoe House Publications
189 Anglesey Road, Burton upon Trent, Staffordshire DE14 3NS
www.glencoehouse.co.uk

Text © 2011 Delora Jones

Photographs on pages 4, 13 and on the outside back cover © 2011 Plain Design Ltd. Photographs on pages 43, 104 (popcorn), 112 (rice), 121 and 218 © 2011 Laura Dexter. All other photographs © 2011 Delora Jones.

Front and back cover designs by Plain Design Ltd, 14a Ashby Road, Burton upon Trent, Staffordshire DE15 0LA. www.plaindesign.co.uk

All rights reserved. No part of this publication may be reproduced, stored in a retrieval system, or transmitted, in any form or by any means, electronic, mechanical, photocopying, recording or otherwise without the prior permission in writing of Glencoe House Publications.

British Library Cataloguing in Publication Data
A catalogue record for this book is available from the British Library.

ISBN 978-0-9533557-2-3

Printed by Healey's Print Group, Ipswich, Suffolk.

This book is dedicated
to the memory of my sister

GLADYS MARY JONES

who helped me in many ways,
including checking sizes and availability
of British foods in American supermarkets.
I've a note she'll get back to me on Rich Tea Biscuits;
I'm still waiting.

Acknowledgements

Measurements for Cooking is a far superior book to what it would have been, thanks to Michele White, my proofreader, whose suggestions transformed the book into a much more user-friendly and easier to understand reference book. Also thanks to Roger Owen, who provided endless computing support and also suggested the book's subtitle.

And many, many thanks to the graphics experts at Plain Design in Burton upon Trent, who transformed my rather pedestrian cover layouts into the eye-catching covers you see now, and who provided many other graphics solutions along the way.

Thanks also to Laura Dexter, who photographed some of the ingredients, and whose creative touches made for much more striking settings.

In addition, over the years whilst compiling this document, many friends and relatives in the US provided answers I could not have found myself, short of a trip to the states, and for this I'd like to especially thank the late Gladys Jones, as well as Anita Montanile, Ronni Stachelek, Jean Ranallo, Mid Sarchioto, Ed Jones and Marty Weiner, Barbara Gare, and Leah and Don Ryel.

Many of the grams-to-cups equivalents in this book are from weighing and measuring the foods myself but other times, especially when weights for American fresh and packaged foods were required, a number of books proved especially helpful, including Barbara Gibbs Ostmann and Jane L. Baker's *Recipe Writer's Handbook*, Polly Clingerman's *The Kitchen Companion* and Rombauer and Becker's *Joy of Cooking*.

TABLE OF CONTENTS

ACKNOWLEDGEMENTS
INTRODUCTION 1
A WORD ABOUT MEASUREMENT EQUIVALENTS 5
    What's volume? What's weight? 5
    Who did the measuring in this book? 6
    Metric vs. Imperial 7
    Imperial vs. US Customary 9
HOW TO CONVERT THE MEASURES in the LIST OF INGREDIENTS 13
    'Americanizing' measures: Converting to a volume (e.g., cups) 14
    'Anglicising' measures: Converting to a weight 15
LIST OF INGREDIENTS and THEIR EQUIVALENT MEASURES 17
SUBSTITUTES & OTHER TRANSFORMATIONS 143
RECIPES 165
MEASUREMENTS CHARTS, CONVERSIONS, &C. 185
    Quick-reference charts & conversion formulas for:
        Weights 185
        Fluid Volume (Fl. Oz.) 191
        Lengths 203
        Temperatures 209
    Food staples: Butter, Flour, Sugar quick reference charts 217
    Food staples: Eggs, Milk, Cream (British v American) 237
    American sizes: cups and cans 243
MEASURING TOOLS & DEFINITIONS, PAN SIZES, &C. 247
BIBLIOGRAPHY 259
INDEX 263

INTRODUCTION

Why a book just about measurements? Aren't there already any number of cookery books containing lists of food measures and equivalents? Well, yes there are, but try finding measures for less common ingredients, such as quinoa, or try finding a common ingredient in the configuration you want. For example, a recipe calls for 2 cups of cooked rice; how much uncooked rice would you need to start with if you don't have cooked rice to hand? Or it calls for 3 cups of cubed pumpkin; what weight of unpeeled pumpkin will give you 3 cups of peeled cubed pumpkin?

Following the publication of *American Cooking in England* in 1998, I've 'Americanized' books for the North American market. Most have been cookery books, and Americanizing these includes converting the weights of ingredients to cups. Finding these conversions typically meant weighing and measuring the ingredients myself. These conversions I'd then compile in a document which, over the years, grew until it had expanded to the length of a book. However, this 'book' remained on my computer and increasingly, I found I needed it in the kitchen. Then the penny dropped: if I needed it in the kitchen, perhaps others did, too — and then the real work started. The *List of Ingredients* section in the book you're now holding is my conversions document, tidied-up so that someone other than me can make sense of it, and reworked so that people in both the UK and North America can use it for their conversions.

The main sections of this book are:

> *A word about measurement equivalents* — This small but important section clarifies the difference between volume and weight. It also looks at the effects of the Metrication Law on

Britain, as well as the differences between the British Imperial and US Customary measurements systems. The fluid ounce: a measure of weight or volume? Not sure? To clear up the understandable confusion, read this section.

List of ingredients — This fairly comprehensive list of ingredients gives the weight and volume equivalents of each ingredient listed, so that people who measure food in cups can do a weight-to-cups conversion, and those who measure food by weight can do the reverse. Invaluable when using a cookbook from 'across the pond'. Also in this section are instructions for making a bouquet garni, a biscuit base (graham cracker crust), tea/coffee, and for cooking wheat grains and reconstituting frozen concentrated orange juice.

Substitutes & other transformations — This section tells you what to do if you don't have a particular item in stock, for example, Baker's chocolate squares, buttermilk, baking powder, self-raising flour, etc. It also says what to do to substitute dried beans for cooked/tinned (and vice versa) and how to calculate amounts for things like whipped-from-unwhipped cream; uncooked-to-cooked rice; etc.

Recipes — To help lighten things up in this reference book, I've included a smattering of recipes, including crêpes, chilli, latkes, and others.

Measurements charts & conversion formulas — This section includes 'quick-reference' charts and conversion formulas for weights, volumes and lengths. There are also oven and air temperatures charts, and helpful tips on food-safety and cooking temperatures.

These are followed by *Food Staples*, with quick-reference charts for butter, flour and sugar — including granulated, brown and icing [confectioners'] sugar, plus egg charts comparing EU, old EEC & US sizes, and milk and cream charts comparing fat contents of British and American milks and creams. Next is the *American Cooking Equivalents* chart for common US cooking measures (e.g., $2/3$ cup), and an *American Can Sizes* chart.

The final section, *Measuring Tools & Definitions, Pan Sizes, &c.,* includes spoon measures, bar measures (e.g., jigger), etc.

I've compiled the measurements in this book to demystify the cup conundrum for British cooks and the metric muddle for the Americans, and to give us all a single source we can grab for quick conversions, and which is likely to have the food or measurement we're looking for.

I hope you find this book as helpful as I do.

Burton upon Trent, November 2011   Delora Jones

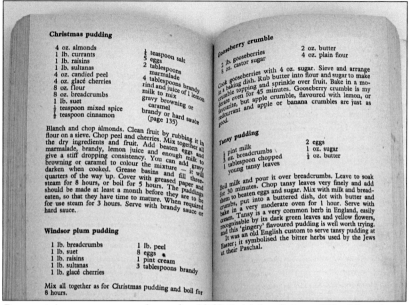

Pre-metric: open pages from the 1963 British edition of Cooking the British Way *by Joan Clibbon.*

A WORD ABOUT MEASUREMENT EQUIVALENTS
What's volume? What's weight?

Volume vs. weight — know which you're using.

Volume: Teaspoons and tablespoons; cups, pints, quarts and gallons; millilitres and litres; and *fluid* ounces are all measures of volume. That is, they measure the amount of three-dimensional space a thing takes up, not how much a thing weighs.

The American measuring cup is based on the volume, i.e., the amount of space, 8 ounces of water takes up, so the American cup is an 8-*fluid*-ounce cup, hence *fluid* ounces are a measure of volume.[1] But you don't use a measuring cup solely to measure water — it may be flour that you're measuring, and although a cup of flour takes up the same amount of space as a cup of water, it weighs much less, only about 130g or so [$4\frac{1}{2}$ oz.]. So don't assume that because it's called an 8-ounce cup, anything that's measured in it will weigh 8 ounces — it's an 8 *fluid* ounce cup (people often drop the key adjective 'fluid'), so a cupful of water will weigh 8 ounces but something else may be a quite different weight.

Another thing to bear in mind when converting volumes is that British and American fluid ounces, pints, quarts and gallons differ (for more information, see *Imperial vs. US Customary* on page 9).

Weight: *Avoirdupois* ounces, pounds, stones, etc., and the metric grams and kilograms are all measures of weight. They measure the heaviness of an item -- not how much space it takes up, and this distinction is very important. If an item is very dense or moist, 8 ounces

---

[1] Eight fluid ounces equals 237ml, normally rounded up to 240 or 250ml.

of it *may* convert to 1 cup as in the case of butter, but if it's something light like Rice Krispies®, 8 ounces converts to over 9 cups!

So the weight-to-volume varies depending upon the ingredient being weighed, and that is why I have done the extensive *List of Ingredients* that starts on page 17: to help convert from one country's method of measure to another — American and Canadian cooks measure by volume, British cooks tend to measure by weight — and to help people who've bought cookery books in another country and have then struggled to convert the measures.

Who did the measuring in this book?

In the *List of Ingredients*, most of the British foods are ones I weighed and measured myself, using a digital kitchen scale and a standard 8-fluid-ounce cup (or 5ml teaspoon or 15ml tablespoon), measured level — not heaped, for their American equivalents.

The American foods in the list were sometimes weighed and measured by myself, other times they're from sources such as the conversion lists in *Joy of Cooking*, *The Recipe Writer's Handbook* or *The Kitchen Companion*, or from other books (see Bibliography, page 259) and, when these sources differed, majority ruled.

You'll notice that in certain instances in the *List of Ingredients*, '(US)' or '(UK)' appears next to a food. This tells you whether the original ingredient or product is from the US or the UK. I've done this for packaged goods such as tins and frozen foods, as they differ from one country to the other, and also for certain types of fresh produce, to give an idea what 'small', 'medium' and 'large' refer to in that country. For example, medium apples in the US might be considered large in the UK.

You may also notice that the equivalents given in the *List of Ingredients* are not always consistent. For example, you may see '1 oz. [28g]' — the exact metric equivalent, or '1 oz. [30g]'— the rounded up metric equivalent. When the exact equivalent is given, it will be for one of the following reasons.

Sometimes it's to show the amounts just as they appear on American or British food products, such as the 142ml on our double-cream pots, and although 142ml is an exactness that could not be measured in your kitchen, it's technically the precise equivalent of a British $\frac{1}{4}$ pint.

Other times I've included exact, rather than rounded-up, gram amounts for the weights of very light ingredients, such as cocoa powder or dried yeast. In these instances, I list the gram weight precisely as it appeared on my scale — sometimes giving a range of weights if I've had more than one result — rather than rounding the weights up or down. This has been in order to keep things in proportion when doubling or trebling that light-weight ingredient in a recipe.

If you notice any errors or suspect a weight or measurement is not correct, please notify me. Contact details are on page 262.

Metric vs. Imperial

In 2000, the Metrication Law[2] came into force in Britain. This law required all UK traders to use metric units for measuring and labelling, and for all pre-packed goods to be marked in metric units, 'and created a general prohibition on the use of Imperial units for use in trade'.[3] There were some exceptions, the most noticeable of which are the retention of the road mile, and of the pint for selling draught beer and cider, and milk (and other beverages) in returnable bottles.

---

[2] *Weights and Measures Act 1985 (Metrication) (Amendment) 1994*
[3] www.consumeradvice.net: Weight and Measures Legislation

However, in my opinion, trying to limit us to only one system disregards the fact that the units of the other system might, in some instances, be more appropriate, for example, when measuring a person's height. Here we use metres, to my mind a much-too-long unit. After all, not many people are taller than 2 metres so why use a unit for heights which will almost always total just 1 and a fraction — how does one visualise that? And centimetres are too small; these could number into the hundreds. Equally, yards are too long and inches too short, which is why, I think, a length such as feet is better suited in this case.[4]

And if weighing something light like yeast, grams rather than fractions of an ounce make most sense. So why shouldn't we use the unit, whether metric or Imperial, which we feel is best suited to the task?

However, I would *not* suggest that the British Imperial and the US Customary measurements systems sit alongside one another. They are much too similar, and where their names agree, their measures differ, for example, fluid ounces, pints and gallons. But between metric and Imperial (or metric and US Customary), there is less scope for confusion.

An Imperial-to-metric side effect

In getting things readied for metrication in Britain, we retooled our tin, jar and bottle sizes to match the rest of Europe's metric-sized ones. We also amended the measures in all new editions of cookery books, but instead of converting 1 pound to something fairly close, like 450 grams, that 454g-pound often jumped to 500g, for no other reason that I could see other than that 500g is a neat, round number, easily doubled to 1kg or trebled to 1.5kg, but here's the rub: altering amounts in this fashion means that that recipe can no longer be relied upon to be multiplied

---

[4] One foot = 30.5cm.

accurately, when the weight of that ingredient in the original recipe was about 50g less than in the newly-metricised recipe. In some cases, such as meat recipes, it won't make too much difference if you were just doubling the 500g — this would come to about $\frac{1}{4}$ pound more meat than if doubling the original recipe, but if quadrupling the recipe, it could make a noticeable difference. And even in doubling the meat recipe, a quarter-pound is roughly one serving of meat, so you might be buying more meat than you really need for that number of servings, not to mention the extra calories.

Imperial vs. US Customary

In my own home, I use metric and Imperial, and sometimes US cups for measuring, but cups is the only American measure I use, as otherwise, there's too much scope for confusion between the Imperial and US Customary measurements systems.

At one time the British, i.e., Imperial, and American measurements systems were the same, but that was some time ago. What these two systems do still have in common are the *avoirdupois* ounce (dry ounce) and pound, and our units of length, i.e., inches, feet, yards and miles. Where the systems differ is in measuring volume.

British and American measures of volume such as the fluid ounce, pint and gallon may go by the same name, but always check which country your cookery book is from as, although the British and American fluid ounce differ only slightly, our pints and gallons differ significantly.

The British fluid ounce (28.41ml) is marginally smaller than the American fluid ounce (29.57ml) and although these differences are too small to measure in the kitchen, they do show up when the ounces accumulate. For example, if we wish to convert one US gallon —

which is 128 US fl. oz. — to litres, we must use the US-fl.-oz. conversion factor (29.57) to arrive at the correct value of 3.78 litres. If instead we had used the British-fl.-oz. conversion factor (28.41), we would get an incorrect value of 3.64 litres. The more gallons you convert using the incorrect factor, then the greater the error becomes.

Which leads us to pints: the Imperial liquid/dry pint, the US liquid pint, and the US dry pint.

The Imperial liquid pint = 20 UK fl. oz. [568ml], exactly the same as the Imperial dry pint.

The US liquid pint = 16 US fl. oz. — nearly a $1/2$ cup smaller than the US dry pint.[5]

So, although neither of the American pints *exactly* equal the British pint, the British pint and the US dry pint are almost the same — about $2^1/_2$ US cups — while the US *liquid* pint, at just 2 US cups, is noticeably different from either, and it's the liquid pint, not the dry pint, that's most commonly used. (The image on the book's cover visually demonstrates the difference between a British pint and a US liquid pint.)

Dry pints are for measuring things like strawberries and raspberries; liquid pints measure things like milk, cream, beer and ice cream and, usually, when a recipe calls for pints it means liquid pints. So if using an American recipe calling for a pint of cream, you'll want to use 2 cups — about $3/_4$ of a British pint. And if using a British recipe calling for a pint of milk, you'll want to use about $2^1/_2$ US cups.

As for quarts, there are 2 pints in 1 quart. So in the Unites States, 2 US dry pints equal 1 US dry quart [1.1 litres] and 2 US liquid pints equal 1

---

[5] The US liquid pint = 28.875 cu. inches [473ml]; the US dry pint = 33.6 cu. inches [551ml or about 18.6 US fl. oz.].

US liquid quart [0.946 litre]. In Britain, 2 Imperial pints equal 1 Imperial quart [1.14 litres], but the quart is not much used in the UK these days, whereas in the US, the liquid quart and half-gallon are commonly used.

As for gallons, there are 4 quarts in 1 gallon (think quarters for quarts). The British gallon at 160 Imp. fl. oz. [4.546 litres] is substantially larger than the American gallon at 128 US fl. oz. [3.785 litres], which is why British pints ($\frac{1}{8}$ Imp. gallon) are larger than American fluid pints ($\frac{1}{8}$ US fl. gallon). Now, if you look at just the number of ounces, the British gallon *appears* to equal $1\frac{1}{4}$ American gallons but when converting large American and British volumes, always bear in mind that the size of our fluid ounces differ so it's best to convert based on their metric equivalents rather than the number of fluid ounces. One and a quarter American gallons is 4.75 litres; the British gallon is 4.546 litres, so when we convert based on the metric volumes, we find our Imperial gallon is actually a little less than — not equal to — $1\frac{1}{4}$ US gallons.

So, just be glad we don't have to deal with these sorts of differences on a daily basis as the scope for error is great. Imperial and metric (or US Customary and metric) sit much more happily side by side than do Imperial and US Customary.

How to Convert the Measures
in the
List of Ingredients

You're American but you've a cookbook using grams...

OR

you're British but you've a cookbook calling for cups...

What to do? *Turn the page for the answers* →

'Americanizing' measures:
Converting to a volume (e.g., cups)

Q: I have a British recipe that calls for grams but I've no scale — how do I convert to American cups?

A: Find the ingredient you want to convert in the LIST OF INGREDIENTS (page 17). In the example below, we use oatmeal. Follow the same steps below for your ingredient, as we have for oatmeal.

OATMEAL

coarse [steel-cut oats, US]   1 cup uncooked = about 138g [5 oz.]

- Divide the volume given (e.g., number of cups or teaspoons or tablespoons, or pieces of fruit, etc.) by the equivalent weight given. In the example above, the volume is 1 — i.e., 1 cup — so, using your kitchen calculator, divide 1 by 138 (the equivalent gram weight of 1 cup coarse oatmeal). This gives you 0.0072463.
- Multiply the resulting figure — 0.0072463 — by the weight you want to convert, such as the weight given in your recipe. Let's say your recipe calls for 85g oatmeal, so multiply 0.0072463 by 85.
- The resulting figure tells you how many cups — or, if the figure is less than 1, what fraction of a cup — you'll need of that ingredient for that recipe.

  In our example, the resulting figure was 0.615, just under $^2/_3$ cup (0.66 = $^2/_3$ cup), so that's what you'll need for your recipe.

> Be consistent with your units of measure, e.g., don't divide a volume by grams and then multiply the result by ounces, and also, don't divide a weight by tablespoons and then multiply by cups.

'Anglicising' measures:
Converting to a weight

Q: I have an American recipe that calls for cups but I've no cup measures — how do I convert to grams or ounces?

A: Find the ingredient you want to convert in the LIST OF INGREDIENTS (page 17). In the example below, we use oatmeal again. Follow the same steps below for your ingredient, as we have for the oatmeal.

OATMEAL
coarse [steel-cut oats, US]   1 cup uncooked = about 138g [5 oz.]

- Divide the weight given by the equivalent volume given (e.g., number of cups, teaspoons or tablespoons, or pieces of fruit, etc.). In the example above, the weight is 138 — i.e., 138 grams — so, divide 138 by the volume, in this case, 1 (1 being the 1 cup). You won't need a calculator for this one: 138 divided by 1 = 138.

- Multiply the resulting figure — in this case, 138 — by the volume you want to convert, such as the volume given in your recipe. Let's say your recipe calls for $^2/_3$ cup oatmeal, so multiply the 138 by $^2/_3$ (i.e., 0.66).

- The resulting figure tells you the weight you'll need of that ingredient for that recipe.
  In our example, the resulting figure was 91 and, as our calculations were based on grams, this tells us that $^2/_3$ cup oatmeal = about 91 grams, so that's what you'll need for your recipe.

Note: Many of the ingredients in the LIST OF INGREDIENTS also give a 100g equivalent so you may find you only ever occasionally need to do the above calculations.

In short:

'Americanizing' measures
converting <u>to a volume</u> (American) from a weight

In this book's LIST OF INGREDIENTS section, find the ingredient you want, take its volume and equivalent weight and do these calculations:

$$\text{volume} \div \text{weight} \rightarrow n$$

n × the weight you want to convert from your recipe → the volume (e.g., number of cups) needed for your recipe

---

'Anglicising' measures
converting <u>to a weight</u> (British) from a volume

In this book's LIST OF INGREDIENTS section, find the ingredient you want, take its weight and equivalent volume and do these calculations:

$$\text{weight} \div \text{volume} \rightarrow n$$

n × the volume (e.g., number of cups) you want to convert from your recipe → the weight needed for your recipe

---

For examples, see previous pages.

LIST OF INGREDIENTS
and
THEIR EQUIVALENT MEASURES

NOTE: throughout this section, the cup measure used is the American cup [237ml / 16 Tbsp.]. Also, 1 pound = 16 ounces = 454g.

ALFALFA SPROUTS	*(US)*	1 cup = about 75g; 100g = about $1\frac{1}{3}$ cups

→ If you can't find alfalfa sprouts, **MUSTARD & CRESS** is similar.

ALLSPICE	*ground*	1 Tbsp. = about 7g

ALMONDS	*ground*	1 cup ground = about 100g
	finely chopped	1 cup finely chopped = about 120g; 100g finely chopped = $\frac{3}{4}$–1 cup
	flaked [slivered, US]	1 cup flaked = about 80g; 100g flaked = about $1\frac{1}{4}$ cups
	whole	1 cup whole almonds = about 130g; 100g whole = about $\frac{3}{4}$ cup

---

ALUM (a mineral compound)	1 level Tbsp. = 7g

AMARANTH (a grain)	*uncooked*	1 cup uncooked = 190–195g; 100g uncooked = about $\frac{1}{2}$ cup
	uncooked to cooked	1 cup uncooked [190g] = about $2\frac{1}{2}$ cups cooked [590g] *(more on amaranth, overleaf)*

---

1 US cup = 16 Tbsp.   1 Tbsp. = 3 tsp.   (1 Irish or old English Tbsp. = 4 tsp.)

	cooked grains	1 cup cooked = about 250g; 100g cooked = $1/3$–$1/2$ cup

→ To figure cooked from uncooked: if using cups, multiply uncooked cups by 2.5; if going by weight, multiply uncooked weight by 3.

ANCHOVIES *finely chopped* 1 Tbsp. chopped tinned anchovies = about 10g

tinned (UK) 50g tin = 30g drained anchovies = $2^2/3$ Tbsp. finely chopped

tinned (US) 2-oz. tin [57g] contains 6 to 8 anchovies

APPLES

FRESH (UK) *grated* 1 cup grated = about 150g; 100g = about $2/3$ cup

peeled, thinly-sliced/cut-up 1 cup sliced/cut-up = about 100g

medium apples, $2^1/2$" [6.5cm] 1 medium apple, cored, chopped = about $1^1/2$ cups; 3 med. apples = 440–500g [1 lb.]

large apples, 3" [7.5cm] 2 large apples = about 500g [1 generous lb.]

Bramleys, peeled to unpeeled 2 medium whole Bramleys, 820g = about 690g peeled & cored = about 7 cups cut up (enough for 1 good crumble)

FRESH (US) *medium apples* 3 medium = about 1 pound

DRIED 1 cup dried = about 90g

28g = 1 oz   57g = 2 oz   85g = 3 oz   100g = 3½ oz   113g = 4 oz   142g = 5 oz

LIST OF INGREDIENTS

APRICOTS	*fresh (US)*	1 lb. fresh = 8–12 whole or 2½ cups sliced or halved; 100g = about 2–3 whole or about ½ cup sliced
DRIED	*whole*	1 cup dried = about 150g; 100g dried = about ⅔ cup or about 12 dried apricots
	chopped	1 cup chopped = about 130g; 100g chopped = about ¾ cup
CANNED	*halves (UK)*	1 cup halves = about 155–180g; 100g halves = about ½–⅔ cup; 411g tin contains 1½ cups drained apricot halves, about 270g; 220g tin contains 1 cup drained apricot halves, 155–160g
	whole (US)	16-/17-oz. can [454/482g] = 6–8 whole apricots

ARTICHOKES		
FRESH	*(US)*	2 medium = about 1 pound
CANNED	*in water (UK)*	100g = about 3 artichoke hearts, or about 1 cup; 390g tin = about 2½ cups drained artichoke hearts, about 240g
	in water (US)	14-oz. jar [397g] = 8–10 medium or 5–7 large hearts
	marinated in oil (US)	6½-oz. jar [184g] = ¾ cup

---

1 US cup = 16 Tbsp.   1 Tbsp. = 3 tsp.   (1 Irish or old English Tbsp. = 4 tsp.)

ASPARAGUS	*fresh, cut up*	100g = about 1 cup 1" pieces; 2 cups pieces = about 230g
	fresh (US)	1 lb. = 16–20 spears or $2\frac{1}{2}$ cups cooked pieces

---

AUBERGINE [eggplant, US]

whole (UK)	1 small-to-medium = 230–285g; 1 medium aubergine = 345–385g; a 350g aubergine = about 305g peeled & topped
finely sliced	1 cup finely sliced = about 85–90g; 100g sliced = 1 heaped cup; a 350g aubergine = about $3\frac{1}{3}$–$3\frac{1}{2}$ cups peeled & finely sliced
raw to cooked	1 cup finely sliced raw aubergine = $\frac{1}{4}$ cup or more cooked & mashed
cooked & mashed	1 cup cooked & mashed = about 235g — for this amount, start with a 365g or so aubergine
whole, medium (US)	1 medium American eggplant = about $1\frac{1}{4}$ lb. [570g]

SMALL AUBERGINES [EGGPLANTS, US]

whole, about $4\frac{1}{2}$" long	100g = about 2 small [11.5cm]
PEA AUBERGINES	1 cup = about 120g; 100g = $\frac{3}{4}$ cup plus 1–2 Tbsp.

→ Pea aubergines (*makua phuong*), called pea eggplants in the US, are pea-sized aubergines that grow in clusters.

28g = 1 oz   57g = 2 oz   85g = 3 oz   100g = 3½ oz   113g = 4 oz   142g = 5 oz

LIST OF INGREDIENTS

AVOCADOS *cut up small cubes* 1 cup cubes = about 130–140g;
100g cubes = about $3/4$ cup

Fuerte, medium (UK) 1 medium Fuerte = about 285g

Hass, small, $3\frac{1}{4}$–$3\frac{1}{2}$" (UK) 1 small Hass, 8–9cm diam. = about 170g = about 115g peeled & stoned = 1 scant cup cubes (this smallish Hass was labelled 'medium')

Hass, med., $4\frac{1}{4}$" diam. (UK) 1 medium Hass, 11cm diam. = about 240g = about 175g peeled & stoned = about $1\frac{1}{3}$ cup cubes

(US) 1 lb. avocados = 2 medium, or about $2\frac{1}{2}$ cups sliced or chopped

---

BACON & HAM

raw back bacon, 7" long 1 slice [18cm] = 37–39g;
6 slices = about 230g;
100g back bacon = about $2\frac{2}{3}$ slices

raw streaky bacon, 10" long 1 slice [25.5cm] = 40–45g;
6 slices = about 260g;
100g streaky = about $2\frac{1}{3}$ slices = about $2/3$–$3/4$ cup finely chopped

AMERICAN BACON (like a thinly-cut streaky bacon)

thin-sliced (US) 1 thin strip = about 13g;
100g = 7–8 thin strips;
1 lb. = 35 thin strips

regular (US) 1 regular strip = about 22–28g;
100g = $3\frac{1}{2}$–$4\frac{1}{2}$ regular strips;
1 lb. = 16–20 regular strips
(more on bacon, overleaf)

---

1 US cup = 16 Tbsp.   1 Tbsp. = 3 tsp.   (1 Irish or old English Tbsp. = 4 tsp.)

	thick-sliced (US)	1 thick strip = about 28–38g; 100g = 2½–3½ thick strips; 1 lb. = 12–16 thick strips
HAM	*regular, cooked (US)*	8 slices crisply cooked = about ½ cup crumbled
	cooked, finely cut	½ cup finely cut = about 60g or about 2 slices; 100g finely cut = ¾ cup plus 1 Tbsp. = about 3⅓ slices
	prosciutto di Parma	4 slices = about 65g; 100g = about 6 slices

BAKING POWDER 1 level Tbsp. = 9–10g

⇨ No baking powder in stock? Don't despair — you may have other ingredients which will do the trick. See *Baking Powder* on page 144 in the *Substitutes & Other Transformations* section.

baking soda, *see* **BICARBONATE OF SODA**

BAMBOO SHOOTS	*matchsticks*	1 cup sliced, tinned bamboo shoots, cut into matchsticks = about 120g; 100g matchsticks = ¾ cup plus 1–2 Tbsp.
	tinned (UK)	220g tin = about 120g drained

BANANAS	*whole*	1 lb. = 3 medium bananas
	whole to sliced	3 medium bananas = about 250g peeled = about 2 cups sliced

28g = 1 oz   57g = 2 oz   85g = 3 oz   100g = 3½ oz   113g = 4 oz   142g = 5 oz

	sliced	1 cup = about 115–130g; 100g = about $3/4$ cup
	mashed	1 cup = about 200g; 100g = about $1/2$ cup
very ripe (brown/black skin)		a 180g very ripe banana = about 145g peeled or $2/3 - 3/4$ cup mashed
DRIED	*dried chips (UK)*	1 cup = about 70g chips; 100g = $1 1/3 - 1 1/2$ cups
	dried slices (US)	1 lb. dried slices = $4 1/2$ cups

---

barley, see **PEARL BARLEY**

BASE MEGENEP (a fresh Balinese spice mixture)

	fresh, homemade	330g = $2 1/2$–3 cups; 100g = $3/4$–1 cup

BASIL   *dried, chopped*   1 Tbsp. = about 2g

---

basmati rice, see **RICE, BASMATI**

BAY LEAVES   *dried* $1/3$ cup dried leaves = about 4g

BEANCURD (TOFU), FRESH (AND LONG-LIFE PACKAGED)

firm tofu, cut into small cubes		1 cup cubed tofu = about 120g; 100g = $3/4$ cup plus 1–2 Tbsp.
	1 freshly-made 'cake'	1 beancurd cake = about 115g
PACKAGED	*long-life (UK)*	soft silken tofu comes in 340g box *(more on beancurd, overleaf)*

---

1 US cup = 16 Tbsp.   1 Tbsp. = 3 tsp.   (1 Irish or old English Tbsp. = 4 tsp.)

chilled firm (UK)	comes in 250g packet
chilled soft (UK)	comes in 300g container
chilled firm (US)	comes in 14-/16-oz. carton [400/454g]
chilled medium-soft (US)	sold in 12-oz. cakes [340g]

→ Fresh beancurd cakes, sold loose at Chinese groceries, should be stored in the fridge, in fresh water, with the water changed every day or so. Long-life tofu can be stored at room temperature until opened.

BEANCURD 'SKINS' & STICKS, DRIED

dried 'skins' (8" x 12" sheets)	1 sheet, 20 x 30cm = about 15g; 100g = 6–7 'skins'
dried sticks, $12\frac{1}{2}"$–13"	100g = about 4 sticks, 32–33cm
dried sticks, broken up	1 cup fragments = about 50g

BEANSPROUTS

fresh mung bean sprouts	2 cups = about 115g; 100g = about $1\frac{3}{4}$ cup

→ Virtually any bean, seed or lentil can be sprouted but in the West, beansprouts are usually from sprouted mung beans while in China they're usually from sprouted soya beans.

→ Although canned beansprouts are available, the canning causes them to lose their crunch so better to use fresh.

BEANS, AZUKI (aduki beans, adzuki beans, red beans)

dried	1 cup = about 180g; 100g dried = $\frac{1}{2}$ cup plus 1 Tbsp.

28g = 1 oz   57g = 2 oz   85g = 3 oz   100g = 3½ oz   113g = 4 oz   142g = 5 oz

	cooked	1 cup = about 210g;
		100g cooked = about $\frac{1}{2}$ cup
	dried to cooked	1 cup dried [180g] =
		about 2 cups cooked [400–420g]

⇨ For conversion formulas for dried-to-cooked and cooked-from-dried beans, and for substituting tinned, see *Beans, Dried* on page 147 in the *Substitutes & Other Transformations* section.

BEANS, BAKED

BRITISH	*tinned*	1 cup = about 210g;
		100g = about $\frac{1}{2}$ cup;
		Heinz brand 415g tin contains
		about $1\frac{1}{2}$ cups
AMERICAN-STYLE	*canned*	15-oz. cans [425g] hold ~$1\frac{3}{4}$ cups;
		28-oz. cans [794g] hold ~3 cups

→ American baked beans come in a sweet thick brown sauce while British Heinz baked beans come in a thinner, less sweet, tomato-based sauce. I would not substitute the American beans for the British beans, especially not in dishes like jacket potato with baked beans, or beans on toast, unless you happen to prefer the stodgier sweet American beans.

BEANS, BLACK-EYED [black-eyed peas, US]

	dried	1 cup = about 165g;
		100g dried = about $\frac{2}{3}$ cup

⇨ For conversion formulas for dried-to-cooked and cooked-from-dried beans, and for substituting tinned, see *Beans, Dried* on page 147 in the *Substitutes & Other Transformations* section.

---

1 US cup = 16 Tbsp.   1 Tbsp. = 3 tsp.   (1 Irish or old English Tbsp. = 4 tsp.)

beans, Boston, *see* **BEANS, HARICOT**

BEANS, BROAD [fava beans, US]

shelled & peeled fresh beans	1 cup shelled peeled beans = about 115–125g (for this amount, start with about 560g pods or about 190g shelled beans [$1\frac{1}{2}$ cups]); 100g = $\frac{3}{4}$ cup plus 1–2 Tbsp. (for this amount, start with about 450g pods)
unshelled pods to shelled	450g pods = about 150g shelled beans [scant $1\frac{1}{4}$ cups] = about 100g peeled beans [scant cup]

→ Although common in England and Italy, you'd not see pods of fresh broad beans in American grocery stores, unless perhaps in Italian neighbourhoods. Depending upon the recipe, lima beans might do as a substitute.

⇨ For broad bean conversion formulas, to figure things like the weight of pods you'd need to start with to yield a particular weight of shelled & peeled broad beans, see *Broad Beans* on page 145 in the *Substitutes & Other Transformations* section.

BEANS, CANNELLINI

dried	1 cup dried = about 170–175g; 100g dried = $\frac{1}{2}$ cup plus 1 Tbsp; 1 pound dried = about $2\frac{2}{3}$ cups
soaked & cooked	1 cup cooked = about 135–140g; 100g cooked = about $\frac{3}{4}$ cup

---

28g = 1 oz   57g = 2 oz   85g = 3 oz   100g = 3½ oz   113g = 4 oz   142g = 5 oz

LIST OF INGREDIENTS *Page 27*

One cup dried cannellini beans yields about $2^3/_4$–3 cups cooked.

	dried to cooked	1 cup dried [170–175g] = about $2^3/_4$–3 cups cooked [385–400g]
TINNED		1 cup tinned beans = about 145g; 100g tinned = about $2/_3$ cup
	(UK)	400g tin (the most common size) = about $1^1/_3$ cups drained beans, about 225–240g; 300g tin = about 1 cup drained
	(US)	comes in a 19-oz. can [540g]

⇨For conversion formulas for dried-to-cooked and cooked-from-dried beans, and for substituting tinned, see *Beans, Dried* on page 147 in the *Substitutes & Other Transformations* section.

---

1 US cup = 16 Tbsp.   1 Tbsp. = 3 tsp.   (1 Irish or old English Tbsp. = 4 tsp.)

BEANS, DRIED
dried beans (most varieties)   1 cup dried = 165–175g;
100g dried = $1/2$–$2/3$ cup;
1 lb. dried = $2\frac{1}{2}$–$2\frac{3}{4}$ cups
soaked & cooked   1 cup cooked = 130–160g;
100g cooked = $2/3$–$3/4$ cup
dried to cooked   1 cup dried [165–175g] = $2\frac{1}{2}$–3 cups cooked;
1 lb. dried [$2\frac{1}{2}$–$2\frac{3}{4}$ cups] = $6\frac{1}{4}$–9 cups cooked

See also individual varieties.

⇨ For conversion formulas for dried-to-cooked and cooked-from-dried beans, and for substituting tinned, see *Beans, Dried* on page 147 in the *Substitutes & Other Transformations* section.

---

beans, garbanzo, *see* **CHICKPEAS**

---

beans, Great Northern, *see* **BEANS, HARICOT**

BEANS, GREEN OR WAX BEANS
FRESH 'FRENCH BEANS'   100g = about 9–12 whole beans, 5–7" long [12–18cm]
cut into $1/2$–1" lengths   1 cup cut-up beans = about 140g;
100g cut-up = about $3/4$ cup;
1 lb. cut-up = about $3\frac{1}{4}$ cups
FROZEN   *cut-up beans (US)*   'French-cut' beans and regular-cut beans each come in 10-oz. pkg. [285g] containing about 3 cups

---

28g = 1 oz   57g = 2 oz   85g = 3 oz   100g = 3½ oz   113g = 4 oz   142g = 5 oz

CANNED	*green beans (US)*	come in $14\frac{1}{2}$-/$15\frac{1}{2}$-oz. cans [410g/440g] containing about $1\frac{3}{4}$ cups

---

BEANS, HARICOT [navy beans, Great Northern beans, US]

	dried	1 cup dried = 175–180g; 100g dried = $\frac{1}{2}$–$\frac{2}{3}$ cup; 1 pound dried = about $2\frac{1}{2}$ cups
	soaked & cooked	1 cup cooked = about 130–150g; 100g cooked = about $\frac{2}{3}$–$\frac{3}{4}$ cup
	dried to cooked	1 cup dried [175g] = about $2\frac{1}{2}$–3 cups cooked [390g]
TINNED		1 cup tinned = about 150–155g; 100g tinned = about $\frac{2}{3}$ cup
	(UK)	420g tin haricot beans = $1\frac{2}{3}$ cups drained, about 255g
	(US)	15-/$15\frac{1}{2}$-oz. can Gt. Northern beans [~425g] = about $1\frac{1}{2}$ cups

→ Haricot beans are also known in the US as pea beans and as Boston beans (they're the bean used in the dish 'Boston baked beans').

⇨ For conversion formulas for dried-to-cooked and cooked-from-dried beans, and for substituting tinned, see *Beans, Dried* on page 147 in the *Substitutes & Other Transformations* section.

BEANS, KIDNEY	*dried*	1 cup dried = 155–165g; 100g dried = $\frac{1}{2}$–$\frac{2}{3}$ cup; 1 pound dried = about $2\frac{3}{4}$ cups *(more on kidney beans, overleaf)*

---

1 US cup = 16 Tbsp.   1 Tbsp. = 3 tsp.   (1 Irish or old English Tbsp. = 4 tsp.)

	soaked & cooked	1 cup cooked = about 135–155g; 100g cooked = about $2/3$–$3/4$ cup
	dried to cooked	1 cup dried [160g] = $2\frac{1}{3}$–$2\frac{1}{2}$ cups soaked & cooked [315–360g]
TINNED		1 cup tinned = about 160g; 100g tinned = about $1/2$–$2/3$ cup
	(UK)	420g tin contains $1\frac{2}{3}$ cups drained, about 270g
	(US)	15-/$15\frac{1}{2}$-oz. can [425g] contains about $1\frac{3}{4}$ cups

→ There are toxins present on the skins of kidney beans. After the dried beans have soaked, give them a 10–15 minute vigorous boiling to render the toxins harmless. Then, reduce the heat and simmer for the remaining 1–$1\frac{1}{2}$ hours, till tender.

⇨ For conversion formulas for dried-to-cooked and cooked-from-dried beans, and for substituting tinned, see *Beans, Dried* on page 147 in the *Substitutes & Other Transformations* section.

BEANS, LIMA	(US)	1 cup = about 150g; 100g = about $2/3$ cup; 1 pound fresh, canned or frozen = about 3 cups

---

beans, navy, also **beans, pea,** *see* **BEANS, HARICOT**

BEANS, PINTO	canned (US)	15-/$15\frac{1}{2}$-oz. can [425g] contains about $1\frac{3}{4}$ cups

---

28g = 1 oz   57g = 2 oz   85g = 3 oz   100g = 3½ oz   113g = 4 oz   142g = 5 oz

⇨ For conversion formulas for dried-to-cooked and cooked-from-dried beans, and for substituting tinned, see *Beans, Dried* on page 147 in the *Substitutes & Other Transformations* section.

BEANS, REFRIED *canned (US)* 16-oz. can contains about $1^3/_4$ cups

---

BEANS, SOYA — DRIED [soybeans, US]

    dried 1 cup dried = 155–160g;
100g = about $^2/_3$ cup;
1 pound = about $2^3/_4$ cups

    soaked & cooked 1 cup cooked = about 135–140g;
100g = about $^3/_4$ cup

    dried-to-cooked 1 cup dried [160g] = about $2^3/_4$–3 cups cooked [370–400g]

⇨ For conversion formulas for dried-to-cooked and cooked-from-dried beans, and for substituting tinned, see *Beans, Dried* on page 147 in the *Substitutes & Other Transformations* section.

BEANS, SOYA — FROZEN (FROM FRESH) [edamame, US]

    shelled 1 cup frozen shelled soya beans (edamame) = about 120–140g;
100g shelled = about $^3/_4$ cup

    still in their pods (US) 1 cup frozen (from cooked) edamame, still in their pods = about 100g — you just thaw, shell and eat these soya beans

---

1 US cup = 16 Tbsp.   1 Tbsp. = 3 tsp.   (1 Irish or old English Tbsp. = 4 tsp.)

beef, *see* **MEAT**

BEER & STOUT

BEER	*bottled & tinned (UK)*	usually in 500ml bottles or tins
	bottled & canned (US)	typically comes in 12-oz. bottles or cans [360ml], though in the US, bottled beer is much more common than canned
STOUT	*tinned*	in both the UK and US, Guinness comes in 440ml tins [15 oz.], but the American cans are labelled 14.9-oz. [440ml]

BEETROOT [beets, US]

raw, whole, 3" wide	one medium-large beetroot [7.5cm] = about 225g
cooked cubed beetroot	2 cups cooked cubed beetroot = about 270g; 100g cubed = about $^3/_4$ cup
canned (US)	$14^1/_2$-/16-/17-oz. can [411g/454g/482g] = about $1^3/_4$–2 cups

---

BICARBONATE OF SODA [baking soda, US]

1 level Tbsp. = about 12g

BISCUIT BASE [cookie-crumb crust; graham cracker crust, US]

biscuit base (UK)   for a 23cm base, combine 150–200g crushed digestives with 70–80g melted butter

---

28g = 1 oz   57g = 2 oz   85g = 3 oz   100g = 3½ oz   113g = 4 oz   142g = 5 oz

graham cracker crust (US)		for a 7" crust, combine $1\frac{1}{2}$–2 cups crushed graham crackers (or other cookies) with $\frac{1}{3}$ cup butter

See also **CRACKERS & CRACKER CRUMBS**.

⇨ To make shortcrust pastry [pie dough, US], see *Shortcrust Pastry* on page 161 in the *Substitutes & Other Transformations* section.

BISCUITS [cookies, US]

BRITISH	*shortbread*	1 biscuit = about 28g; 100g = 3–4 shortbread biscuits
	plain digestives	1 biscuit = about 15g; 100g = 6–7 digestive biscuits
AMERICAN	*vanilla wafers*	1 wafer = 3–4g; 1 cup = about 55g [2 oz.]; 100g = about 26–27 wafers [$1\frac{3}{4}$–2 cups]
	graham crackers	come in 16-oz. box containing 33 sheets (66 squares); there are 2 squares to a sheet and 1 sheet weighs about 14g [$\frac{1}{2}$ oz.]; 100g = 14–15 squares

See also **BISCUIT BASE** [crumb crust], above, for making digestive biscuit or graham cracker or other cookie-crumb crusts.

BLACKBERRIES	*fresh (US)*	1 cup = about 130g; 100g = about $\frac{3}{4}$ cup; 1 lb. = about $3\frac{1}{2}$ cups *(more on blackberries, overleaf)*

---

1 US cup = 16 Tbsp.   1 Tbsp. = 3 tsp.   (1 Irish or old English Tbsp. = 4 tsp.)

	frozen (US)	12-oz. pkg. [340g] frozen blackberries = about $1\frac{3}{4}$ cups
	canned (US)	15-oz. can [425g] = about $1\frac{3}{4}$ cups

(Source: Ostmann & Baker)

BLACKCURRANTS, REDCURRANTS

1 cup = about 100g;
1 lb. = about $4\frac{1}{2}$ cups;

BLACKPOOL ROCK, CANDY CANES

Blackpool rock, 7" stick	18cm stick = about 30g
7" candy cane	1 candy cane = about 30g

BLUEBERRIES

	fresh (UK)	1 cup = about 125g; 100g = about $\frac{3}{4}$ cup
	frozen (US)	10-oz. pkg. [283g] = $1\frac{1}{2}$ cups
	canned (US)	15-oz. can [425g] = about $1\frac{1}{2}$ cups
	pie filling (US)	20-/21-oz. can [567/595g] = about $2\frac{1}{3}$ cups, enough for a 9" pie [23cm]

---

bok choy, *see* **PAK CHOI**

---

bouillon cubes, *see* **STOCKS, BROTHS, BOUILLONS, CONSOMMÉS**

BRAN (e.g., **WHEATBRAN**, OATBRAN)

wheatbran	1 cup = about 62g;
	100g = about $1\frac{2}{3}$ cups

28g = 1 oz   57g = 2 oz   85g = 3 oz   100g = 3½ oz   113g = 4 oz   142g = 5 oz

BRAZIL NUTS	*shelled*	1 cup = about 125g; 100g = about $^3/_4$ cup

BREAD	*1-lb. granary loaf*	1 slice = 30–32g; 100g = about 3 slices; 1 loaf = about 14–15 slices
	bread made in breadmaker	$^1/_2$ large loaf = about 440g
	1-lb. standard-sliced loaf (US)	1 slice = 25–32g; 100g = 3–4 slices; 1 loaf = 14–18 slices
	1-lb. thin-sliced loaf (US)	1 thin slice = 16–19g; 100g = 5–6 thin slices; 1 loaf = 24–28 thin slices

BREADCRUMBS — DRIED

HOMEMADE	*fine dried*	1 cup fine crumbs = about 78g; 100g dried = about $1^1/_4$ cups
PACKAGED	*dry Italian (US)*	1 cup Italian = about 115g; 100g Italian = $^3/_4$ cup plus 2 Tbsp; 24-oz. cylindrical package [680g] contains about 6 cups
	panko breadcrumbs (dried)	1 cup panko = about 43g; 100g panko = about $2^1/_3$ cups
	1 slice dried bread (US)	1 slice dry American bread yields about $^1/_3$ cup dry crumbs

→ Note differences between weights of 1 cup dried homemade, dried packaged Italian and dried panko breadcrumbs.

---

1 US cup = 16 Tbsp.   1 Tbsp. = 3 tsp.   (1 Irish or old English Tbsp. = 4 tsp.)

BREADCRUMBS & CUBES — FRESH

BREADCRUMBS

soft homemade, torn up — 1 cup torn up small = about 58g; 100g = about 1 3/4 cups

blitzed in blender — 1 cup coarsley blitzed = about 52g; 100g = 1 3/4–2 cups

from shop-bought bread (US) — 1 slice, blitzed in blender = about 1/2 cup

BREAD CUBES

from dense homemade bread — 1 cup cubed = about 52g; 100g = 1 3/4–2 cups

from shop-bought bread (US) — 1 slice = 1 scant cup cubed

---

bread soda, *see* **BICARBONATE OF SODA**

BREWER'S YEAST — 1 level Tbsp. = about 10g

BROCCOLI *fresh (UK)* — 1 lb. = 1 large or 2 small bunches

fresh florets, cut up — 1 heaped cup florets = 60g; 100g = 1 3/4–2 cups cut-up florets

fresh (US) — 1 pound = 1 bunch or 6 cups chopped & cooked

frozen (US) — 10-oz. pkg. [283g] = 2 1/2 cups chopped

---

broth, *see* **STOCKS, BROTHS, BOUILLONS, CONSOMMÉS**

BRUSSELS SPROUTS *fresh* — 1 cup = about 100g; 1 pound = 4–4 1/2 cups;

28g = 1 oz   57g = 2 oz   85g = 3 oz   100g = 3½ oz   113g = 4 oz   142g = 5 oz

LIST OF INGREDIENTS *Page 37*

      fresh, 1 stick of sprouts   holds about 750–850g sprouts (about 7–8 cups), but this will vary

      frozen (US)   10-oz. pkg. [283g] contains 18–24 sprouts, or $1\frac{1}{2}$–2 cups

---

BUCKWHEAT GROATS [kasha, US]

      dried $\frac{1}{3}$ cup dried = about 55g; 100g = about $\frac{1}{2}$ cup plus 2 Tbsp.

BULGUR [bulgar, bulghur] *dried*   1 cup = about 170g; 100g = about $\frac{1}{2}$ cup plus $1\frac{1}{2}$ Tbsp.

      dried to cooked   1 cup dried = about $2\frac{3}{4}$–3 cups cooked

---

BUTTER, LARD, SUET, SHORTENING

      butter or lard   1 Tbsp. = 15g;
1 stick (US) = $\frac{1}{2}$ cup [113g];
1 cup = 225g = 2 sticks butter;
50g = $3\frac{1}{2}$ Tbsp;
100g = $\frac{1}{2}$ cup minus 1 Tbsp. = 1 stick minus 1 Tbsp;
1 lb. = 2 cups = 4 sticks butter

      butter (UK)   250g block = 1 cup plus 2 Tbsp.

      butter (US)   1-lb. box contains 4 sticks [2 cups]

      whipped butter (US)   100g = $\frac{2}{3}$ cup; 16-oz. pkg. = 3 cups

      shredded suet (UK)   100g = 1 cup minus 1 Tbsp; 250g box = $2\frac{1}{3}$ cups

      (more on shortening, overleaf)

---

1 US cup = 16 Tbsp.   1 Tbsp. = 3 tsp.   (1 Irish or old English Tbsp. = 4 tsp.)

soft vegetable shortening (US)   100g = about ½ cup;
1 pound = 2⅓–2½ cups

→ Crisco is a soft vegetable shortening.

⇨ For quick reference, see the **BUTTER CHART**, page 219.

BUTTERMILK POWDER   *(US)*   12-oz. container [340g] buttermilk powder will make the equivalent of 15 cups buttermilk [3.75 qt./3.54L]

→ To reconstitute, dissolve 4 Tbsp. powder in 1 cup water [240ml] for each cup of buttermilk called for.

⇨ Recipe calls for buttermilk but no buttermilk or buttermilk powder in stock? You might have a suitable substitute to hand — see *Buttermilk* on page 148 in the *Substitutes & Other Transformations* section.

CABBAGE, SPRING OR HISPI   1 leaf = about 30g
     hispi cabbage (UK)   1 cup cored, sliced = about 40–45g;
100g sliced = about 2½ cups;
4 cups cored, sliced = about 165g

CABBAGE, WHITE [green cabbage, US]
     shred (thinly sliced)   1 cup thinly sliced = 55–60g;
100g = about 1⅔–1¾ cups
     marinated or coleslaw   1 cup coleslaw = about 100g
     whole (UK)   1 average-sized head weighs about 1.1–1.2kg [2½–2¾ lb.]
     whole (US)   1 small head = about 1 lb;
1 medium head = about 2 lb. [900g]

28g = 1 oz   57g = 2 oz   85g = 3 oz   100g = 3½ oz   113g = 4 oz   142g = 5 oz

	shredded (US)	1 small head, cored and shredded = $3\frac{1}{2}$–$4\frac{1}{2}$ cups, or 2 cups cooked

CAKE, SHOP-BOUGHT
    Golden Syrup Cake (UK)   100g = about 1 cup crumbled cake
$2\frac{3}{4}$" x $2\frac{3}{4}$" x 2" slab of cake
[7 x 7 x 5cm] = about 140g =
about $1\frac{2}{3}$ cups crumbled cake

---

candy canes, *see* **BLACKPOOL ROCK, CANDY CANES**

---

canteloupe, *see* **MELON**

---

candied fruit, candied peel, *see* **MIXED PEEL**

CAPERS   1 Tbsp. capers = about 10g

CARAWAY SEEDS   1 Tbsp. caraway seeds = about 7g

CARROTS
    grated   1 cup grated = about 135g;
100g grated = $\frac{3}{4}$ cup

    finely chopped   1 cup = about 120g;
100g = about $\frac{3}{4}$ cup plus 1 Tbsp.

    chopped or sliced   1 cup chopped/sliced = 115–130g;
100g chopped/sliced = $\frac{2}{3}$–$\frac{3}{4}$ cup;
1 lb. = $3\frac{1}{2}$–4 cups chopped/sliced

    cubes   1 cup cubes = about 115g;
100g cubes = $\frac{3}{4}$ cup plus 2 Tbsp.
(more on carrots, overleaf)

---

1 US cup = 16 Tbsp.   1 Tbsp. = 3 tsp.   (1 Irish or old English Tbsp. = 4 tsp.)

	1" pieces	1 cup pieces = 120–150g; 100g pieces = $^2/_3$–$^3/_4$ cup; 1 lb. pieces = 3–3$^3/_4$ cups
WHOLE	*small carrots, 4–6"*	3 small carrots, 10–15cm long = about 100g
	medium-sized carrots	3 medium carrots = 230–300g; 100g = 1–1$^1/_3$ medium carrots; 1 lb. = 5–6 medium carrots
	baby carrots (US)	1 lb. = 3$^1/_2$ cups, about 20 carrots per cup
PACKAGED	*frozen (US)*	10-oz. pkg. [285g] = 1$^1/_2$–2 cups
	canned (US)	13$^1/_2$-/15-oz. can [382/425g] = about 1$^1/_2$ cups sliced

⇨ For conversion formulas for finding the weight of trimmed carrots from the weight of untrimmed, and vice versa, see *Carrots* on page 149 in the *Substitutes & Other Transformations* section.

CASHEWS   1 cup = about 120g;
                     100g = about $^3/_4$ cup plus 1 Tbsp.

---

cassia, *see* **CINNAMON** and **CASSIA**

CAULIFLOWER
FRESH	*1$^1/_4$" florets*	1 cup florets [3cm] = about 75g; 100g florets = about 1$^1/_3$ cups
	one medium head	with leaves on = about 900g [2 lb.]; with leaves off = about 500g; leaves off & cored = about 400g

---

28g = 1 oz   57g = 2 oz   85g = 3 oz   100g = 3½ oz   113g = 4 oz   142g = 5 oz

FROZEN	*frozen (US)*	10-oz. pkg. [285g] = 1½ cups florets

CELERIAC	*cut into ½" cubes*	1 cup cubes [1.3cm] = about 100g
	cut into thick matchsticks	1 cup 'matchsticks' = about 80g; 100g = about 1¼ cups
	whole (UK)	one average celeriac = about 700–900g [1½–2 lb.]
	unpeeled to peeled	one unpeeled 700g celeriac = about 500g peeled

⇨ For conversion formulas for finding the weight of peeled celeriac from the weight of unpeeled, and vice versa, see *Celeriac* on page 150 in the *Substitutes & Other Transformations* section.

CELERY	*chopped or sliced*	2 med. ribs = about 1 cup chopped; 100g = about ¾ cup chopped
	1" lengths	100g = 1 heaped cup
	1 medium bunch	1 medium bunch, with leafy ends sliced off = about 650g [1½ lb.] or about 4½ cups chopped
	1 large bunch	1 large bunch = about 1kg [2¼ lb.]

CELERY SEEDS, CELERY SALT, etc.

celery seeds	1 Tbsp. = about 7g
celery salt	1 Tbsp. = about 14g
dried celery flakes	1 Tbsp. = 2–3g

---

1 US cup = 16 Tbsp.   1 Tbsp. = 3 tsp.   (1 Irish or old English Tbsp. = 4 tsp.)

CEREALS, BREAKFAST

	Cornflakes	1 cup = about 25g;
		100g = about 4 cups
	Cornflake crumbs	1 cup crumbs = about 85g;
		100g crumbs = 1 cup plus 3 Tbsp.
	Malt Bites (like Chex)	1 cup = about 60g;
		100g = about $1\,2/3$ cups
	Rice Krispies	1 cup = 23–24g;
		100g = 4–$4\,1/3$ cups;
		6 cups = 140–145g — this is the amount called for in 1 recipe of Rice Krispies Treats (page 184)

CHARD   *chopped*   1 cup chopped = about 75g;
100g = about $1\,1/3$ cups;
900g chard [2 lb.] = about 12 cups chopped stems and shredded leaves

---

CHEESE

	blue cheese	1 cup crumbled = about 115g;
		100g = about $3/4$ cup plus 2 Tbsp.
	Cheddar, shredded	1 packed cup = about 90g;
		100g = 1 packed cup plus 2 Tbsp;
		1 lb. = about $4\,1/2$–5 packed cups
	cottage cheese, cream cheese	see SOFT CHEESES, below
	feta, cubed	1 cup cubes = about 125g;
		100g = about $3/4$ cup;
		200g packet = a heaped $1\,1/2$ cups cubes
	Gruyère	see *Swiss, shredded*, below

28g = 1 oz   57g = 2 oz   85g = 3 oz   100g = 3½ oz   113g = 4 oz   142g = 5 oz

LIST OF INGREDIENTS   *Page 43*

One hundred grams of fresh shredded Parmesan ($1^1/_3$ cups), 100g of fresh finely-grated Parmesan ($1^1/_2$ cups) and 100g shop-bought finely-grated 'hard' cheese (1 scant cup).

mozzarella, shredded (US)	same as for *Swiss, shredded,* below
paneer, $^1/_4$" cubes	1 cup cubes [6mm] = 120–125g; 100g = about $^3/_4$ cup; 277g packet = about $2^1/_3$ cups
Parmesan	see HARD CHEESES, below
ricotta	see SOFT CHEESES, below
Swiss, shredded (US)	1 cup shredded = about 115g; 100g = about 1 cup minus 2 Tbsp; 1 lb. = about 4 cups

HARD CHEESES

Parmesan, fresh, shredded	1 cup shredded = 75–80g; 100g shredded = $1^1/_3$ cups *(more on cheeses, overleaf)*

---

1 US cup = 16 Tbsp.   1 Tbsp. = 3 tsp.   (1 Irish or old English Tbsp. = 4 tsp.)

Parmesan, fresh, finely grated		1 cup finely-grated fresh = 66–68g; 100g finely-grated fresh = 1½ cups
packaged, finely grated		1 cup shop-bought finely-grated 'hard' cheese = about 110–115g; 100g shop-bought finely-grated 'hard' cheese = 1 cup minus 2 Tbsp.

→ Note differences between weights of fresh shredded and fresh finely-grated Parmesan, and also between the fresh finely-grated Parmesan and the shop-bought finely-grated 'hard' cheese.

SOFT CHEESES		1 cup cream cheese, cottage cheese or ricotta = 225g; 100g = ½ cup minus 1 Tbsp.
	packaged (UK)	*cream cheese*: the 200g container is the most common size; *cottage cheese*: comes in 250g and 650g containers; *ricotta*: comes in 250g tub
	packaged (US)	*cream cheese*: the 8-oz. package [227g] is the most common size; there's also a 3-oz. size [85g]; *cottage cheese*: comes in 16-oz. and 24-oz. tubs [454g & 680g]; *ricotta cheese*: comes in 15-oz. & 32-oz. tubs [425g & 900g]

CHERRIES

FRESH	*sweet cherries*	100g = about ⅔ cup with stems, unpitted or about ½–⅔ cup pitted;

28g = 1 oz   57g = 2 oz   85g = 3 oz   100g = 3½ oz   113g = 4 oz   142g = 5 oz

DRIED	*glacé*	1 lb. = about 3 cups with stems, unpitted or about $2\frac{1}{2}$–3 cups pitted 1 cup glacé cherries = about 140g; 100g = about $\frac{3}{4}$ cup
CANNED		
	tart pitted cherries (US)	16-oz. can [454g] = about $1\frac{1}{2}$ cups
	cherry pie filling (US)	20-/21-oz. can [570/600g] = about $2\frac{1}{3}$ cups, enough for one 9" pie [23cm]
MARASCHINO CHERRIES		30 cherries = 1 scant cup; 100g = 21–24 cherries, or about $\frac{3}{4}$ cup
	cocktail cherries (UK)	225g jar holds 29–30 cherries, 125–135g drained weight
	maraschino cherries (US)	10-oz. jar [285g] holds about 30 cherries; the 16-oz. jar [454g] holds about 40–50 cherries

(Source for US measures: Ostmann & Baker)

CHESTNUTS

DRIED		1 cup dried = about 130–135g; 100g dried = about $\frac{3}{4}$ cup
	soaked or cooked	same as for dried, above
	dried to cooked	1 cup dried = about 2 cups cooked; 100g dried = about 200g cooked
FRESH (UK)	*unpeeled*	1 cup unpeeled [about 8 chestnuts] = about 115–130g; *(more on chestnuts, overleaf)*

---

1 US cup = 16 Tbsp.   1 Tbsp. = 3 tsp.   (1 Irish or old English Tbsp. = 4 tsp.)

		100g unpeeled [6–7 chestnuts] = about $^3/_4$ cup;
		$^1/_2$ lb. unpeeled [14–15 chestnuts] = $1^3/_4$–2 cups
	peeled	1 cup peeled = about 130–135g;
		100g peeled = about $^3/_4$ cup
	unpeeled to peeled	$1^1/_2$ cups unpeeled [180–195g] = about 1 cup peeled;
		125g unpeeled = about 100g peeled;
		$^1/_2$ lb. unpeeled [225g] = about $6^1/_2$ oz. peeled [180–190g]
PACKAGED (US)		
	canned whole	10-oz. can [285g] holds about 25 whole chestnuts
	canned puree	10-oz. can [285g] = about $1^1/_3$ cups puree, equal to about 25 whole chestnuts

➔ Trouble finding dried chestnuts? Try a Chinese grocery.

⇨ For conversion formulas for dried-to-cooked, and for substituting dried for fresh unpeeled chestnuts (and vice versa), see *Chestnuts* on page 151 in the *Substitutes & Other Transformations* section.

---

chicken, *see* **POULTRY**

CHICKPEAS [garbanzo beans]

	dried	1 cup dried = about 170g;
		100g dried = $^1/_2$ cup & 2 Tbsp.
	cooked	1 cup cooked = about 140g;
		100g cooked = about $^3/_4$ cup

28g = 1 oz   57g = 2 oz   85g = 3 oz   100g = 3½ oz   113g = 4 oz   142g = 5 oz

LIST OF INGREDIENTS

PACKAGED	*dried to cooked*	1 cup dried [170g] yields about 2½ cups cooked [345g]
	tinned	1 cup tinned = about 130–140g; 100g tinned = about ¾ cup
	tinned (UK)	400g tin holds a heaped 1½ cups, drained weight about 235g
	canned (US)	comes in 15-oz. cans [425g]

⇨ For conversion formulas for dried-to-cooked and cooked-from-dried chickpeas, and for substituting tinned, see *Beans, Dried* on page 147 in the *Substitutes & Other Transformations* section.

CHILLIES [chiles or chilies, US]

FRESH	*finely chopped*	¼ cup chopped = about 30g; 10g = 1 Tbsp. & 1 tsp.
	thin whole chillies	1 cup = about 58g, or 34 chillies; 10g = about 6 chillies = about 1¼ Tbsp. seeded, thinly sliced [2½–3" long / 6.5–7.5cm long]
	1" wide chillies	3 chillies, 2¼" long = about 80g; 10g = about ⅓ of a chilli [2.5 wide x 5.5cm long]
DRIED	*bird's eye chillies*	10g = about ¼ cup tiny chillies (these chillies, also called Thai chillies, are just ½" long [1cm])
	large red chillies	10g = about 2 large dried chillies
CANNED (US)	*whole*	4-oz. can green, whole chillies [115g] = about 3 chillies
		(more on chillies, overleaf)

---

1 US cup = 16 Tbsp.   1 Tbsp. = 3 tsp.   (1 Irish or old English Tbsp. = 4 tsp.)

	chopped	4½-oz. can green, chopped chillies [125g] = about ½ cup; 7-oz. can green, chopped chillies [200g] = about 1 cup

CHILLI FLAKES [red pepper flakes, US]

1 Tbsp. = about 5g

CHILLI POWDER [chili powder, US]

1 Tbsp. = about 7g

CHIVES

FRESH	*chopped*	10g chopped = a ¼ cup
	cut into 1½" lengths [4cm]	10g cut up = about ½ cup
	whole	a small-to-medium handful chives = about 20g
DRIED	*chopped, freeze-dried*	1 Tbsp. = about 2g

CHOCOLATE

	grated into shavings	1 cup shavings = about 80g; 100g = about 1¼ cups
	finely chopped	1 cup finely chopped = about 140g; 100g = a scant ¾ cup
	broken into small pieces	1 cup broken up = about 170g; 100g = ⅔ cup broken up pieces
	Green & Black's bars	comes in 100g bars in UK and US; 10g = about 3 small squares from 100g bar

---

28g = 1 oz   57g = 2 oz   85g = 3 oz   100g = 3½ oz   113g = 4 oz   142g = 5 oz

LIST OF INGREDIENTS *Page 49*

large chocolate bars (UK)	the really large British chocolate bars weigh 200g
Cadbury Flake	6" flake [15cm] = about 34g; 100g = 3 flakes
CHOCOLATE CHIPS	1 cup chips = about 160g; 100g chips = about $^2/_3$ cup
packet (UK)	100g packet contains about $^2/_3$ cup
package (US)	12-oz. bag [340g] (most common size) contains just over 2 cups; 6-oz. bag [170g] contains about 1 cup chips

➜ One batch of chocolate chip cookies calls for 1 cup of chocolate chips or one 6-oz. bag but if making them in England, you'll need to buy two of the 100g packets to have enough.

CHOCOLATE SQUARES (US)	
Baker's Chocolate	1 square = 1 ounce [28g]; 1 square, grated = about $^1/_4$ cup
1 package Baker's Chocolate	8-oz. box [227g] contains eight 1-oz. squares [28g]

➪ Baker's brand semisweet chocolate squares and unsweeted chocolate squares are a staple of American kitchens, but not of English kitchens. No Baker's chocolate in stock? Don't despair — you may have other ingredients which will do the trick. See *Baker's Chocolate Squares* on page 144 in the *Substitutes & Other Transformations* section.

CHORIZO	*cut-up dried*	1 cup cut up = about 125g; 100g = about $^3/_4$ cup *(more on chorizo, overleaf)*

---

1 US cup = 16 Tbsp.   1 Tbsp. = 3 tsp.   (1 Irish or old English Tbsp. = 4 tsp.)

	soft chorizo links	2 soft Spanish chorizo links = about 140g

See also **PEPPERONI** and **SAUSAGE, FRESH BRITISH**.

---

chutney, *see* **PRESERVES**

---

cilantro, *see* **CORIANDER LEAVES**

CINNAMON, CASSIA (similar to cinnamon) and **CLOVES**

	ground	1 Tbsp. = about 6g; 10g = about 1½ Tbsp. plus ½ tsp; 1 oz. = about ¼ cup plus 2 tsp.
CINNAMON STICKS, 2⅓"		1 stick, 6cm long = 3–3.5g; 10g = about 3 sticks
CASSIA BARK	*broken up*	½ cup broken bark = about 25–30g
	2" piece bark [5cm]	1 piece bark = about 4g
WHOLE CLOVES		1 Tbsp. = about 5g; 10g = about 2 Tbsp; 1 oz. = about ⅓ cup

---

citrons, *see* **MIXED PEEL**

CLAMS

	fresh (US)	1 dozen in shell = about 1⅓ cups shucked
	canned (US)	6½-oz. can shelled clams [185g] = about ¾ cup

→ Clams are not commonly sold in the UK but mussels are and they're usually a good substitute.

→ I've not seen clam juice in British supermarkets.

CLEMENTINES and **SATSUMAS**		1 small-medium = about 70–75g; 1 medium-large = about 100–115g; 1 pound = about 4–6 medium

---

cloves, *see* **CINNAMON, CASSIA** and **CLOVES**

COCKLES	*shelled, cooked*	1 cup = about 140g; 100g cooked = about $^3/_4$ cup

---

COCOA POWDER, UNSWEETENED		1 cup cocoa powder = about 100g
	packaged (UK)	125g container holds about $1^1/_3$ cups
	packaged (US)	8-oz. tin [227g] holds about $2^1/_4$–$2^1/_3$ cups

---

COCONUT	*shredded fresh*	1 cup = about 70g; 100g = a scant $1^1/_2$ cups
	small half-coconut	half a small coconut = about 100g
DESICCATED (DRIED)	*grated*	1 cup finely grated = about 75g; 100g grated = about $1^1/_3$ cups
finely sliced 'flakes' or 'chips'		1 cup flaked coconut = 40–50g

⇨ To make coconut cream or coconut milk, see *Coconut cream and coconut milk* on page 153 in the *Substitutes & Other Transformations* section.

---

1 US cup = 16 Tbsp.   1 Tbsp. = 3 tsp.   (1 Irish or old English Tbsp. = 4 tsp.)

coconut: creamed coconut blocks, *see page 154*

COCONUT CREAM & COCONUT MILK
    tinned coconut milk (UK)   400ml tin holds $1^{3}/_{4}$ cups
    canned coconut milk (US)   comes in 13.5-/14-oz. cans
                                              [400/414ml]

⇨Tinned coconut cream, sometimes called thick coconut milk, can be hard to find. There is a canned product sold in the US called Cream of Coconut, but this is a sweetened coconut cream used in desserts and cocktails; it is not a suitable substitute for the coconut cream used in Thai cooking. However, you can make your own. To make your own coconut cream or coconut milk, see *Coconut cream and coconut milk* on page 153 in the *Substitutes & Other Transformations* section.

COFFEE   *ground beans*   1 cup ground = about 80g;
                                         100g ground = about $1^{1}/_{4}$ cups
                     whole beans   1 cup espresso beans = about 75g;
                                           100g beans = about $1^{1}/_{3}$ cups

→ For brewing fresh coffee ('filter coffee'): Allow 2 level Tbsp. ground coffee per cup of water [10g coffee per 240ml water].

---

consommé, *see* **STOCKS, BROTHS, BOUILLONS, CONSOMMÉS**

CORIANDER LEAVES [cilantro, US]
    FRESH   *chopped leaves*   1 Tbsp. finely chopped = about 3g;
                                            $^{1}/_{3}$ cup finely chopped = about 13g;
                                            10g = about 4 Tbsp.
           whole leaves (no stems)   1 cup leaves = about 15–20g

---

28g = 1 oz   57g = 2 oz   85g = 3 oz   100g = 3½ oz   113g = 4 oz   142g = 5 oz

LIST OF INGREDIENTS

	coriander stalks & leaves	26g bag (from supermarket) yields about 13g leaves (1 cup) = $1/3$ cup finely chopped;
		125g bag (from Pakistani grocery) yields about 40g leaves (2 cups) = $3/4$–1 cup finely chopped
DRIED	*dried leaves*	1 Tbsp. = about 1.5g;
		$1/4$ cup = about 6g

→ For the fresh leaves, use the above measures only as a rough guide; their weight will vary based on the amount of moisture they retain.

CORIANDER SEEDS	*ground*	1 Tbsp. = about 4.25g;
		10g = about $2 1/2$ Tbsp.
	whole	1 Tbsp. = 4.75g;
		10g = about 2 Tbsp.

CORN [sweetcorn, UK]

	fresh, on the cob	1 medium ear yields about $1/2$ cup kernels;
		2–$2 1/2$ lbs. corn on the cob yields about 2 cups kernels
	fresh baby corn cobs	10 baby cobs = about 120g;
		100g = about 1 cup
	tinned	1 cup kernels = about 140g;
		100g = about $3/4$ cup
	frozen (US)	10-oz. package frozen kernels [285g] = about 2 cups

---

cornflakes, *see* **CEREALS, BREAKFAST**

---

1 US cup = 16 Tbsp.   1 Tbsp. = 3 tsp.   (1 Irish or old English Tbsp. = 4 tsp.)

CORNFLOUR [cornstarch, US] 1 Tbsp. = about 6.25g;
$\frac{1}{4}$ cup = about 25g;
10g = about 1 Tbsp. plus 2 tsp.

→ To substitute for cornflour when thickening a sauce:
If using wheat flour instead of cornflour, use twice the amount called for. For example, if 1 Tbsp. of cornflour is called for, use 2 Tbsp. wheat flour. This is because cornflour has twice the thickening power of wheat flour.

CORNISH GAME HENS (US) 1 Cornish game hen = about
$1\frac{1}{4}$ lbs. [570g] = 1 serving

→ If unavailable, guinea fowl makes a similar-sized substitute.

CORNMEAL [polenta] 1 cup = about 150g;
100g = about $\frac{2}{3}$ cup

cornstarch, *see* **CORNFLOUR**

COURGETTES [zucchini, US]
fresh, whole, 8" long 1 courgette [20.5cm] = 200–225g =
$1\frac{1}{2}$ cups sliced = 2 cups grated
fresh, grated 1 cup = about 85g;
100g grated = 1 cup plus 3 Tbsp.
fresh, sliced $\frac{1}{4}$" thick 1 cup slices [6mm] = 105–120g;
100g sliced = about 1 cup

→ What's large? One stuffed zucchini [courgette] recipe called for large zucchini, 10" long, 2" wide [25cm, 5cm]; another called for

28g = 1 oz   57g = 2 oz   85g = 3 oz   100g = 3½ oz   113g = 4 oz   142g = 5 oz

large zucchini, 7" long [18cm]. Courgettes are harvested at about 6" long so I wouldn't call 7" large, but I would 10".

COUSCOUS

uncooked to cooked

1 cup = about 170g;
100g = about $1/2$–$2/3$ cup
$1/3$ cup [55g] uncooked 'quick-cooking' couscous = about 1 cup cooked

---

CRABMEAT

tinned
fresh, flaked
fresh, in shell (US)

$1/2$ cup = about 115g
1 pound flaked = about 3–$3 1/2$ cups
a 1-lb. crab (in shell) yields about 1–$1 1/2$ cups crabmeat

→ In the UK, crabmeat includes both white and brown meat; in the US, typically it's just the white meat that's sold.

CRACKERS & CRUMBS

cream crackers (UK)

10 crackers = about 80g;
100g = about 12 crackers

saltines (US)

100g = about 30 crackers

FINE CRUMBS

1 cup fine crumbs (crushed in food processor) = about 100g
(this applies to cream crackers, saltines, digestives and graham crackers)

matzoh crumbs (US)

6 matzoh sheets = about 1 cup crumbs or matzoh meal
(more on crackers, overleaf)

---

1 US cup = 16 Tbsp.   1 Tbsp. = 3 tsp.   (1 Irish or old English Tbsp. = 4 tsp.)

matzoh, cont.	(can substitute British water biscuits for use in recipes)
graham cracker crumbs (US)	15 graham cracker squares [about 100g] = about 1 cup fine crumbs
vanilla wafer crumbs (US)	1 cup fine crumbs = about 110g

⇨ Also see *Cornflake crumbs* under **CEREALS, BREAKFAST**, page 42.

CRANBERRIES & CRANBERRY JUICE

fresh cranberries, packaged	100g = 1 heaped cup; 12 oz. bag = $3\frac{3}{4}$ cups; 300g bag = $3\frac{1}{4}$ cups

CRANBERRY JUICE COCKTAIL (CRANBERRY FRUIT JUICE DRINK)

flip-top box (UK)	a 1-litre box = about $4\frac{1}{4}$ cups
bottled (US)	a 48-fl.-oz. bottle = 6 cups

CREAM

1 cup = 215g
100g = $\frac{1}{2}$ cup minus $\frac{1}{2}$ Tbsp.

unwhipped to whipped	10 fl. oz. unwhipped double cream [$\frac{1}{2}$ UK pint or 285ml] expands to 17 fl. oz. softly whipped [485ml]

BRITISH CONTAINERS (the pints below are Imperial: 20 fl. oz.)

single cream (~19% fat)	170ml container = $\frac{3}{4}$ cup; 284ml container [$\frac{1}{2}$ UK pint] = about $1\frac{1}{4}$ cups
double cream (48% fat)	142ml container [$\frac{1}{4}$ UK pint] = $\frac{2}{3}$ cup minus 1 Tbsp; 170ml container = $\frac{3}{4}$ cup; 285ml container [$\frac{1}{2}$ UK pint] = about $1\frac{1}{4}$ cups

---

28g = 1 oz   57g = 2 oz   85g = 3 oz   100g = 3½ oz   113g = 4 oz   142g = 5 oz

LIST OF INGREDIENTS *Page 57*

AMERICAN CONTAINERS (the pints below are American: 16 fl. oz.)
half & half (~11% fat)	comes in 1-pint cartons [470ml] and 1-quart [945ml] cartons
light cream* (18–30% fat)	comes in $\frac{1}{2}$-pint cartons [240ml]
sour cream (at least 18% fat)	comes in 8-oz., 1-lb. and $1\frac{1}{2}$-lb. round tubs [225/454/680g]
heavy cream (36–40% fat) (aka whipping cream)	comes in 8-oz. and 1-pint cartons [240/470ml]

➔ *The only size of light cream I could find in the US was the $\frac{1}{2}$-pint size. In America, Half & Half seems to have replaced light cream, although its fat content is almost half that of light cream.

⇨ Also see **CREAM CHART**, page 241.

⇨ For conversion formulas for finding the volume of whipped cream from unwhipped, and vice versa, see *Cream* on page 154 in the *Substitutes & Other Transformations* section.

CREAM OF TARTAR   1 Tbsp. = 9–10g

➔ Cream of tartar is a white powdered acid used in baking powder. It's from the tartar deposits that have crystallised inside wine barrels.

⇨ Also see *Baking powder* on page 144 in the *Substitutes & Other Transformations* section.

CROÛTONS	*homemade*	cup = about 55g; 100g = about $1\frac{3}{4}$ cups
	packaged (US)	$5\frac{1}{2}$-oz. pkg. [155g] = $3\frac{1}{2}$ cups; 40-oz. pkg. [1.1kg] = $24\frac{1}{2}$ cups

---

crumb crusts, *see* **BISCUIT BASE**

---

1 US cup = 16 Tbsp.   1 Tbsp. = 3 tsp.   (1 Irish or old English Tbsp. = 4 tsp.)

CUCUMBERS
    ENGLISH $1/2$ English cuke = about 160g;
                                                  1 English cuke = about 320g;
                                                  100g = about $1/3$ English cuke
                             peeled & grated $1/2$ English cuke = 1 rounded cupful;
                                                    1 cup grated = about 120g;
                                                  100g grated = about $3/4$–1 cup
                    peeled & finely sliced   1 cup sliced = about 150g;
                                                  100g = about $2/3$ cup
                         cut into $1/2$" pieces   same as for sliced, above
    AMERICAN   *1 medium*   1 medium = about $1/2$ pound [227g]
                    sliced or finely chopped   1 medium = about 2 cups sliced or finely chopped

---

CUMIN   1 Tbsp. seeds (or ground) = 6–7g
                                 ground cumin   10g = about 1 Tbsp. plus 2 tsp.
                                               seeds   10g = about $1\frac{1}{2}$ Tbsp

---

CURRANTS, DRIED $1/2$ cup = about 65g;
                                                  100g = about $3/4$ cup

---

CUSTARD [vanilla pudding, US]
    CUSTARD POWDER   *(UK)*   75g sachet = about $2/3$ cup powder = $1\frac{3}{4}$–2 cups reconstituted custard
                    instant vanilla pudding (US) $1/2$ cup powder, reconstituted, makes 2 cups pudding (4 servings)
    READY-MADE   *(UK)*   comes in 396g tins and 1kg boxes
                    dairy-free soya custard (UK)   Alpro-brand comes in 525g boxes

---

28g = 1 oz   57g = 2 oz   85g = 3 oz   100g = 3½ oz   113g = 4 oz   142g = 5 oz

	vanilla pudding (US)	Jello-brand vanilla pudding 6-packs contain six $3\frac{1}{2}$-oz. servings [100g]

→ In the US, custard is usually called vanilla pudding.

DATES, DRIED

WITH PITS [STONES, UK]		
	dense & meaty dates	1 cup = about 170g; 100g = about $\frac{1}{2}$–$\frac{2}{3}$ cup; 1 lb. = about $2\frac{1}{2}$ cups
	small, dryish dates	1 cup = about 100g [about 15 dates]
PITTED [STONED, UK]		
	dense & meaty dates	1 cup pitted (about 23 meaty dates) = about 135g; 100g pitted = about $\frac{3}{4}$ cup
	small, dryish dates	1 cup pitted = about 90g
WITH-PITS TO PITTED		1 cup with pits = scant cup pitted (regardless of whether meaty or dryish dates)
READY-TO-EAT (REHYDRATED)		1 cup chopped = about 140g; 100g chopped = about $\frac{3}{4}$ cup

→ The density, dryness and size of dried dates affect their weight. A cup of dense & meaty pitted dates was 135g whilst a cup of withered parched pitted dates was just 90g, so I've listed both types, above, to make you aware of this. Many American books list 1 pound of dates with pits as equalling $2\frac{1}{2}$ cups; this is based on meaty dense dates so if the dates you're using are mummified and mean, use the 'dryish dates' equivalents above.

---

1 US cup = 16 Tbsp.   1 Tbsp. = 3 tsp.   (1 Irish or old English Tbsp. = 4 tsp.)

digestive biscuit base, *see* BISCUIT BASE

DILL   *seeds*   1 Tbsp. = 6–7g
                 dried dill weed   1 Tbsp. = about 2g

Doritos, *see* TORTILLA CHIPS

---

eggplant, *see* AUBERGINE

EGGS

   BRITISH (EU)   *whole eggs*   1 medium egg = 53–63g;
                                        1 large egg = 63–73g
                    whites, large   1 large white = about 36–42g;
                                          1 cup = about 6 large whites;
                                          100g = about $2\frac{1}{2}$–3 large whites
                    yolks, large   1 large yolk = about 15–19g;
                                           1 cup = about 8–9 large yolks;
                                          100g = about $5\frac{1}{2}$–6 large yolks
   AMERICAN   *whole eggs*   1 medium egg = about $1\frac{3}{4}$–2 oz. [50–57g];
                                          1 large egg = about 2–$2\frac{1}{4}$ oz. [57–64g];
                                          1 cup = about 5–7 large eggs
                    whites, large   1 large white = about 2 Tbsp;
                                          1 cup = about 8–10 large whites
                    yolks, large   1 large yolk = about 1 Tbsp;
                                          1 cup = about 12–14 large yolks

(Source for American egg measures: USDA and Ostmann & Baker.)

28g = 1 oz   57g = 2 oz   85g = 3 oz   100g = 3½ oz   113g = 4 oz   142g = 5 oz

→ One large American egg is closer in weight to 1 medium British egg, so bear this in mind when converting recipes for or from the US.

→ To check, before breaking, if a raw egg is rotten, place it in water. If it floats, it's rotten.

→ When cracking open a raw egg, if some of the shell falls into the bowl along with the egg, use a piece of shell to retrieve it.

→ If your hard-boiled egg is difficult to peel and the shell breaks off in little bits, it's a sign the egg is fairly fresh.

⇨ For complete charts of the old and new EEC egg sizes, and of American egg sizes and weight per dozen, see pages 238 and 239.

FENNEL SEEDS		1 Tbsp. = 6–7g
FENUGREEK LEAVES	*dried*	1 Tbsp. = 1–2g
FIGS	*fresh*	3 medium fresh figs = about 100g; 1 lb. = about 12 medium fresh figs
	dried, chopped	1 cup chopped = about 150g; 100g chopped = about $^2/_3$ cup
	dried, whole	4 dried figs = about 60g or $^1/_2$ cup; 100g = about 6–7 dried figs
FISH	*dry salt cod*	100g dry salt cod, soaked & cooked = a scant $^1/_2$ cup; 340g dry salt cod, soaked & cooked = about $1^1/_2$ cups flaked
AMERICAN	*fish fillets*	1 avg. fillet = 4–5 oz. [115–140g] *(more on fish, overleaf)*

1 US cup = 16 Tbsp.   1 Tbsp. = 3 tsp.   (1 Irish or old English Tbsp. = 4 tsp.)

fish steaks   1 average fish steak = 6–8 oz. [225–285g]

See also **CLAMS, MUSSELS, LOBSTER, SHRIMPS & PRAWNS, &c.**

---

flaxseeds, *see* **LINSEEDS**

FLOUR — IN GENERAL

The weight of a volume of flour (e.g., 1 cup) can vary due to many things: how much the flour has settled, how humid the air is, etc. The weights given below are the averaged-out weights these flours weighed the day I measured them, based on a number of weighings. However, where you see '*(US)*' after the flour, those volumes are based on the average cups per pound, as given in many American cookery books.

---

flour, all purpose, *see* **FLOUR, PLAIN**

FLOUR, CAKE   *(US)*   1 pound cake flour = about $4\frac{1}{2}$–5 cups sifted

→ Cake flour (or pastry flour) is a soft-wheat flour with less gluten than plain flour, so is good for cake- and pastry-making but not for bread-making as the bread would be too crumbly. I've not seen cake flour in British supermarkets and I believe it's now not too common in American ones as well. If you've no cake flour in stock, then for every cup of cake flour called for, use 1 cup minus 2 Tbsp. plain flour [all-purpose flour].

⇨ Sometimes 'cake flour' refers to a self-raising flour. To make your flour a self-raising flour, see *Flour, self-raising* on page 155 in the *Substitutes & Other Transformations* section.

28g = 1 oz   57g = 2 oz   85g = 3 oz   100g = 3½ oz   113g = 4 oz   142g = 5 oz

FLOUR, PLAIN [all-purpose, US]

   plain flour (UK)   1 level cup = about 128–140g
           (avg. per cup = 132g);
           100g = about $^3/_4$ cup;
           1 lb. plain flour = $3\frac{1}{4}$–$3\frac{1}{2}$ cups

   all-purpose flour (US)   1 lb. all-purpose = about $3\frac{1}{2}$ cups
   strong [bread] flour (UK)   1 level cup = about 132–150g
           (avg. per cup = 140g);
           100g = a scant $^3/_4$ cup;
           1 lb. strong flour = 3–$3\frac{1}{2}$ cups

⇨ For quick reference charts for weights of plain [all-purpose] and strong [bread] flours, see **FLOUR CHART**, page 222. The plain flour weights will be correct for plain self-raising flour as well.

⇨ Also see **FLOUR — IN GENERAL**, page 62.

FLOUR, SELF-RAISING [self-rising, US]

   self-raising flour   weights are the same as for plain flour (see above)

⇨ No self-raising flour? Don't worry — you may already have in stock what you need to make your own. See *Flour, self-raising* on page 155 in the *Substitutes & Other Transformations* section.

FLOUR, VARIOUS TYPES

   gram (chickpea) flour   1 level cup = about 125g;
           100g = a heaped $^3/_4$ cup;
           1 lb. gram flour = about $3^2/_3$ cups

           (more on flour, overleaf)

---

1 US cup = 16 Tbsp.   1 Tbsp. = 3 tsp.   (1 Irish or old English Tbsp. = 4 tsp.)

potato flour   1 level cup = about 152g;
100g = about $2/3$ cup;
1 lb. potato flour = about 3 cups

rice flour   1 level cup = about 127g;
100g = about $3/4$ cup;
1 lb. rice flour = $3\frac{1}{2}$–$3\frac{3}{4}$ cups

rye flour (US)   1 level cup = about 111–118g;
100g = 1 scant cup;
1 lb. rye flour = $3\frac{3}{4}$–4 cups

tapioca flour   1 level cup = about 110g;
100g = 1 scant cup;
1 lb. tapioca flour = about 4 cups

➔ For other flours, see **CORNFLOUR** [cornstarch, US]; **FLOUR, CAKE**; **FLOUR, PLAIN** [all-purpose, US]; **FLOUR, SELF-RAISING** [self-rising, US]; **FLOUR, WHOLEMEAL** [wholewheat, US]

➪ Also see **FLOUR — IN GENERAL**, page 62.

FLOUR, WHOLEMEAL [wholewheat, US]

wholemeal flour* (UK)   1 cup = about 130g;
100g = about $3/4$ cup;
1 lb. wholemeal = about $3\frac{1}{2}$ cups
(same weights as for plain flour)

➔ *Wholewheat and wholemeal flour should weigh roughly the same.

➪ Also see **FLOUR — IN GENERAL**, page 62.

---

fromage frais, *see* **YOGURT**

28g = 1 oz   57g = 2 oz   85g = 3 oz   100g = 3½ oz   113g = 4 oz   142g = 5 oz

LIST OF INGREDIENTS *Page 65*

GALANGAL
    FRESH *pounded*   10g pounded to a paste = 1 Tbsp.
    peeled, finely sliced $\frac{1}{4}$ cup sliced = about 20–25g;
    100g sliced = $1-1\frac{1}{3}$ cups
    peeled, finely chopped $\frac{1}{4}$ cup chopped = about 25g;
    100g chopped = about 1 cup
    unpeeled to peeled   100g unpeeled = about 75g peeled
    & trimmed = $\frac{3}{4}$–1 cup finely sliced
    or a full $\frac{3}{4}$ cup finely chopped

GARLIC   *sliced*   1 clove [5g] = $2\frac{1}{2}$–3 tsp. sliced;
    10g sliced = about $5\frac{1}{4}$–6 tsp.
    finely chopped [minced, US]   1 clove [5g] = 2 tsp. chopped;
    10g chopped = about $4\frac{1}{2}$ tsp.
    whole, medium-large clove   1 unpeeled clove = 5–6g
    $2\frac{1}{4}$" bulb [5.5cm], unpeeled   1 bulb garlic = about 50g
    unpeeled to peeled   a 47g bulb = about 40g peeled = 6
    Tbsp. (and a bit) finely chopped
    DRIED   *garlic powder*   1 Tbsp. garlic powder = about 9g
    garlic salt   1 Tbsp. garlic salt = about 14g

→ Equivalents: $\frac{1}{4}$ tsp. garlic powder is equal in potency to $\frac{3}{4}$ tsp. finely chopped fresh garlic — about $\frac{1}{2}$ medium-large clove.

GELATINE [gelatin, US]
    BRITISH GELATINE (for gelling 20-fluid-ounce pints)
    powdered beef gelatine   13g sachet, about 4 tsp, will set
    1 UK pint [580ml];
    70g box contains 6 sachets
    (more on gelatine, overleaf)

---

1 US cup = 16 Tbsp.   1 Tbsp. = 3 tsp.   (1 Irish or old English Tbsp. = 4 tsp.)

powdered Vege-gel	6g sachet, about 2¼ tsp, will set 1 UK pint [580ml]; 25g box contains 4 sachets
leaf gelatine, 7.3 x 11cm	4 leaves, about 10g, will set 1 UK pint [580ml]
AMERICAN GELATINE (for gelling 16-fluid-ounce pints)	
Knox-brand unflavored	¼-oz. envelope [7g], about 3 tsp, will set 1 US pint [480ml]; 1-oz. box contains 4 envelopes
gelatine sheets, 4" x 9"	4 sheets [10 x 23cm] will set 1 US pint [480ml] but gelatine sheets are not easy to find in the US. Surfas, a restaurant-supply store, sell them (surfasonline.com); other gourmet & bakery supply shops may also carry them.

→ Different pints, different packets: The British pint is 20 fluid ounces; the American pint is 16. So, one British gelatine packet containing 4 teaspoons will gel 1 Imperial pint (20 fl. oz.), and one American packet containing 3 teaspoons will gel 1 US pint (16 fl. oz.). Therefore, if you're in the US but cooking from a British recipe which calls for a 13g packet gelatine (4 teaspoons), use 1⅓ American packets to give you the equivalent amount. And if you're in the UK but cooking from an American recipe which calls for one packet gelatine, use just 3 teaspoons from your British packet for the equivalent amount. And mind you use the correct-sized pint, too!

GINGER, DRIED

powdered (ground)	1 Tbsp. = about 5g

28g = 1 oz   57g = 2 oz   85g = 3 oz   100g = 3½ oz   113g = 4 oz   142g = 5 oz

LIST OF INGREDIENTS

| | *dried pieces* | 1 Tbsp. = about 7g |

→ Equivalents for ginger powder: 1¼ tsp. powdered ginger is equal in potency to about 1 Tbsp. fresh, grated ginger.

GINGER, FRESH

	peeled, shredded	1 Tbsp. shredded = 8–9g (for this, start with an unpeeled marble-sized piece, about 12g); 100g shredded = about ¾ cup
peeled, finely sliced/chopped		1 Tbsp. = about 6–8g; 10g = 1½–2 Tbsp. (for this, start with an unpeeled marble-sized piece, about 15g); 100g = 1 scant cup
unpeeled to peeled & trimmed		100g unpeeled = about 85g peeled = about 11–14 Tbsp. finely sliced, or 14 Tbsp. finely chopped
marble-sized piece		1 unpeeled 12–15g marble-sized piece = 8–12g peeled = 1½–2 Tbsp. finely chopped, or about 1 Tbsp. shredded
larger pieces		2¼" x 1" piece unpeeled ginger, about 25g = about 2½–3½ Tbsp. peeled and finely chopped; 2½" x 1½" piece unpeeled ginger, about 40g = about 4½–5½ Tbsp. peeled and finely chopped

---

1 US cup = 16 Tbsp.   1 Tbsp. = 3 tsp.   (1 Irish or old English Tbsp. = 4 tsp.)

GINGER, PICKLED OR CANDIED

pickled, sliced $1/2$ cup = about 85g;
50g = about $4\frac{1}{2}$–5 Tbsp.

stem (preserved) ginger   3 balls ginger = about 50g = about $1/3$ cup finely chopped

candied, chopped (US)   1 oz. [28g] = about 2 Tbsp.

GLYCERINE, LIQUID $1/4$ cup = about 50g

GOLDEN NEEDLES (dried tiger lily buds, dried lily flowers)
10g = 21–22 buds or about $1/3$ cup;
1 cup, around 65 buds = about 30g

GOLDEN SYRUP   1 teaspoon = 6–7g;
1 Tbsp. = about 20g;
100g = 5 Tbsp. [about $1/3$ cup];
1 cup = about 330g

→ Quick reference: here are some typical golden syrup weights called for in British recipes: 30g = $1\frac{1}{2}$ Tbsp.; 75g = $3\frac{3}{4}$ Tbsp. [scant $1/4$ cup]; 150g = about 7 Tbsp. [scant $1/2$ cup]; 175g = about 8 Tbsp. [$1/2$ cup]; 350g = about 1 cup. Or does your recipe use millilitres rather than grams? If so, bear in mind that millilitres (ml) are a measure of volume, not of weight, and one tablespoon holds 15ml so divide your ml amount by 15 to get the equivalent number of tablespoons.

GOOSEBERRIES   1 cup = about 115g;
100g = $3/4$–1 cup

28g = 1 oz   57g = 2 oz   85g = 3 oz   100g = 3½ oz   113g = 4 oz   142g = 5 oz

LIST OF INGREDIENTS

graham cracker crust, *see* **BISCUIT BASE**

GRAPEFRUIT	*fresh, whole*	1 medium grapefruit weighs about 310–450g [$^3/_4$–1 lb.]
	fresh, juiced	1 medium grapefruit yields about $^2/_3$–1 cup juice [150–240ml]
	fresh, grated peel (zest)	some books say 1 medium grapefruit yields 3–4 Tbsp. zest but my 310g grapefruit yielded a scant 1 Tbsp. zest, so bear this in mind
TINNED	*(UK)*	1 cup segments = about 150g; 411g tin = about $1^1/_3$–$1^1/_2$ cups segments, about 225g drained; 540g tin = 290–320g drained
	(US)	16-oz. can [454g] = about 2 cups sections

GRAPES   *whole or halved*   1 cup = about 150g; 100g = about $^2/_3$ cup or 25 grapes; $^1/_2$ lb. grapes = about $1^1/_2$ cups or 56 grapes

---

ham, *see* **BACON & HAM**

HAZELNUTS   1 cup = about 130g; 100g = about $^3/_4$ cup

HEMP SEEDS   1 Tbsp. = about 7g

---

1 US cup = 16 Tbsp.   1 Tbsp. = 3 tsp.   (1 Irish or old English Tbsp. = 4 tsp.)

HERBS

FRESH	*finely chopped*	1 Tbsp. chopped = about 1.5–3g; 1 cup chopped = about 25–50g (based on finely chopped mint leaves: 25–30g/cup, and coriander leaves [*cilantro*]: 40–50g/cup)
	whole mint leaves	1 cup mint leaves = about 15g; 1 packed cup = about 20g; 1 handful = about 15–25g
	leaves on stalks	100g stalks yields 2–2$\frac{1}{3}$ fairly packed cups of leaves, 40–45g (based on mint stalks, nettle stalks)
DRIED	*crumbled leaves*	1 Tbsp. = about 1.5–2g; $\frac{1}{4}$ cup = about 6–8g (based on dried basil, parsley, oregano, mint, dill weed)
	needle leaves (e.g., thyme)	1 Tbsp. = about 3g; $\frac{1}{4}$ cup = about 13g

→ Note: In general, 1 teaspoon dried herb has the potency of 1 tablespoon chopped fresh herb (3 teaspoons).

→ For a bouquet garni, tie together (for easy removal from soup or stew) 3–4 sprigs parsley, 2 sprigs thyme and a small bay leaf.

For dried herbs, see also **BAY LEAVES, CHIVES, FENUGREEK LEAVES**

HONEY 1 teaspoon = 5–6g;
1 Tbsp. = 17–18g;
$\frac{1}{4}$ cup = about 70g;
100g = 5$\frac{1}{2}$–6 Tbsp.

28g = 1 oz   57g = 2 oz   85g = 3 oz   100g = 3½ oz   113g = 4 oz   142g = 5 oz

LIST OF INGREDIENTS *Page 71*

→ For a quick reference for honey amounts often called for in British recipes: 85ml = about 5½ Tbsp. [⅓ cup]; 100ml = about 6½ Tbsp; 125ml = about 8 Tbsp. [½ cup]. Millilitres (ml) are a measure of volume, not of weight; there are 15ml per tablespoon so the preceeding equivalents were arrived at by dividing the ml amount by 15 to get the equivalent number of tablespoons. Do the same for any other ml amounts called for.

HORSERADISH

ready-prepared sauce   1 Tbsp. = about 14g; 10g = about 2 tsp.

→ Equivalents: 2 Tbsp. bottled sauce is equal in potency to about 1 Tbsp. grated fresh horseradish.

HOT DOGS (also called frankfurters, weiners)

packaged (US)   16-oz. pkg. [454g] contains 8 to 10 hot dogs

See also **SAUSAGES**.

ICE CREAM   *(UK)*   comes in 500ml tubs or 'pots', and 1-litre plastic containers; a 2-litre size [70 UK fl. oz./68 US fl. oz.] is becoming common now, too

tubs (US)   Häagen Dazs and Ben & Jerry's come in 1-pint tubs [16 fl. oz.]

waxed-card cartons (US)   the ½-gallon waxed-box carton [64 fl. oz./1.9L] is the most common size   *(more overleaf)*

---

1 US cup = 16 Tbsp.   1 Tbsp. = 3 tsp.   (1 Irish or old English Tbsp. = 4 tsp.)

waxed cartons, cont. also comes in 1-quart cartons [32 fl. oz./950ml], but see note, below.

→ The American $\frac{1}{2}$-gallon ice cream containers [64 fl. oz./1.9L] from makers such as Breyer's, Edy's and Mayfield Dairies shrank to a $1\frac{3}{4}$-quart size [56 fl. oz./1.7L] to counter, they said, the price-rise of its ingredients, but then it shrank even further, to a $1\frac{1}{2}$-quart size [48 fl. oz./1.4L]. However, half-gallon containers of other American ice cream brands, such as Stewart's, currently remain the full, 64-fluid-ounce American half-gallon.

ICE   *1 cube*   1 cube = 28g (from an American normal-sized ice cube tray)

---

jam, *see* **PRESERVES**

JELLO [jelly, UK]
  jelly cubes (UK)   135g packet contains a block of 12 jelly cubes, which will gel 1 Imp. pint liquid [20 fl. oz.]
  powdered jello (US) 3-oz. pkg. [85g] contains $\frac{1}{2}$ cup powder which will gel 1 US pint liquid [16 fl. oz.]

See also **GELATINE**.

→ What Americans call 'jelly' is what the Brtitish would call a clear jam — it's what is spread on peanut butter and jelly sandwiches. What Americans call 'jello' is what the British call 'jelly', the gelatine dessert; Americans do not spread jello on sandwiches.

28g = 1 oz   57g = 2 oz   85g = 3 oz   100g = 3½ oz   113g = 4 oz   142g = 5 oz

LIST OF INGREDIENTS   *Page 73*

JUNIPER BERRIES	*dried*	1 Tbsp. = about 5–6g; 10g = a scant 2 Tbsp.

KALE	*leaves from fresh stalks*	100g kale on stalks = about $2\frac{1}{2}$–3 cups chopped leaves; $\frac{3}{4}$ lb. kale on stalks yields about 9–10 cups chopped leaves

kombu, *see* **SEAWEED**

lard, *see* **BUTTER, LARD, SUET, SHORTENING**

LASAGNE

BRITISH	*dried, packaged*	sold in 375g boxes, the lasagne sheets are typically flat, with no frilled edges, and usually measure $6\frac{1}{2}$" x $3\frac{1}{4}$" [16.5 x 8cm]
AMERICAN	*dried, packaged*	sold in 1-lb. boxes containing about 17 strips of lasagne with frilled edges; the strips normally measure 10" x $2\frac{1}{4}$" [25.5 x 5.5cm]

→ Note: British lasagne is usually the 'no pre-cook' variety; most American lasagne requires that you cook it first but check the package as the no-pre-cook variety is now also being sold in the US.

LEEKS	*thinly shred (sliced)*	1 cup thinly shred = about 55–65g; 100g thinly shred = $1\frac{1}{2}$–$1\frac{3}{4}$ cups *(more on leeks, overleaf)*

---

1 US cup = 16 Tbsp.   1 Tbsp. = 3 tsp.   (1 Irish or old English Tbsp. = 4 tsp.)

	1-inch-thick leek	1 medium leek, 16" long including green ends = about 200g; 100g = $\frac{1}{2}$ medium leek
	trimmed	200g leek = about 115g, with base & green ends trimmed off = about $1\frac{3}{4}$–2 cups thinly sliced

LEMONGRASS

	finely sliced or chopped	1 Tbsp. sliced = about 5g
	one 8" stalk [20.5cm]	1 stalk = about 20g = about $\frac{1}{4}$ cup finely sliced or chopped

LEMONS

MEDIUM	*whole*	1 medium lemon = 115–140g
	juiced	1 medium lemon yields about 2–3 Tbsp. juice
	grated peel (zest)	1 medium lemon yields about 2–3 tsp. grated peel
MEDIUM-LARGE	*whole*	1 med.-large lemon, about $3\frac{1}{2}$" long x $2\frac{3}{4}$" [9 x 7cm] = 200–230g
	juiced	1 medium-large lemon yields about 5 Tbsp. juice
	grated peel (zest)	1 medium-large lemon yields about 2 Tbsp. grated peel [~13g]
PRESERVED LEMON		1 tsp. finely chopped = about 4g

→ Lemons vary greatly in size, as does the amount of juice you get from two similar-sized lemons so the amounts above are a rough guide to what's expected from these sized fruits.

28g = 1 oz   57g = 2 oz   85g = 3 oz   100g = 3½ oz   113g = 4 oz   142g = 5 oz

LIST OF INGREDIENTS *Page 75*

LENTILS AND SPLIT PEAS

MOST VARIETIES	*dried*	1 cup dried = 165–200g; 100g dried = $1/2$–$2/3$ cup; 1 lb. dried = $2\frac{1}{4}$–$2\frac{3}{4}$ cups
	dried-to-cooked	1 cup dried = about 3 cups cooked; 100g dried = $1\frac{3}{4}$–2 cups cooked

GREEN LENTILS & GREEN SPLIT PEAS

	green lentils	1 cup dried = 165–175g; 100g = $1/2$ cup & 1–2 Tbsp. [9–10 Tbsp.]
	green split peas	1 cup dried = about 190g; 100g = about $1/2$ cup [8 Tbsp.]
	mung beans, whole	same as for *green split peas*, above (also known as green gram beans and *moong dal*, though *moong dal* usually refers to split mung beans; they're the seed of the plant *Phaseolus aureus*)
Puy lentils [French lentils]		same as for *green split peas*, above
	mung beans, split	see *moong dal, split* below
RED LENTILS	*split*	1 cup dried = 170–185g; 100g = $1/2$ cup & 1 Tbsp. or so [$8\frac{1}{2}$–$9\frac{1}{2}$ Tbsp.] (also known as pink lentils, *Masar dal* and *Masoor dal*)

YELLOW LENTILS & YELLOW SPLIT PEAS

	channa dal	1 cup dried = about 180g; 100g = $1/2$ cup & 1 Tbsp. [9 Tbsp.]

(more on lentils, overleaf)

---

1 US cup = 16 Tbsp.   1 Tbsp. = 3 tsp.   (1 Irish or old English Tbsp. = 4 tsp.)

	(*channa dal* are hulled and split *kala channa* [black chickpeas], a variety of chickpea from the plant *Cicer arietinum*)
yellow lentils (toor dal)	same as for *channa dal*, above (also known as *arhar dal* and *toover dal*; it is the seed of the pigeon pea plant *Cajanus cajan*)
moong dal, split	1 cup dried = about 200g; 100g = about $\frac{1}{2}$ cup [8 Tbsp.] (these are hulled, split mung beans and require no pre-soaking)
yellow split peas	same as for *moong dal, split*, above (dried split yellow peas are from the pea plant *Pisum sativum*)

→ There are many different types of lentils and split peas so be sure you're using the ones you want as some don't need to be soaked beforehand, and the cooking times can vary. This is especially true of yellow lentils and dried yellow split peas which cover a wide range, including yellow split mung beans (*moong dal*) and yellow split chickpeas (*channa dal*), and these are not interchangeable in recipes — *channa dal* takes longer to cook — so be sure the ones you're cooking are the right ones for your recipe.

LETTUCE

BRITISH	*flat lettuce*	1 head flat lettuce = 180–200g = about 6 cups leaves; 100g torn leaves = about 3–3$\frac{1}{2}$ cups, fairly packed

---

28g = 1 oz   57g = 2 oz   85g = 3 oz   100g = 3½ oz   113g = 4 oz   142g = 5 oz

LIST OF INGREDIENTS *Page 77*

		(also known as *Boston* or *butterhead* lettuce in the US)
	little Gem lettuce	1 head = 115–150g = 3–4 cups leaves
		(*little Gem* lettuces are like mini *romaine* and are often sold in pairs)
	Cos lettuce	1 head = about 400g = about 12 cups torn-up leaves
		(called *romaine* lettuce in the US)
AMERICAN	*iceberg*	1 head = about 18–20 oz. [510–570g] = about 10–11 cups loosely-packed leaves

---

LIMES   *whole, medium*   one 2" lime [5cm] = about 70g

fresh, juiced   1 medium lime yields a good 2 Tbsp. juice

fresh, grated peel (zest)   1 medium lime yields about $1\frac{1}{2}$–2 tsp. grated peel

---

LINSEEDS [flaxseeds]   1 Tbsp. = about 8g;
$\frac{1}{4}$ cup = about 33g;
100g = $\frac{3}{4}$ cup [12 Tbsp.]

LIQUORICE ROOT [licorice root, US]

one 8" piece [20.5cm] = about 5g

LOBSTER   *(US)* $1\frac{1}{2}$-lb. live lobster [680g] = about $1\frac{1}{4}$ cups cooked meat

---

1 US cup = 16 Tbsp.   1 Tbsp. = 3 tsp.   (1 Irish or old English Tbsp. = 4 tsp.)

LOTUS ROOT	*dried*	3 pieces = about 28g; 100g = about 10–11 pieces

lox, *see* **SALMON, SMOKED**

LYCHEE NUTS	*tinned, peeled*	1 cup tinned lychees = 115–125g; 100g = about $\frac{3}{4}$–1 cup
	tinned (UK)	567g tin of lychees in syrup contains a good 2 cups drained lychees [about 250g], and the syrup fills about $1\frac{1}{4}$ cups

MACE	*ground (shop-bought)*	1 Tbsp. = about 6g
	1 blade, ground	1 blade mace, ground in mortar = a full $\frac{1}{2}$ teaspoon

→ Mace is the membrane that covers nutmeg, hence their similarity; use one in place of the other if you don't have the one that's called for.

MANGE-TOUT & SUGAR SNAP PEAS

	mange-tout [snow peas, US]	a small handful = about 60g; a very large handful = about 170g; 100g = about 25 mange-tout, or about $1\frac{1}{2}$ small handfuls
	sugar snap peas	1 heaped cup = 100g or about 25 sugar snap peas

MANGOES	1 medium = about $\frac{3}{4}$ lb. [340g] = 1 *very* heaped cup $\frac{3}{4}$" pieces [2cm]

28g = 1 oz   57g = 2 oz   85g = 3 oz   100g = 3½ oz   113g = 4 oz   142g = 5 oz

LIST OF INGREDIENTS *Page 79*

TINNED		1 cup drained slices = about 170g; 100g drained = about $1/2$–$2/3$ cup
	(UK)	425g tin contains about 230–250g drained slices = $1\frac{1}{3}$ – $1\frac{1}{2}$ cups
CRYSTALLISED MANGO		1 cup crystallised mango chunks = about 100g

---

MARJORAM   *fresh leaves*   1 Tbsp. leaves = about 1g
                   fresh 4" sprigs   three 10cm sprigs = about 5g; leaves from these sprigs = about 2g
     dried, crumbled (shop-bought)   1 Tbsp. dried = about 1.75g

→ With fresh herbs, the weight of one sprig to another, and the number of leaves from the sprigs, can vary considerably so use the weights above as a rough guide only.

MARSHMALLOWS

LARGE MARSHMALLOWS		1 cup large = about 35g; 100g large = $2\frac{3}{4}$–3 cups
	(UK)	300g bag contains $8\frac{1}{2}$–9 cups, or about 56 large marshmallows — however, the 2 bags I weighed each contained about 28g less than what was claimed (but still enough for 1 recipe Rice Krispies Treats)
	(US)	10-oz. bag [283g] contains about 40–45 large marshmallows (enough for 1 recipe of Rice Krispies Treats, page 184); *(more on marshmallows, overleaf)*

1 US cup = 16 Tbsp.   1 Tbsp. = 3 tsp.   (1 Irish or old English Tbsp. = 4 tsp.)

(US), cont.	16-oz. bag [454g] contains 60–70 large marshmallows
MINIATURE MARSHMALLOWS	1 cup miniature = about 40g; 100g miniature = about $2\frac{1}{2}$ cups
(UK)	comes in a 200g bag
(US)	$10\frac{1}{2}$-oz. bag [298g] has enough for 1 recipe Rice Krispies Treats

→ The large marshmallows from Aldi in England were the same length as American marshmallows — $1\frac{1}{4}$" [3cm] — but less wide, hence a difference in the number of marshmallows per bag.

→ In the UK, large marshmallows are usually coloured and flavoured rather than white, aimed more at the kids' snack market than the cook's ingredients market. But beware, marshmallows are not low in calories — 25g large marshmallows (about 4) contain about 84 calories [kcal], so a snack to be given in small measure.

MARZIPAN (rolled icing)	1 cup = about 300g; 100g = about $\frac{1}{3}$ cup
packaged (UK)	comes in 250g block and 454g box

MAYONNAISE	1 cup = 227g; 100g = 7 Tbsp. [scant $\frac{1}{2}$ cup]

MEAT	
BEEF *cooked, finely chopped*	1 cup = about 150g; 100g chopped = about $\frac{2}{3}$ cup; 1 lb. chopped = about 3 cups
raw, minced [ground, US]	1 cup minced = about 227g;

28g = 1 oz   57g = 2 oz   85g = 3 oz   100g = 3½ oz   113g = 4 oz   142g = 5 oz

LIST OF INGREDIENTS *Page 81*

raw, cubed for stew	100g minced = a scant $\frac{1}{2}$ cup; 1 pound minced = about 2 cups same as for *raw, minced*, above
flank steak (US)	1 steak = $1\frac{1}{4}$–$1\frac{1}{2}$ lb. [570–680g]

See also **BACON & HAM; POULTRY**.

MELON *melon balls* $\frac{1}{2}$ cup melon balls = about 100g
2" wedge from $4\frac{3}{4}$" melon 5 cm wedge from 12cm round melon = about 100g
whole 6" canteloupe (US) 1 whole canteloupe, 15cm = about 3 lbs. [1.36kg]

MILK, FRESH $\frac{1}{4}$ cup [4 Tbsp.] = 50g
(UK) comes in UK-pint bottles [570ml], and in plastic 1-litre bottles
(US) most common sizes are US-$\frac{1}{2}$-gallon & 1-gallon containers [1.9L & 3.78L]; also sold in US-quart & US-pint sizes [950ml & 470ml]

MILK, DRIED $\frac{1}{4}$ cup [4 Tbsp.] = about 19g;
10g = about 2 Tbsp;
50g = about $\frac{2}{3}$ cup
packaged dried skimmed (UK) 198g tub makes about 2.2 litres milk [~4 UK pts. or $2\frac{1}{3}$ US qts.]
packaged instant nonfat (US) 9.6-oz. pkg. [272g] contains about 4 cups powder and makes about 3 qts. milk [~2.8L or 5 UK pints]
(more on dried milk, overleaf)

---

1 US cup = 16 Tbsp.   1 Tbsp. = 3 tsp.   (1 Irish or old English Tbsp. = 4 tsp.)

→ To reconstitute: Place 50g powder [$^2/_3$ cup] in a measuring jug and fill with water to the 570ml level [1 UK pint / $2^1/_2$ cups].

MILK, CANNED & 'LONGLIFE'		1 cup evaporated milk = 220–225g; 100g = $^1/_2$ cup minus 1 Tbsp.
BRITISH	*evaporated milk*	410g tin contains about $1^2/_3$ cups; 170g tin contains about $^2/_3$–$^3/_4$ cup (they usually come in a 3-pack)
	condensed milk	comes in 397g tins
	goat's milk, longlife	comes in 1-litre boxes
	soya milk, longlife	comes in 1-litre boxes
AMERICAN	*evaporated milk*	comes in 5-oz. & 12-oz. cans [140g & 340g]
	sweetened condensed milk	comes in 14-oz. cans [400g]
	goat milk	comes in 12-oz. cans [340g]
	soy milk, longlife	comes in 1-qt. boxes [~1L]

→ 'Longlife' milk does not require refrigeration *prior to* opening, but it should be refrigerated after opening.

MILLET	*millet grains*	1 cup = about 185–200g; 100g = about $^1/_2$ cup
	millet flakes	1 cup = about 105g

MINCEMEAT	1 cup = about 225g; 100g = $^1/_2$ cup minus 1 Tbsp; 1 lb. = about 2 cups

---

28g = 1 oz   57g = 2 oz   85g = 3 oz   100g = 3½ oz   113g = 4 oz   142g = 5 oz

LIST OF INGREDIENTS

MINT LEAVES

FRESH	*finely chopped*	1 Tbsp. finely chopped = 1.5–2g; $\frac{1}{4}$ cup [4 Tbsp.] = about 6g; 1 cup chopped = about 24–30g; 10g chopped = about $\frac{1}{3}$ cup
	whole mint leaves	1 packed cup = about 20g; 25g = about 1 good handful leaves
	stalks with leaves, 12–15"	50g = about 6–7 stalks with leaves, 30–38cm long; leaves from these stalks = about 20–21g or 1 fairly-packed cup
DRIED	*very finely chopped*	1 Tbsp. dried = 1.5g; 10g = about 6 Tbsp. plus 2 tsp.

→ Note: For fresh mint leaves, use the above measures only as a rough guide; the weight of fresh mint leaves is affected by the amount of moisture they retain, which varies.

MISO (a soya bean paste)   1 level Tbsp. = about 16g;
10g = about 2 teaspoons

MIXED PEEL [citrons, candied fruit, candied peel, US]

		1 cup = about 130–140g; 100g = about $\frac{3}{4}$ cup
	packaged candied fruit (US)	8-oz. pkg. [227g] = about $1\frac{1}{2}$ cups chopped

---

MUESLI   *shop-bought*   1 cup = about 100g
           homemade   1 cup = about 110–115g

---

1 US cup = 16 Tbsp.   1 Tbsp. = 3 tsp.   (1 Irish or old English Tbsp. = 4 tsp.)

mung beans, *see* LENTILS AND SPLIT PEAS

MUSHROOMS, FRESH
   BUTTON MUSHROOMS (small cultivated or white mushrooms)
      finely sliced or shredded   1 cup sliced = about 60–70g;
                                     100g sliced = about $1\frac{1}{2}$–$1\frac{2}{3}$ cups
                            whole   1 cup whole = 55–70g;
                                       100g whole = about $1\frac{1}{2}$–$1\frac{3}{4}$ cups
   FLAT MUSHROOMS — flat mushrooms are like portobello but lighter coloured & less strongly flavoured
      chopped flat mushrooms   1 cup chopped = about 65g;
                                        100g = about $1\frac{1}{2}$ cups
                      thinly sliced   1 cup thinly-sliced, pressed into the cup = about 50–60g;
                                        100g sliced = about $1\frac{2}{3}$–2 cups
      whole 3–4" caps, with stalks   weights vary widely:
                                        a 3" cap [7.5cm] weighed ~ 45g;
                                        a $3\frac{1}{2}$" cap [9cm] weighed ~ 60g;
                                        a denser 4" cap weighed 114g;
                                        so 100g = $\frac{1}{2}$–1 flat mushroom, and 1 lb. could hold anywhere from 4–10 caps
                whole, de-stalked   100g whole = about 88g de-stalked
   PACKAGED MUSHROOMS
      whole portobellos (US)   16-oz. pkg. = 3 very large caps
      sliced portobellos (US)   7-oz. pkg. sliced portobellos [200g] = 12–14 slices, $\frac{1}{4}$-in. thick [0.5cm]

28g = 1 oz   57g = 2 oz   85g = 3 oz   100g = 3½ oz   113g = 4 oz   142g = 5 oz

MUSHROOMS, TINNED OR BOTTLED

BUTTON MUSHROOMS	*sliced*	1 cup tinned sliced = about 145g; 100g = about $^2/_3$ cup
	whole (UK)	290g tin whole button mushrooms = 1 heaped cup drained, about 145g
	(US)	4-oz. jar [115g] = about $^2/_3$ cup; 7-oz. can/jar [200g] = about 1 cup
STRAW MUSHROOMS	*halves*	1 cup tinned halves = about 130g; 100g = about $^3/_4$ cup
	(UK)	425g tin straw mushroom halves = about $1^1/_2$ cups drained, about 210g

---

MUSHROOMS & FUNGUS, DRIED

CHINESE MUSHROOMS	*dried*	1 cup = about 22–24g; 50g = about 17–18 dried caps
SHIITAKE	*dried*	1 cup = about 28g; 10g dried = about $^1/_3$ cup
WOOD EARS*	*dried*	1 cup = about 15–18g; 10g = about $^1/_2$–$^2/_3$ cup

➔ *Wood ears, a dried black fungus, are also known as cloud ears, tree ears, *mo er*, *mu er*, *won yee*, as well as other names.

MUSSELS	*in shells (UK)*	$1^1/_2$ lb. [680g] = about 30 mussels; 4 lb. [1.8kg] = about 75 mussels; 1kg = about 40–45 mussels

➔ Suggested quantity per person is 1 pound (about 18–20 mussels).

---

1 US cup = 16 Tbsp.   1 Tbsp. = 3 tsp.   (1 Irish or old English Tbsp. = 4 tsp.)

MUSTARD	*prepared (wet)*	1 Tbsp. = about 15g;
		10g wet = about 2 teaspoons
	dried (powdered)	1 Tbsp. dried = about 5g;
		10g dried = about 2 Tbsp.
SEEDS	*whole*	1 Tbsp. = about 9g;
		10g seeds = $3\frac{1}{3}$ teaspoons

NECTARINES	*(US)*	1 lb. = 3–4 medium or about $2\frac{1}{2}$ cups sliced

---

NOODLES

   FRESH NOODLES

thin Chinese egg noodles	1 cup fresh = about 95–100g
$\frac{1}{8}$"-wide Chinese egg noodles	1 cup fresh = about 120–130g; 100g fresh = about $\frac{3}{4}$ cup
fresh to cooked $\frac{1}{8}$"-wide	1 cup fresh = $1\frac{1}{2}$ cups cooked; 100g fresh = about 180g cooked; 500g bag fresh [about 4 cups] = about 900g cooked [about 6 cups]
cooked $\frac{1}{8}$"-wide	1 cup cooked (from fresh) = about 140–150g; 100g cooked = about $\frac{2}{3}$–$\frac{3}{4}$ cup
udon noodles	1 cup fresh [about 100g] = about 1 cup cooked [about 125g]; 100g cooked = about $\frac{3}{4}$ cup

   DRIED NOODLES

medium-sized egg noodles	100g dried = about $2\frac{2}{3}$ cups cooked; 4 oz. dried = about 3 cups cooked

---

28g = 1 oz   57g = 2 oz   85g = 3 oz   100g = 3½ oz   113g = 4 oz   142g = 5 oz

pappardelle (UK)	1 pappardelle nest = about 42g; 100g dried = about $2\frac{1}{2}$ nests; 250g packet contains 6 dried nests
rice sticks ($\frac{1}{4}$" wide noodles)	250g dried = about 475g cooked [about $2\frac{3}{4}$ cups], so figure the cooked weight = about double the dried weight; 1 cup cooked = about 155–180g; 100g cooked = about $\frac{1}{2}$–$\frac{2}{3}$ cup
rice vermicelli*	100g dried [about $1\frac{3}{4}$–$2\frac{1}{4}$ cups] = about $1\frac{2}{3}$–$1\frac{3}{4}$ cups soaked [about 145–180g]; 4 oz. dried, broken up vermicelli [about 2–$2\frac{1}{2}$ cups] = about 2 cups soaked [about 175–205g]
spaghetti	100g dried = $1\frac{1}{2}$–$1\frac{3}{4}$ cups cooked; 4 oz. dried = $1\frac{3}{4}$–2 cups cooked

See also **PASTA**.

→ For Shanghai noodles, use the measures given for udon noodles.

→ *Rice vermicelli, also called *sen mee*, are fine rice noodles used in the Thai dish *pad Thai*.

⇨ For information on cooking noodles, see *Pasta & noodles* on page 156 in the *Substitutes & Other Transformations* section.

NUTMEG, GROUND   1 Tbsp. = about 7g;
10g nutmeg = about 4 teaspoons

---

1 US cup = 16 Tbsp.   1 Tbsp. = 3 tsp.   (1 Irish or old English Tbsp. = 4 tsp.)

nuts, *see individual nuts, e.g.,* **PEANUTS, CASHEWS, HAZELNUTS**, etc.

OATS

    OATMEAL*

	coarse [steel-cut oats, US]	1 Tbsp. uncooked = about 8g;
		1 cup uncooked = about 138g;
		10g = about 4 teaspoons;
		100g = about $3/4$ cup
	medium oatmeal	1 cup uncooked = about 145g;
		100g = about $2/3$ cup
ROLLED OATS (old-fashioned)		1 cup uncooked = about 95g

→ *OATMEAL above refers to whole oat grains (groats) that have been cut into pieces — it does not refer to rolled oats or instant oatmeal (in the US, rolled oats are often called 'oatmeal'). Oatmeal comes in a variety of grades in the UK, including fine, medium and, perhaps the most common, coarse or pinhead oatmeal (called steel-cut oats, Scottish oatmeal and Irish oatmeal in the US).

OILS   *olive oil*   1 Tbsp. = about 10g;
                                            50g = 5 Tbsp. [~$1/3$ cup]

→ If you deep-fry in olive oil, you may re-use the oil up to around 5 times. Just strain it and store it in a cool place out of the light such as a cool pantry or cupboard, or garage or fridge. If the oil becomes dark and starts to smell rancid, it's time to get rid of it.

OKRA   *cut into $1/2$–$3/4$" rings*   1 cup rings, 1.3–2cm = 60–65g;
                                                100g rings = about $1\,2/3$ cups;
                                               190g rings = about 3 cups

---

28g = 1 oz   57g = 2 oz   85g = 3 oz   100g = 3½ oz   113g = 4 oz   142g = 5 oz

LIST OF INGREDIENTS   *Page 89*

Coarse or pinhead oatmeal on the left, rolled oats on the right. They are not interchangeable in recipes without first adjusting their cooking times — coarse oatmeal takes much longer to cook than rolled oats, but is worth the time.

	whole pods	250g = about 40 okra pods = about 190g topped & tailed
BABY OKRA	*baby pods*	8 pods, about 28g = about $\frac{1}{3}$ cup; 100g = about $1–1\frac{1}{3}$ cups
PACKAGED	*frozen (US)*	10-oz. pkg. [285g] = about $1\frac{1}{2}$ cups chopped
	canned (US)	$14\frac{1}{2}$-/$15\frac{1}{2}$-oz. can [410/440g] = about $1\frac{3}{4}$ cups

---

1 US cup = 16 Tbsp.   1 Tbsp. = 3 tsp.   (1 Irish or old English Tbsp. = 4 tsp.)

OLIVES, BLACK (ripe)	*chopped*	1 cup chopped olives = about 115g; 100g chopped = about $3/4$–1 cup
	whole, pitted [stoned, UK]	1 cup pitted olives = about 100g
	with pits [stones, UK]	1 cup olives with pits = about 130g or, with pits removed, about $2/3$ cup cut-up pieces [85g]; 100g with pits = about $3/4$ cup, or about $1/2$ cup after pits are removed
BRITISH	*olive halves*	410g tin = about 235g drained
	whole stoned	230g jar = a good cupful, ~100g; 330g jar = $1\,3/4$–2 cups, ~180g
AMERICAN	*chopped*	$4\,1/4$-oz. can [120g] = about $2/3$ cup
	sliced	$2\,1/4$-oz. can [64g] = about $1/2$ cup
	whole pitted medium olives	6-oz. can [170g] = about 55 olives
	whole pitted colossal olives	$5\,3/4$-oz. can [163g] = about 25 colossal olives
	whole pitted super-colossal	$5\,3/4$-oz. can [163g] = about 18 super-colossal olives

(Source for American measures: Ostmann & Baker.)

OLIVES, GREEN [Spanish, US]

chopped/sliced stuffed olives	1 cup chopped/sliced = about 120g; 100g = $3/4$–1 cup
whole green, stuffed	1 cup stuffed olives = about 125g; 100g = a good $3/4$ cup
olive tapenade (bottled)	$1/3$ cup tapenade = about 65g; 100g = about 8 Tbsp. [$1/2$ cup]

28g = 1 oz   57g = 2 oz   85g = 3 oz   100g = 3½ oz   113g = 4 oz   142g = 5 oz

LIST OF INGREDIENTS *Page 91*

BRITISH		290g jar = about $1\frac{1}{3}$–$1\frac{1}{2}$ cups olives, about 175g drained
AMERICAN	*Spanish, stuffed*	7-oz. jar [200g] = about 65 olives
	Spanish, with pits	5-oz. jar [140g] = about 20 olives

(Source for American measures: Ostmann & Baker.)

ONIONS	*grated*	1 cup grated = about 160g (about 1 onion, $2\frac{3}{4}$–3"); 100g grated = about 10 Tbsp. [$\frac{1}{2}$ cup plus 2 Tbsp.]
	chopped	1 cup chopped = about 115g, (about $\frac{2}{3}$ of an onion, $2\frac{3}{4}$"); 100g chopped = about 13–14 Tbsp. [1 cup minus 2–3 Tbsp.]
	sliced	1 cup sliced = 130–160g; 100g sliced = about 10–13 Tbsp. [$\frac{1}{2}$ cup plus 2–5 Tbsp.]
SMALL, $1\frac{1}{4}$" [3cm]		1 small, unpeeled = about 50g; 100g = 2 small onions
MEDIUM, $2\frac{1}{2}$" [6.5cm]		1 medium, unpeeled = 115–140g; 100g = $\frac{3}{4}$ medium onion; 4 unpeeled, about 570g = about 510g peeled = about $4\frac{1}{3}$ cups chopped
MEDIUM-LARGE, 3" [7.5cm]		1 unpeeled = about 170–185g; 100g = $\frac{1}{2}$–$\frac{2}{3}$ medium-large onion; 185g unpeeled = about 175g peeled = about $1\frac{1}{2}$ cups chopped = $1\frac{1}{3}$–$1\frac{1}{2}$ cups sliced *(more overleaf)*

---

1 US cup = 16 Tbsp.   1 Tbsp. = 3 tsp.   (1 Irish or old English Tbsp. = 4 tsp.)

COCKTAIL ONIONS [pearl or baby onions, US]
    whole 1 cup = about 115g;
        100g = about $3/4$–1 cup

WHOLE PICKLING ONIONS [small white boiling onions, US]
    whole 1 cup = 11–12 onions = 115–140g;
        100g = about 8–10 pickling onions

AMERICAN ONIONS & ONION PRODUCTS
 white or yellow onions, fresh 1 lb. = 2 large or 3 med. US onions
    onion powder $1/2$ Tbsp. onion powder = about 5g

➔ Equivalents: $1/2$ Tbsp. onion powder is equal in potency to 1 small onion. One Tbsp. dehydrated minced onion is, after rehydrating, equal to $1/4$ cup [4 Tbsp.] minced fresh onion, or about 1 small onion.

ORANGE JUICE CONCENTRATE $1/4$ cup concentrate [60ml],
          reconstituted = 1 cup [240ml]
    frozen can* (US) 12-fl.-oz. can [360ml] = 6 cups
          reconstituted [1.4L / $2\frac{1}{2}$ UK pints];
          6-fl.-oz. can [180ml] = 3 cups
          reconstituted [700ml / $1\frac{1}{4}$ UK pints]

➔ *To reconstitute: add 3 cans cold water to the can of concentrate.
➔ Frozen concentrated orange juice is not something easily found in the UK — Sainsbury's carried it briefly in the 1990s but I've not seen it here since. High-juice orange squash is probably our closest equivalent, although that is only about 40% juice.

ORANGES   *fresh zest* 1 Tbsp. weighs between 6–11g
       dried zest 1 Tbsp. dried zest (from 1 orange)
          didn't even register 1 gram

28g = 1 oz 57g = 2 oz 85g = 3 oz 100g = 3½ oz 113g = 4 oz 142g = 5 oz

LIST OF INGREDIENTS

MEDIUM		*whole*	1 medium = about 155–230g
		juiced	1 med. orange yields about 75–120ml juice [5–8 Tbsp; $1/3$–$1/2$ cup]
		grated peel (zest)	according to many sources, the zest from one medium orange = 1–3 Tbsp, but I've found it to be closer to 1–$1\frac{1}{2}$ Tbsp.
MEDIUM-LARGE		*whole*	1 medium-large = about 265–300g, and measures about 3" [7.5cm]
		juiced	1 medium-large orange yields about 150ml juice [$1/4$ UK pint; $2/3$ cup]
		grated peel (zest)	1 medium-large orange yields about $1\frac{1}{2}$ Tbsp. zest
MANDARIN ORANGES		*tinned*	1 cup segments = about 150g; 100g = about $2/3$ cup
		(UK)	312g tin = about $1\frac{1}{4}$ cups segments (175–185g), and $3/4$–1 cup syrup
		(US)	11-oz. can [310g] = about $1\frac{1}{4}$ cups; 15-oz. can [425g] = about $1\frac{3}{4}$ cups

See also **CLEMENTINES** and **SATSUMAS**.

OREGANO	*dried, crumbled*	1 Tbsp. = 1–2g; $1/4$ cup [4 Tbsp.] = about 7g

---

OYSTERS	*tinned smoked (UK)*	$1/3$ cup = 5 small oysters = about 55–60g
	fresh shucked (US)	100g shucked = about $1/3$–$1/2$ cup; 1 lb. shucked = about 2 cups

---

1 US cup = 16 Tbsp.   1 Tbsp. = 3 tsp.   (1 Irish or old English Tbsp. = 4 tsp.)

PAK CHOI [bok choy, US]		4 small bunches = about 150g; 100g = $2\frac{1}{2}$–3 small bunches
PAPAYAS	*fresh (US)*	1 medium = about 1 lb; 100g = about $\frac{1}{4}$ papaya
	crystallised chunks (UK)	1 cup crystallised = about 135g; 100g = about $\frac{3}{4}$ cup
PAPRIKA [*pimentón*, Spain]		1 Tbsp. = 5–6g
Parmesan, *see* **CHEESE**		
PARSLEY		
FRESH	*finely chopped*	1 Tbsp. chopped = 1.5–2g; 1 cup finely chopped in blender = about 26g; 10g chopped = about 6 Tbsp.
	stalks & leaves	28g stalks & leaves yield $\frac{1}{3}$ cup finely chopped leaves [~10g]
DRIED	*parsley flakes*	1 Tbsp. dried = about 1.5g; $\frac{1}{4}$ cup [4 Tbsp.] = about 6g
PARSNIPS	*cut up (UK)*	1 cup cork-sized pieces = about 105–125g
	medium, 7" (UK)	1 parsnip, 18cm = about 190–280g; 4 medium parsnips = about 950g [2 lb., 2 oz.]; 100g = about $\frac{1}{2}$ medium parsnip

LIST OF INGREDIENTS *Page 95*

unpeeled to peeled (UK)	4 medium parsnips [950g] = about 775g peeled & trimmed = about $6\frac{1}{2}$–$7\frac{1}{2}$ cups cork-sized pieces
medium (US)	4 medium parsnips = 1 pound = $2\frac{1}{2}$ cups cooked, chopped

→ How long have they spent in storage? The weight of a parsnip varies according to how fresh it is — if it's spent months in storage, it will have lost moisture and weight. Fresh 7-inch parsnips bought in season (autumn-winter) weighed about 200–300g each, whilst *two* parsnips, bought in June (so they'll have spent some months in storage), weighed 240g — about 120g each, so you can see how much moisture-weight can leach out over time. Also notice above the difference between the UK and US weights of parsnips; the UK ones I weighed myself in late autumn whilst the US weight is from a book (and more than one book gives this weight). Either the American ones are thinner and/or shorter or have spent longer in storage — or a bit of both.

→ I don't know why but parsnips are to the US what cranberries are to the UK — they show up around Thanksgiving/Christmas time, and then they pretty much disappear from the shelves.

PASTA SHAPES	*fusilli* (UK)*	1 cup dried [~65g] = $1\frac{3}{4}$ cups plus 2 Tbsp. cooked [~145g]; 100g dried [about $1\frac{1}{2}$ cups] = $2\frac{3}{4}$ cups plus 2 Tbsp. cooked [~220g]; 1 cup cooked fusilli = 75–80g; 100g cooked = about $1\frac{1}{4}$ cups *(more on pasta, overleaf)*

1 US cup = 16 Tbsp.   1 Tbsp. = 3 tsp.   (1 Irish or old English Tbsp. = 4 tsp.)

macaroni (US)	1 cup dried [115–120g] = $2\frac{1}{3}$ cups plus 1 Tbsp. cooked [275–290g]; 100g dried [$\frac{3}{4}$ cup plus 2 Tbsp.] = about 2 cups cooked [230–240g]; 1 cup cooked macaroni = 115–120g; 100g cooked = ~$\frac{3}{4}$ cup & 2 Tbsp.
penne** (UK)	1 cup dried 'quills' [80–90g] = $1\frac{3}{4}$–2 cups cooked [170–190g]; 100g dried [about $1\frac{1}{4}$ cups] = 2–$2\frac{1}{2}$ cups cooked [210–235g]; 1 cup cooked penne = 90–95g; 100g cooked = ~1 cup & 2 Tbsp.

See also **NOODLES**.

→ For shells and bows [farfalle], use the measures given for fusilli.

→ *Fusilli is a spiralled spaghetti, similar to spirals [gemelli, US] and to rotini [corkscrew], but rotini are fatter than fusilli.

→ **Penne are diagonally cut tubes of pasta, called mostaccioli in the US, and quills in Canada.

⇨ For information on cooking pasta, see *Pasta & noodles* on page 156 in the *Substitutes & Other Transformations* section.

PASTRY, FILO [phyllo, US]
    BRITISH FILO PASTRY SHEETS
        frozen   270g packet holds 6 sheets, 500 x 240mm each [20" x 10"]
    AMERICAN PHYLLO DOUGH SHEETS AND SHELLS
        frozen (Pepperidge Farms)   1-lb. pkg. contains 22 sheets, 14" x 18" each [355 x 455mm]

28g = 1 oz   57g = 2 oz   85g = 3 oz   100g = 3½ oz   113g = 4 oz   142g = 5 oz

LIST OF INGREDIENTS *Page 97*

	frozen (Athens brand)	1-lb. pkg. contains 40 'fillo' sheets, 9" x 14" each [230 x 355mm], with 20 sheets per twin-pack roll
	frozen shells (Athens brand)	2.1-oz. freezer box [60g] contains 15 baked 'mini fillo shells'

PASTRY, PUFF

BRITISH	*frozen blocks*	1kg freezer packet holds two 500g blocks of pastry dough for rolling
AMERICAN	*frozen sheets*	17.3-oz. package [490g] holds 2 ready-to-bake sheets
	frozen shells	10-oz. package [285g] contains 6 ready-to-bake shells

---

PASTRY, SHORTCRUST [pie dough, US]

BRITISH	*frozen blocks*	1kg packet holds two 500g blocks of shortcrust pastry for rolling — enough for four 8" or three 9" single-crust pies [20.5/23cm]
AMERICAN	*frozen crusts*	10-oz. package [285g] contains two 9" ready-made pie crusts [23cm]; 12-oz. package [340g] contains two 9" deep-dish pie crusts
	refrigerated crusts	15-oz. package [425g] contains two 9" ready-made pie crusts

⇨To make your own shortcrust pastry [pie dough, US], see *Shortcrust Pastry* on page 161 in the *Substitutes & Other Transformations* section.

---

1 US cup = 16 Tbsp.   1 Tbsp. = 3 tsp.   (1 Irish or old English Tbsp. = 4 tsp.)

PASTRY, STRUDEL

Although some recipes call for ready-made strudel pastry dough (or 'strudel leaves'), I have not found strudel leaves in either British or American supermarkets or shops. Prepared strudels, yes, but not the raw pastry dough with which to make one. Use filo [phyllo] pastry dough instead.

PEACHES		
	sliced	1 cup slices = about 165–190g; 100g slices = about $1/2$–$2/3$ cup
	medium, $2\frac{1}{2}$" (UK)	1 peach, 6.5cm = about 160g = about $2/3$–$3/4$ cup blanched, stoned, sliced [about 125g]; 3 peaches [6.5cm] = 450–500g = about $2\frac{1}{2}$–$2\frac{2}{3}$ cups blanched, stoned, sliced [about 410g]
	medium (US)	1 lb. = 3–4 medium
	canned (US)	16-oz. can [454g] = 6–10 halves or 2 cups sliced

---

PEANUT BUTTER   1 cup = about 225g;
100g = about 7 Tbsp. [$1/2$ cup minus 1 Tbsp.]

→ To make from scratch: 2 cups peanuts will make about 1 cup peanut butter.

PEANUTS		
	finely chopped	1 cup = about 100g
	whole	1 cup = about 135g; 100g = about $3/4$ cup

28g = 1 oz   57g = 2 oz   85g = 3 oz   100g = 3½ oz   113g = 4 oz   142g = 5 oz

LIST OF INGREDIENTS *Page 99*

	in shell	1 lb. in shell = 2–2¼ cups peanuts

PEARL BARLEY [barley, US]   1 cup dried = about 185g;
100g = a good ½ cup

PEARS   *Conference pears (UK)*   1 medium = about 155–190g;
3 medium = about 465–565g
[1–1¼ lb.];
4 small = about 360–480g
[¾–1 lb.]

medium pears (US)   1 pound = about 3 medium pears = about 2 cups sliced or chopped

canned (US)   16-oz. can [454g] contains about 6–10 halves

DRIED   *'ready-to-eat'*   1 cup, fully packed = about 165g;
100g dried = about ⅔ cup;
1 lb. dried pears = about 3 cups

PEAS   *fresh, shelled*   1 cup shelled = about 155g;
100g = about ⅔ cup

fresh, in pod   1 lb. in pod = about 1 cup shelled

frozen   1 cup frozen = about 125g;
100g = about ¾ cup

frozen box (US)   10-oz. box [283g] contains about 1½–2 cups

canned (US)   15-/17-oz. can [425–480g] contains 1¾–2 cups

(more on peas, overleaf)

---

1 US cup = 16 Tbsp.   1 Tbsp. = 3 tsp.   (1 Irish or old English Tbsp. = 4 tsp.)

	DRIED	1 cup dried peas = about 170g; 100g dried = $9\frac{1}{2}$ Tbsp. [$\frac{1}{2}$ cup plus $1\frac{1}{2}$ Tbsp.]
PECANS	*chopped*	1 cup chopped = about 105g
	pecan halves	1 cup halves = about 115g; 100g = $\frac{3}{4}$ cup plus 2 Tbsp; 1 lb. halves = about 4 cups
	in shell	100g in shell = about $\frac{1}{2}$ cup pecans; 1 lb. in shell = $2-2\frac{1}{4}$ cups pecans

PEPPERS, SWEET — FRESH [bell peppers, US]

	finely chopped	1 cup finely chopped = about 110g; 100g = $\frac{3}{4}$ cup plus $1\frac{1}{2}$ Tbsp.
	thinly sliced	1 cup thinly sliced = about 75g; 100g sliced = about $1\frac{1}{3}$ cups
	medium, $3\frac{1}{2}$" long x $2\frac{5}{8}$"	1 medium pepper, 9 x 7cm [125g] = 1 cup finely chopped [110g]
	large (US)	1 large = about 6–8 oz. [170–225g] = $1\frac{1}{3}$–$1\frac{2}{3}$ cups chopped

⇨ For the roasted & peeled red peppers sold in jars, see **PIMIENTOS**.

PEPPERCORNS	*whole black*	1 Tbsp. = about 8g; $\frac{1}{4}$ cup = about 31g; 50g = about $6\frac{1}{2}$ Tbsp.
	ground black	1 Tbsp. = about 7g; $\frac{1}{4}$ cup = about 28g; 50g = about $6\frac{1}{4}$ Tbsp.

28g = 1 oz   57g = 2 oz   85g = 3 oz   100g = 3½ oz   113g = 4 oz   142g = 5 oz

LIST OF INGREDIENTS *Page 101*

SZECHUAN PEPPERCORNS		1 Tbsp. = about 2.5g; 10g = about $3\frac{1}{2}$ Tbsp.
GREEN PEPPERCORNS	*in brine in jar*	1 Tbsp. = about 11g; 50g = about $4\frac{1}{2}$ Tbsp.

PEPPERONI $1\frac{1}{2}$" thick x $1\frac{1}{2}$" long piece of pepperoni [4 x 4cm] = about 60g = about 30 thin slices

---

PESTO $\frac{1}{4}$ cup [4 Tbsp.] = about 50g

PICKLES *whole gherkin* one $2\frac{1}{4}$" gherkin [5.5cm] = about 20g = about 3 Tbsp. sliced

sliced gherkin $\frac{1}{4}$ cup [4 Tbsp.] sliced = about 25g; 10g sliced = about $1\frac{1}{2}$ Tbsp.

---

pickled vegetables, *see* **PRESERVED VEGETABLES**

---

pie crusts and **pie dough**, *see* **PASTRY, FILO** [phyllo]; **PASTRY, PUFF**; **PASTRY, SHORTCRUST**

pie crusts *see also* **BISCUIT BASE** [cookie-crumb crust]

PIMIENTOS *roasted, in a jar* $\frac{1}{2}$ cup chopped = about 80–95g; 100g chopped = about $\frac{1}{2}$ cup

(US) 2-oz. jar [60g] = about $\frac{1}{4}$ cup finely chopped or sliced;

(more on pimientos, overleaf)

---

1 US cup = 16 Tbsp.   1 Tbsp. = 3 tsp.   (1 Irish or old English Tbsp. = 4 tsp.)

(US), cont.   4-oz. jar [115g] = about $\frac{1}{2}$ cup finely chopped or sliced

⇨ For fresh sweet peppers, see **PEPPERS, SWEET — FRESH**.

PINE NUTS $\frac{1}{2}$ cup = about 65g; 100g = about $\frac{3}{4}$ cup

---

PINEAPPLE

FRESH	*cubed*	1 cup cubed = about 125–150g; 100g cubed = about $\frac{2}{3}$–$\frac{3}{4}$ cup
	whole	one medium = about 1.1–1.8kg [$2\frac{1}{2}$–4 lb.]
	1 whole, cut into cubes	a 1.2kg pineapple = about 4 cups cubes [565g]; a 1.6kg pineapple [$3\frac{1}{2}$ lb.] = about 5–6 cups cubes
	whole, unpeeled to peeled	the peeled, cored weight will likely be less than half the unpeeled weight: a 1.2kg pineapple [$2\frac{3}{4}$ lb.], peeled & cored = about 565g [$1\frac{1}{4}$ lb.]
TINNED	*rings, $\frac{3}{8}$″ thick*	4 rings, 1cm thick = 140–150g; 100g = $2\frac{1}{2}$–3 rings
	cut into cubes	4 rings = about 1 cup cubes; 100g cubes = about $\frac{2}{3}$ cup
	(UK)	220g tin contains 4 rings
	(US)	8-oz. can [227g] contains 4 rings; 20-oz. can [570g] contains 10 rings

---

28g = 1 oz   57g = 2 oz   85g = 3 oz   100g = 3½ oz   113g = 4 oz   142g = 5 oz

LIST OF INGREDIENTS

PLUMS	*sliced*	1 cup sliced plums = about 155–165g; 100g sliced = a scant $^2/_3$ cup
BRITISH	*stoned & sliced*	450g small plums (greengage, Victorias, opals) = about 420–425g, stoned = about $2^1/_3$–$2^1/_2$ cups sliced
	fresh damson plums	damsons are very small plums: 1 damson = about 6–10g; 100g = $^3/_4$–1 cup or about 12–13 damsons; 1 UK pint [$2^1/_2$ cups] = about 290g damsons or about 35–36 damsons
	fresh greengage plums	1 greengage = about 27–38g; 100g = about $2^1/_2$–4 greengages; 1 lb. = about 12–16 greengages
	fresh opal plums	1 opal plum = about 31–44g; 100g = about 2–3 opals; 1 lb. = about 10–14 opal plums
	fresh Victoria plums	1 Victoria = about 40–50g; 100g = about 2–3 Victorias; 1 UK pint [$2^1/_2$ cups] = about 7 Victorias [300–340g]; 1 lb. = about 7–10 Victorias (about 10 on average)
AMERICAN	*fresh*	1 pound = about 6–8 large plums
	canned	$15^1/_2$-/16-oz. can [440-454g] = 9 med. plums or 3 cups sliced

(more on plums, overleaf)

---

1 US cup = 16 Tbsp.   1 Tbsp. = 3 tsp.   (1 Irish or old English Tbsp. = 4 tsp.)

Measurements for Cooking

28g = 1 oz   57g = 2 oz   85g = 3 oz   100g = 3½ oz   113g = 4 oz   142g = 5 oz

LIST OF INGREDIENTS *Page 105*

→ The above weights & sizes of these plums are just an average. Some smaller greengage plums bought later in the season had 21 plums to the pound, and some damsons on Derby Market were nearly as small as grapes, so treat the above as only a very rough guide.

→ Greengages and opals are both similar in size to Victorias but, as of this writing, cost about half as much.

polenta, *see* **CORNMEAL**

POMEGRANATES	*whole (US)*	1 medium = about 4 oz. [115g]
	seeds (US)	1 medium = $\frac{1}{2}$–$\frac{3}{4}$ cup seeds

POPCORN	*unpopped kernels*	$\frac{1}{3}$ cup kernels = about 60g; 100g = about $\frac{1}{2}$ cup kernels
	unpopped to popped	$\frac{1}{3}$ cup unpopped [60g] = about 7–8 cups popped (*see photo, page 104*)
	popped	50g popped = 7–8 cups [1.7–2L]; 1 litre popped = about 27g

→ In 2010, an article in the *Times* about cinema snacks, reported that a large 'salted' popcorn had 1,779 calories [kcal], but this is

(see overleaf)

Top photo: *A selection of British plums: greengages on left and opals on right — about $1\frac{1}{4}$–$1\frac{1}{2}$" wide [4cm], and tiny damsons below.*
Bottom photo: *$\frac{1}{3}$ cup popcorn kernels yields about 7–8 cups popped corn which, if dry-popped, has about 190 calories (before butter is added, that is — read note, above).*

---

1 US cup = 16 Tbsp. 1 Tbsp. = 3 tsp. (1 Irish or old English Tbsp. = 4 tsp.)

misleading. The *Joy of Cooking* says one cup of *un*buttered popped popcorn [240ml] has 25 calories. By extension, one British gallon of unbuttered popcorn [4.55 litres] has 474 calories. So if one tub of cinema popcorn is roughly one Imperial gallon, that means the remaining 1,305 calories are from the fat, used in the cooking process and/or poured over the popcorn. One tablespoon butter [15g] = about 100 calories, so 1,305 calories equals about $^3/_4$ cup butter (or other fat — I expect they use something cheaper than butter). The *Times* article's implication was that we have been wrong in viewing popcorn as a low-calorie food but the truth is that any enormous amount of a low-calorie food which is then processed in fat and/or drowned in fat will no longer be low in calories.

POPPY SEEDS		1 Tbsp. = 7–8g; $^1/_4$ cup = about 30g; 50g = 6 Tbsp. plus 2 teaspoons
POTATOES		1 lb. unpeeled = 3 cups peeled, grated [about 400g]
	raw, grated	1 cup grated = about 135g; 100g grated = about $^3/_4$ cup
	raw, thinly sliced	1 cup thinly sliced = 110–125g; 100g thinly sliced = $^3/_4$–1 cup; 1 lb. thinly sliced = about $3^3/_4$ cups
	raw, $^3/_8$" cubes	1 cup cubes [0.9cm] = about 140g; 100g cubes = about $^2/_3$–$^3/_4$ cup
	cooked, mashed	1 lb. cooked = 2 cups mashed; 100g cooked = scant $^1/_2$ cup mashed

---

28g = 1 oz   57g = 2 oz   85g = 3 oz   100g = 3½ oz   113g = 4 oz   142g = 5 oz

LIST OF INGREDIENTS

BRITISH WHOLE POTATOES

Wilja potatoes, $2\frac{1}{4}$–$2\frac{1}{2}$"	1 lb. = 4 medium [5.5–6.5cm]; 100g = about 1 medium Wilja
baking potatoes, 3 x 4"	1 potato, 7.5 x 10cm = 370–400g
small new potatoes	1 lb. small = about $3\frac{1}{3}$–$3\frac{1}{2}$ cups; 100g small = about $\frac{3}{4}$ cup
tiny potatoes, 1–$1\frac{1}{2}$"	1 lb. = about 21 potatoes, 2.5–4cm; 100g = about 4–5 tiny potatoes

AMERICAN WHOLE POTATOES

red potatoes	1 lb. = 4 medium
white potatoes	1 lb. = 3 medium
baking potatoes	1 lb. = 1 large baking potato

PACKAGED POTATO PRODUCTS

dried potato flakes (US)	$\frac{1}{3}$ cup flakes makes about $\frac{1}{2}$ cup mashed

(Source for American measures: Ostmann & Baker.)

POTATOES, SWEET		
	sliced	1 cup thinly sliced = about 135g; 100g thinly sliced = about $\frac{3}{4}$ cup
	$\frac{1}{2}$" cubes	1 cup cubes [1.3cm] = about 115g; 100g = about $\frac{3}{4}$–1 cup cubes
	whole, medium	1 medium = about 230g; 100g = $\frac{1}{2}$–$\frac{2}{3}$ medium; 1 lb.= 2 medium
	whole, large, $4\frac{1}{2}$" x 3"	1 large, 11 x 7cm = about 330g; 100g = $\frac{1}{3}$ large sweet potato; 1 lb. = $1\frac{1}{3}$ large

---

1 US cup = 16 Tbsp.   1 Tbsp. = 3 tsp.   (1 Irish or old English Tbsp. = 4 tsp.)

POULTRY	*cooked, chopped*	100g = about $2/3$ cup chopped; 1 lb. = about 3 cups chopped chicken or turkey
	chicken breast (UK)	1 breast [140g] = about $3/4$–1 cup cubed
	chicken breast (US)*	1 whole breast [285g] = about $1\,1/2$–2 cups cubed
	whole chicken	$2\,1/2$–$3\,1/2$-lb. chicken [1.1–1.6kg] = about $2\,1/2$–3 cups cooked meat (cubed or chopped); 4–5-lb. chicken [1.8–2.3kg] = about 5 cups cooked meat (cubed or chopped)
	chicken livers, cut-up	1 cup chicken livers = about 235g; 100g livers = $1/2$ cup minus 1 Tbsp.

➔ *In the US, with poultry (e.g., chicken), 'breast' traditionally refers to the upper front of their body and a 'whole breast' is comprised of both sides of their upper front whilst a half-breast is just one side. It's important to know this when ordering chicken breasts from a butcher to avoid ending up with twice the amount you intended.

---

prawns, *see* **SHRIMPS & PRAWNS**

PRESERVED VEGETABLES

preserved Chinese vegetable   1 Tbsp. = about 7g;
$1/4$ cup = about 30g;
50g = $1/2$ cup minus 1 Tbsp.

➔ Preserved Chinese vegetable is preserved cabbage.

28g = 1 oz   57g = 2 oz   85g = 3 oz   100g = 3½ oz   113g = 4 oz   142g = 5 oz

LIST OF INGREDIENTS

PRESERVES 1 Tbsp. = about 18g
100g = about $\frac{1}{3}$ cup;
1 cup = about 290g

→ Preserves include things like jams, jellies, marmalades, chutneys.

---

prosciutto, *see* **BACON & HAM**

PRUNES [sometimes called dried plums in the US]

pitted [stoned] 100g pitted prunes = 12–13 prunes = $\frac{3}{4}$ cup

with pits, then pitted 1 cup large prunes with pits [145g] = scant cup pitted [110g]; 100g with stones = about $\frac{1}{2}$ cup stoned [about 75g]

packaged, with pits (UK) 250g packet = about 23 large prunes or a heaped $1\frac{1}{2}$ cups = $1\frac{1}{2}$ cups pitted, about 200g

packaged, pitted (US) 12-oz. package [340g] = about 54 pitted prunes or $2\frac{1}{2}$ cups

---

pudding, vanilla, *see* **CUSTARD**

---

puff pastry, *see* **PASTRY, PUFF**

PUMPKIN SEEDS 1 Tbsp. = about 9g;
$\frac{1}{2}$ cup = about 70g;
10g = about $3\frac{1}{2}$ teaspoons;
50g = 5 Tbsp. plus 2 teaspoons

---

1 US cup = 16 Tbsp.   1 Tbsp. = 3 tsp.   (1 Irish or old English Tbsp. = 4 tsp.)

PUMPKINS & WINTER SQUASH

PUMPKIN	$\frac{1}{2}$" cubes	1 cup cubes [1.3cm] = 115–135g; 100g peeled = $\frac{3}{4}$–1 cup cubes
	large chunk, 4" x 7"	1 unpeeled 480g chunk [10cm x 18cm] = about 400g peeled = about $3\frac{1}{2}$ cups cubes
	whole, $8\frac{1}{2}$" x $6\frac{1}{2}$" (UK)	1 pumpkin, 21.5cm x 16.5cm = about 3.9kg [$8\frac{1}{2}$ lb.]
	whole, medium (US)	1 medium pumpkin weighs about 3–5 lb. [1.4–2.27kg]
	canned pumpkin puree (US)	15-/16-oz. can [425/455g] contains $1\frac{3}{4}$–2 cups, enough for one 9" pie [23cm]; 29-oz. can [820g] contains about $3\frac{1}{2}$ cups, enough for two 9" pies
WINTER SQUASH	mashed	4 cups peeled cubed winter squash = about 2 cups mashed
	whole butternut squash	1 squash, 970g [2 lb., 2 oz.] = about 670g peeled & seeded [$1\frac{1}{2}$ lb.] = about 5–$5\frac{1}{2}$ cups cubed

---

quark (the cheese, not the meat substitute), *see* **YOGURT**

QUINOA	whole grains	1 cup = about 170g; 100g = $\frac{1}{2}$ cup plus $1\frac{1}{2}$ Tbsp.
	quinoa flakes	1 cup = about 100g

28g = 1 oz   57g = 2 oz   85g = 3 oz   100g = 3½ oz   113g = 4 oz   142g = 5 oz

RADISHES	whole (UK)	100g = 7–8 radishes with tops
	sliced (US)	12 whole radishes (about 1 bunch) = about 1 cup sliced
	Chinese radish	1 large = about 800g [$1^3/_4$ lb.]
	mooli [daikon, US], cut up	1 cup mooli, cut into matchsticks = about 150g;
		100g = about $^2/_3$ cup matchsticks

RAISINS		1 cup = about 140g;
		100g = about $^3/_4$ cup

RASPBERRIES	fresh	1 cup = 120–150g;
		100g = $^2/_3$–1 scant cup;
		1 lb. = 3–$3^3/_4$ cups

→ The weight of raspberries or any berries will vary depending upon how much moisture they hold. One cup of small frozen raspberries I weighed came to just 85g, whilst the frozen raspberries listed in *Food Lover's Companion* work out to 162g/cup; and my fresh raspberries came to 120g/cup, whilst the fresh raspberries listed in *Recipe Writer's Handbook* work out to about 150g/cup – hence the wide range above.

---

redcurrants, *see* **BLACKCURRANTS, REDCURRANTS**

RHUBARB	$^3/_4$" pieces	1 cup of 2cm pieces = 105–110g
	stewed	1 cup stewed = about 195–200g;
		100g stewed = about $^1/_2$ cup;
		(more on rhubarb, overleaf)

---

1 US cup = 16 Tbsp.   1 Tbsp. = 3 tsp.   (1 Irish or old English Tbsp. = 4 tsp.)

Above: 1 lb. British rhubarb stalks (left) = about 4 cups peeled, cut up rhubarb (right). Below: 1 cup uncooked short-grain rice (right) = about $3\frac{1}{2} - 4$ cups cooked rice (left).

28g = 1 oz   57g = 2 oz   85g = 3 oz   100g = 3½ oz   113g = 4 oz   142g = 5 oz

LIST OF INGREDIENTS *Page 113*

	stewed, cont.	1 lb. unpeeled rhubarb = about 2 cups peeled & stewed
	fresh stalks (UK)	1 lb. unpeeled = about 3 stalks = about 4 cups peeled & cut-up (*see photo, page 112*)
	fresh stalks (US)	1 lb. = 4 to 8 stalks
PACKAGED	*frozen (US)*	12-oz. pkg. [340g] = $1\frac{1}{2}$ cups

RICE, BASMATI	*uncooked*	1 cup uncooked = 170–180g; 100g = $\frac{1}{2}$ cup plus 1 Tbsp.
	cooked (absorption method*)	1 cup light fluffy rice = 110–120g, but weights varied (see below); 100g cooked = a generous $\frac{3}{4}$ cup, on average
	uncooked to cooked (absorption method)	1 cup uncooked = on average, $3\frac{1}{2}$–$4\frac{1}{2}$ cooked cups [520–560g] though it can make as much as 5 or even $5\frac{1}{2}$ cups cooked

*This rice was cooked in a soup pot, so not a heavy-based pan.

→ Cooked weights vary depending upon how moist or dry the cooked rice turns out: some drier cooked rice was 105g/cup whilst some moister rice was 155g/cup and higher, and the only difference had been in the pan being used — the cooking times and rice-to-water ratios were the same (heavier-based pans produced moister rice). All the above rice was cooked using 1 part rice to 2 parts water.

⇨ For conversion formulas for uncooked-to-cooked rice and vice versa, see *Rice* on page 158 in the *Substitutes & Other Transformations* section. For how to cook rice, see *Rice, cooking methods* on page 159.

---

1 US cup = 16 Tbsp.   1 Tbsp. = 3 tsp.   (1 Irish or old English Tbsp. = 4 tsp.)

RICE, BROWN	*uncooked*	1 cup uncooked = 190–200g; 100g = about ½ cup
	cooked (absorption method)	1 cup cooked = about 135g; 100g cooked = about ¾ cup
	uncooked to cooked (absorption method)	1 cup uncooked [200g] = 3¼–3⅔ cups cooked [450–500g]; 100g uncooked = about 1⅔–1¾ cups cooked [225–250g]

⇨ For conversion formulas for uncooked-to-cooked rice and vice versa, see *Rice* on page 158 in the *Substitutes & Other Transformations* section. For how to cook rice, see *Rice, cooking methods* on page 159.

RICE, LONG-GRAIN	*uncooked*	1 cup uncooked = about 180g; 100g = ½ cup plus 1 Tbsp.
	cooked (absorption method)	1 cup cooked in pan = 125–140g; 1 cup cooked in rice cooker = 120–125g; 100g cooked = about ¾ cup
	uncooked to cooked (absorption method*)	1 cup uncooked = 4–4⅓ cups cooked in a pan [525–575g], or about 3½ cups cooked in a rice cooker [about 420g]; 100g uncooked = 2–2½ cups cooked

➔ *Both the rice cooked in the pan and the rice cooked in the rice cooker used the absorption method, but the rice cooked in the pan used 1 part rice to 2 parts water, and in the rice cooker used 1 part rice to 1¾ parts water. For how to cook rice, see *Rice, cooking methods* on page 159.

28g = 1 oz 57g = 2 oz 85g = 3 oz 100g = 3½ oz 113g = 4 oz 142g = 5 oz

→ Long-grain rice includes basmati rice and Thai jasmine rice.
See also **RICE, BASMATI**.

⇨ For conversion formulas for uncooked-to-cooked rice and vice versa, see *Rice* on page 158 in the *Substitutes & Other Transformations* section.

RICE, SHORT-GRAIN *uncooked*	1 cup uncooked = 185–190g; 100g = a good $\frac{1}{2}$ cup
cooked (absorption method)	1 cup cooked in pan = 125–140g; 1 cup paella rice cooked in rice cooker = 100–125g; 100g cooked = $\frac{3}{4}$–1 cup
uncooked to cooked (absorption method)	1 cup uncooked = $3\frac{3}{4}$–4 cups cooked in a pan [490–500g], or about $3\frac{1}{2}$ cups cooked in a rice cooker* [about 425g]; 100g uncooked = $1\frac{3}{4}$–$2\frac{1}{4}$ cups cooked

→ *Both the rice cooked in the pan and the rice cooked in the rice cooker used the absorption method, but the rice cooked in the pan used 1 part rice to $1\frac{1}{2}$ parts water, and was cooked the Japanese way, as described in *The Wagamama Cookbook*, whilst the rice cooked in the rice cooker used 1 part rice to $1\frac{3}{4}$ parts water; cooked according to manufacturer's instructions. For how to cook rice, see *Rice, cooking methods* on page 159.

→ Short-grain rice includes risotto [Arborio], arroz Calasparra, paella rice, pudding rice, sushi rice, etc.

(more on rice, overleaf)

---

1 US cup = 16 Tbsp.   1 Tbsp. = 3 tsp.   (1 Irish or old English Tbsp. = 4 tsp.)

⇨ For conversion formulas for uncooked-to-cooked rice and vice versa, see *Rice* on page 158 in the *Substitutes & Other Transformations* section.

---

rice, white, *see* **RICE, BASMATI; RICE, LONG-GRAIN** and **RICE, SHORT-GRAIN**

RICE, WILD *uncooked to cooked*   1 cup uncooked = 3–4 cups cooked; 100ml uncooked = 300–400ml cooked

→ Wild rice is not an actual rice but grains from a marsh grass.

RICE FLAKES   1 cup = about 110g; 100g = 1 cup minus 1½ Tbsp.

Rice Krispies, *see* **CEREALS, BREAKFAST**

ROSEMARY

FRESH	*chopped leaves*	5g fresh leaves [about 4 Tbsp.] = 1½ Tbsp. chopped
	12" sprig [30cm]	1 sprig weighs about 8g; leaves from this sprig = about 5g or about ¼ cup [4 Tbsp.]
DRIED		1 Tbsp. = about 3g

→ As with many herbs, rosemary sprigs can be thinly- or thickly-leaved, so the amount of leaves from one sprig can vary considerably. Use the above measures as a rough guide only.

28g = 1 oz   57g = 2 oz   85g = 3 oz   100g = 3½ oz   113g = 4 oz   142g = 5 oz

LIST OF INGREDIENTS *Page 117*

ROSEHIPS 1 cup, before topping and tailing = about 100g

ROUX *prepared roux* 1 Tbsp. roux = about 15g;
$\frac{1}{4}$ cup [4 Tbsp.] roux = about 58g;
35g roux = about 3 Tbsp.

→ Roux is a cooked flour & butter [or other fat] mixture used for thickening sauces and gravies. Americans use equal volumes of butter & flour for a roux; British cookery books call for equal weights of each, but regardless, it's the amount of flour which will determine the thickness of the sauce: for a medium sauce or gravy, use 2 Tbsp. flour per cup of liquid [240ml]; for a heavy, stiff sauce, use 3 Tbsp.

→ To thicken 1 UK pint hot liquid [$2\frac{1}{2}$ US cups]: make a roux from 30g butter & 30g flour — or use 48g already prepared roux [3 Tbsp. & 1 tsp.], made from equal weights of butter & flour.

→ To thicken 1 US cup hot liquid [240ml]: make a roux made from 2 Tbsp. butter & 2 Tbsp. flour [about 27g butter & 17g flour] — or use 3 Tbsp. already prepared roux [36g], made from equal volumes of butter & flour.

→ To make a roux: melt the butter in a pan, add the flour, and stir for a couple of minutes or until the mixture has lightly browned. Then slowly add the hot liquid and stir to make your gravy or sauce.

---

rutabaga, *see* **SWEDE**

---

1 US cup = 16 Tbsp.   1 Tbsp. = 3 tsp.   (1 Irish or old English Tbsp. = 4 tsp.)

SAFFRON	*packaged (UK)*	the tiny clear plastic boxes hold 1g saffron threads [about 2 tsp.]
	packaged (US)	$1/20$-oz. vial [1.4g] contains about 1 Tbsp. saffron

SAGE		
FRESH	*chopped leaves*	1 Tbsp. = about 1.5g; $\frac{1}{2}$ cup chopped = about 12g
	leaves	$\frac{1}{2}$ cup packed leaves = about 11g; 20g = $3/4$–1 cup = 1 large handful
	7" stalks	1 bushy 18cm stalk = about 15g; leaves from this stalk = about 11g or a fairly packed $\frac{1}{2}$ cup
DRIED	*dried leaves*	1 Tbsp. = about 2g
	rubbed sage (powdered)	1 Tbsp. = about 2.5g

→ With fresh herbs, the weight of one sprig to another, and the number of leaves from the sprigs, can vary considerably so use the weights above as a rough guide only.

SALMON	*tinned (UK)*	comes in 213g tins [160g drained, scant cup] & 418g tins
	canned (US)	comes in 6-oz. cans [170g], about $2/3$ cup; $7\frac{1}{2}$-oz. cans [212g], about 1 cup; and $14^3/_4$-oz. cans [418g], about $1^3/_4$ cups

LIST OF INGREDIENTS

SALMON, SMOKED [lox, US]
    sliced into julienne strips $\frac{1}{4}$ cup [4 Tbsp.] strips = about 45g;
        100g = about $\frac{1}{2}$ cup plus 1 Tbsp.
    packet (UK)   114g packet = $\frac{2}{3}$ cup sliced strips

---

SALT
  FINE   *sea salt*   1 level teaspoon = 5g;
    10g = about 2 teaspoons;
    $\frac{1}{4}$ cup = 60–67g
  COARSE   *sea salt*   1 level teaspoon = 4g;
    10g = about $2\frac{1}{2}$ teaspoons;
    $\frac{1}{4}$ cup = 48–55g
    kosher salt   1 level teaspoon = 3g;
    10g = about $3\frac{1}{3}$–$3\frac{3}{4}$ teaspoons;
    $\frac{1}{4}$ cup = 32–36g
    packaged kosher salt (US)   Diamond Crystal brand comes in 13-oz. containers [368g] and 3-lb. boxes [1.4kg]

→ The current recommended daily limit of salt intake in our diet is 6g, equal to $1\frac{1}{4}$ teaspoons fine salt or 2 teaspoons coarse kosher salt.

SARDINES   *tinned (UK)*   comes in 120g tins, drained weight = about 90g
    canned (US)   comes in $3\frac{3}{4}$-oz. cans [106g] containing about 20 pieces

---

1 US cup = 16 Tbsp.   1 Tbsp. = 3 tsp.   (1 Irish or old English Tbsp. = 4 tsp.)

SAUSAGE, FRESH BRITISH

	average sized	6 sausages = about 290g [10 oz.]; 100g = about 2 avg. sausages; 1 lb. = 9–10 sausages
	slightly larger than average	6 slightly larger sausages = about 350g [$3/4$ lb.]; 100g = about $1\,3/4$ larger sausages; 1 lb. = 7–8 sausages
	fat Cumberland sausages*	6 fat Cumberland sausages = about 660g [$1\,1/2$ lb.]; 100g = about 1 fat sausage; 1 lb. = 4 sausages

→ *These fat Cumberland sausages were about $1\,1/2$" thick x 5–6" long [4cm x 12–15cm], a similar size to Italian sausages sold in the US.

See also **CHORIZO, PEPPERONI**.

---

scallions, *see* **SPRING ONIONS**

SCALLOPS	*bay scallops (US)*	bay scallops are little: 100g = 16–22 bay scallops; 1 lb. = 75–100 bay scallops
	sea scallops (US)	sea scallops are large: 100g = 6–7 sea scallops; 1 lb. = about 30 sea scallops

→ American sea scallops are roughly the same size scallops as those sold by British fishmongers.

---

seafood, *see* **CLAMS, MUSSELS, LOBSTER, SHRIMPS & PRAWNS, &c.**

28g = 1 oz   57g = 2 oz   85g = 3 oz   100g = 3½ oz   113g = 4 oz   142g = 5 oz

LIST OF INGREDIENTS *Page 121*

One bowl of carrageen seaweed (7g), and one semi-closed fistful of carrageen (also 7g). Seven grams carrageen [$1/4$ ounce] is enough to set one recipe carrageen moss pudding: $1 1/2$ UK pints milk [850ml] or about 4 US cups.

SEAWEED

ARAME *(Eisenia bicyclis)*		1 cup = about 21g;
		10g = about $1/2$ cup
	packaged (UK)	50g box contains about $2 1/3$ cups
CARRAGEEN (Irish moss)		1 semi-closed fistful = about 7g
KOMBU	*5" strips*	4 dried 12.5cm strips = about 24g
NORI	*sheets (UK)*	1 sheet = 3–4 g;
		10g = 3 sheets, $8 1/4$ x $7 1/2$"
		[21 x 19cm] or 8 x 8" [20 x 20cm]

---

seeds, *see* **CARAWAY SEEDS, CORIANDER SEEDS,** etc.

1 US cup = 16 Tbsp.   1 Tbsp. = 3 tsp.   (1 Irish or old English Tbsp. = 4 tsp.)

SESAME SEEDS		1 Tbsp. = 8–9g; $\frac{1}{2}$ cup = 70g; 50g = $5\frac{2}{3}$ Tbsp; 100g = about $\frac{3}{4}$ cup
SHALLOTS	*peeled, sliced*	1 Tbsp. sliced = 6–7g; $\frac{1}{3}$ cup sliced = about 35g; 100g sliced = about 1 cup
	finely chopped [minced, US]	1 Tbsp. chopped = about 9–10g; $\frac{1}{3}$ cup finely chopped = about 45g; 100g finely chopped = $\frac{3}{4}$ cup minus 1 Tbsp. [11 Tbsp.]
SMALL ($1-1\frac{1}{4}$")		1 unpeeled shallot, 3cm = 13–14g; 100g = 7–8 small unpeeled shallots
	unpeeled to peeled	114g small, unpeeled = about 100g peeled = 1 cup sliced
MEDIUM		1 medium, unpeeled = 28–31g; 100g = 3–4 medium, unpeeled
LARGE	*unpeeled to peeled*	1 large, unpeeled = about 53g = about 43g peeled = about 5 Tbsp. finely chopped; 100g = $1\frac{3}{4}$–2 large unpeeled shallots = about $\frac{2}{3}$ cup peeled & chopped

shortcrust pastry, *see* **PASTRY, SHORTCRUST**

shortening, *see* **BUTTER, LARD, SUET, SHORTENING**

28g = 1 oz   57g = 2 oz   85g = 3 oz   100g = 3½ oz   113g = 4 oz   142g = 5 oz

LIST OF INGREDIENTS

SHRIMPS & PRAWNS [miniature shrimp & shrimp, US]

    PRAWNS [shrimp, US]

cooked, coarsely chopped	1 cup chopped = about 170g; 100g = $\frac{1}{2}$ cup plus $1\frac{1}{2}$ tbsp.
cooked, whole (UK)	1 cup cooked = about 130g; 100g = about $\frac{3}{4}$ cup
raw to cooked	divide in half your raw unpeeled weight to get your approximate cooked peeled weight

    DRIED SHRIMPS [DRIED MINIATURE SHRIMP, US]

from Oriental grocery store	1 Tbsp. = 4–5g; $\frac{1}{4}$ cup [4 Tbsp.] dried shrimps = about 18g; 10g = about 2 Tbsp.

    AMERICAN SHRIMP COUNTS

miniature shrimp	100g = about 22 miniature; 1 lb. = about 100 miniature
small shrimp	100g = 11 or more small; 1 lb. = 50 or more small
medium shrimp	100g = about 9–11 medium; 1 lb. = 45–50 medium
large shrimp	100g = about 6–8 large; 1 lb. = 31–35 large
extra large shrimp	100g = about 5–7 extra large; 1 lb. = 26–30 extra large
jumbo shrimp	100g = about 4–6 jumbo; 1 lb. = 21–25 jumbo

(more on shrimp, overleaf)

---

1 US cup = 16 Tbsp.   1 Tbsp. = 3 tsp.   (1 Irish or old English Tbsp. = 4 tsp.)

extra jumbo shrimp	100g = about 3–5 extra jumbo; 1 lb. = 16–20 extra jumbo
colossal shrimp	100g = about 2–4 colossal; 1 lb. = 10–15 colossal
extra colossal shrimp	100g = less than 3 extra colossal; 1 lb. = less than 10 extra colossal

→ American shrimp are graded by 'count', that is, the number of shrimp likely to be in a pound, so the smaller the count, the bigger the shrimp. However, depending upon which book or web site you consult, the count can vary considerably. Most of the counts given above are from John Mariani's book *The Encyclopedia of American Food & Drink*, and they are all for unpeeled raw shrimp.

→ Shrimp or prawn — which is it? To the British, they're all prawns, except for the very tiny ones; these, they call 'shrimps' ['minature shrimp', US]. To the Americans, they're all shrimp, but distinguished by a particular size classification (miniature, large, jumbo, etc.).

---

snow peas, *see* **MANGE-TOUT & SUGAR SNAP PEAS**

---

soda, baking *see* **BICARBONATE OF SODA**

SOUP *canned condensed (US)* $10^3/_4$-oz. can [300g] = $1^1/_4$ cups condensed soup = $2^1/_2$ cups reconstituted soup [1 UK pint]

See also **STOCKS, BROTHS, BOUILLONS, CONSOMMÉS**.

28g = 1 oz   57g = 2 oz   85g = 3 oz   100g = 3½ oz   113g = 4 oz   142g = 5 oz

LIST OF INGREDIENTS

soya beans [soybeans, US], *see* **BEANS, SOYA**

---

spelt grains, *see* **WHEAT GRAINS & SPELT GRAINS**

---

spices, *see individual spices, e.g.,* **ALLSPICE, CINNAMON**, etc.

SPINACH	*fresh shredded leaves*	1 cup shredded = 50–60g; 100g shredded = about $1^3/_4$ cups
	fresh whole leaves	50g = 1 scant cup [1 large handful]
	fresh whole leaves & stems	1 lb. with stems = 10–12 cups, stems removed = ~$1^1/_2$ cups cooked = $^1/_2$–$^3/_4$ cup cooked, squeezed dry
FROZEN	*chopped (UK)*	100g frozen = about 43g defrosted and squeezed dry [about $3^1/_4$ Tbsp.]
	packaged chopped (UK)	907g bag = 285g defrosted and squeezed dry [$1^3/_4$ cups]; 1kg bag = 425g defrosted and squeezed dry [2 cups]
	packaged (US)*	10-oz. pkg. [283g] = 1–$1^1/_4$ cups cooked, drained = $^1/_2$ cup plus 1 Tbsp. chopped, squeezed dry
TINNED		1 cup tinned = 220–235g; 100g tinned = scant $^1/_2$ cup
	tinned spinach puree (UK)	395g tin = about $1^3/_4$ cups
	canned spinach (US)	14-oz. can [400g] = about $1^1/_2$ cups

→ *To substitute for a 10-oz. box frozen spinach called for in an American recipe, use 285g frozen, or about 1 lb. fresh, or about 1 cup cooked, or about $^1/_2$ cup cooked, chopped and squeezed dry.

---

1 US cup = 16 Tbsp.   1 Tbsp. = 3 tsp.   (1 Irish or old English Tbsp. = 4 tsp.)

split peas, *see* LENTILS AND SPLIT PEAS

SPRING ONIONS [scallions or green onions, US]
- *finely sliced* — $\frac{1}{2}$ cup finely sliced = about 35g; 10g = about $2-2\frac{1}{2}$ Tbsp.
- *whole* — 1 spring onion = about 15–25g; 1 oz. = 1–2 spring onions; 50g = 2–4 spring onions
- *1 bunch (UK)* — 1 bunch (7–8 spring onions) = about 130–170g

---

sprouts, *see* ALFALFA SPROUTS, BEANSPROUTS, BRUSSELS SPROUTS

SQUASH, SUMMER *fresh* 1 lb. = about 3 medium = about $2\frac{1}{2}-3$ cups sliced; 100g = about $\frac{1}{2}-\frac{2}{3}$ cup sliced

See also **COURGETTES** [zucchini, US].

---

squash, winter, *see* PUMPKINS & WINTER SQUASH

STOCKS, BROTHS, BOUILLONS, CONSOMMÉS
READY-MADE STOCKS & BROTHS
- *chilled fresh (UK)* — comes in 500g pots [about 2 cups]
- *packaged ready-made (UK)* — comes in 500g & 500ml sealed 'bags' [about 2 cups]
- *packaged concentrated (UK)* — comes in 100g sealed 'bags' [about $\frac{1}{2}$ cup] & 160ml sealed 'bags' [about $\frac{2}{3}$ cup]

28g = 1 oz   57g = 2 oz   85g = 3 oz   100g = 3½ oz   113g = 4 oz   142g = 5 oz

canned broth (US)	$14\frac{1}{2}$-fl. oz. can [~400ml / $1\frac{3}{4}$ cups] is the most common size; also comes in $10\frac{1}{2}$-fl.-oz. can [310ml], and 48-/$49\frac{1}{2}$-fl.-oz. can [1.4L]

STOCK CUBES, BOUILLON CUBES & BOUILLON GRANULES

stock cubes (UK)	1 cube will make 500ml stock [about 2 cups]; they come in 66g boxes with 6 cubes, and 80g boxes with 8 cubes
bouillon cubes (US)	1 cube will make 2 cups stock [470ml / about $\frac{3}{4}$ UK pint]; they come in 2.2-oz. boxes [63g] with 6 cubes
bouillon granules (US)	1 level teaspoon granules will make 1 cup bouillon [240ml]; bouillon granules come in a 3.3-oz. container [95g]
beef 'base' (US)	1 level teaspoon beef base will make 1 cup stock [240ml]; it comes in an 8-oz. jar [225g]

→ Canned chicken broth is very common in the US but not in the UK.

→ To make chicken stock, combine in a large pot: 1 chicken carcass (or roasted bones); plus unpeeled cut-up veg such as: 1 large onion, quartered; 2 celery stalks; 1 large carrot; 1 large garlic clove, crushed; 1 well-washed leek; plus seasoning such as: 1 tsp. salt; 2 tsp. dried parsley (or 6 sprigs fresh); $\frac{1}{2}$ tsp. thyme; 1 bay leaf; 6 peppercorns. Add water to cover, bring to boil, then simmer, partially covered 2–3 hours. Let cool then strain through muslin.

---

1 US cup = 16 Tbsp.   1 Tbsp. = 3 tsp.   (1 Irish or old English Tbsp. = 4 tsp.)

stout, *see* BEER & STOUT

STRAWBERRIES	*sliced*	1 cup sliced = about 140g; 100g sliced = about $3/4$ cup
BRITISH	*fresh, whole*	1 cup = about 100g; 1 lb. = 4–$4\frac{1}{2}$ cups average-sized
AMERICAN	*fresh*	1 basket = 1 US dry pint [550ml or ~1 UK pint]
	frozen	10 oz. [285g] = about $1\frac{1}{2}$ cups

STUFFING [dressing, US — also, stuffing]

AMERICAN, PACKAGED   6-oz. pkg. [170g] = about 3 cups

→ When stuffing a bird, figure on about $1/2$ cup of stuffing per pound of poultry [120ml per 450g].

---

suet, *see* BUTTER, LARD, SUET, SHORTENING

SUGAR, BROWN SOFT

	light brown (lt. muscovado)	1 packed cup light = 200–210g; 100g = about $1/2$ cup
	dark brown (dk. muscovado)	1 packed cup dark = 190–200g; 100g = about $1/2$ cup
	molasses sugar	1 packed cup dk. brown molasses sugar = 210–240g; 100g = a $1/2$ cup minus $1/2$–$1\frac{1}{2}$ Tbsp.
PACKAGED	*lt. brown (UK)*	500g box = $2\frac{1}{3}$–$2\frac{1}{2}$ cups firmly packed

---

28g = 1 oz   57g = 2 oz   85g = 3 oz   100g = 3½ oz   113g = 4 oz   142g = 5 oz

LIST OF INGREDIENTS

lt. brown (US)	16-oz. package [454g] = about $2\frac{1}{4}$ cups firmly packed
dk. brown soft sugar (UK)	500g box/bag = $2\frac{1}{2}$–$2\frac{2}{3}$ cups muscovado sugar, firmly packed, or 2–$2\frac{1}{3}$ cups molasses sugar

⇨ For quick volume-to-weight reference, see the **WHITE GRANULATED SUGAR & BROWN SUGAR CHART**, on page 228.

---

sugar, **caster** and **sugar cubes** and **sugar, granulated**, see **SUGAR, WHITE**

---

sugar, confectioners', see **SUGAR, ICING**

SUGAR, ICING [confectioners' sugar, US]

UNSIFTED	(weights will vary)	1 cup unsifted = 130–150g; 100g unsifted = $\frac{2}{3}$–$\frac{3}{4}$ cup
	unsifted to sifted	1 cup unsifted = $1\frac{1}{8}$–$1\frac{1}{4}$ cups sifted; 100g unsifted = $\frac{3}{4}$–$\frac{7}{8}$ cup sifted
	and the reverse	1 cup sifted = $\frac{3}{4}$–$\frac{7}{8}$ cup unsifted; 100g sifted = $\frac{2}{3}$–$\frac{3}{4}$ cup unsifted
SIFTED	(weights will vary)	1 cup sifted = 110–120g; 100g sifted = about $\frac{7}{8}$ cup
PACKAGED	(UK)	500g box = $3\frac{1}{3}$–$3\frac{3}{4}$ cups unsifted, or 4–$4\frac{1}{2}$ cups sifted
	(US)	1-lb. package = 3–$3\frac{1}{2}$ cups unsifted, or $3\frac{3}{4}$–$4\frac{1}{4}$ cups sifted

⇨ Read about icing sugar on page 231 and, for quick reference, refer to the **ICING SUGAR CHART**, on page 232.   *(more overleaf)*

---

1 US cup = 16 Tbsp.   1 Tbsp. = 3 tsp.   (1 Irish or old English Tbsp. = 4 tsp.)

⇨ For conversion formulas for unsifted-to-sifted icing sugar, and vice versa, see *Sugar* on page 161 in the *Substitutes & Other Transformations* section.

---

sugar snap peas, *see* MANGE-TOUT & SUGAR SNAP PEAS

SUGAR, VARIOUS OTHER TYPES

	palm sugar	50g = $1\frac{1}{2}$–$1\frac{3}{4}$" cube [4–4.5cm]
	sliced sugar	2 pieces, 5" x 1" x $\frac{1}{2}$" [12.5 x 2.5 x 1cm] = about 140g

---

SUGAR, WHITE (granulated sugar)

GRANULATED		1 cup = about 200g;
		100g = about $\frac{1}{2}$ cup
	packaged (UK)	500g bag = about $2\frac{1}{2}$ cups
	packaged (US)	1-lb. package = about $2\frac{1}{4}$ cups;
		4-lb. bag [1.8kg] = about 9 cups;
		5-lb. bag [2.27kg] = about $11\frac{1}{4}$ cups
CASTER [superfine, US]		1 cup = about 180g;
		100g = $\frac{1}{2}$ cup & 1 Tbsp.
	packaged (UK)	500g bag = about $2\frac{3}{4}$ cups
SUGAR CUBES		1 Tate & Lyle cube = about 4g;
		1 Silver Spoon cube = about 3g;
		1 American cube = about 4.75g
	10 cubes	10 Tate & Lyle cubes = about 38g or about 3 Tbsp. sugar;
		10 Silver Spoon cubes = about 30g or about $2\frac{1}{2}$ Tbsp. sugar;
		10 American cubes = about 48g or

28g = 1 oz   57g = 2 oz   85g = 3 oz   100g = 3½ oz   113g = 4 oz   142g = 5 oz

packaged (UK)	about ¼ cup sugar [4 Tbsp.] 500g Tate & Lyle box contains 126 cubes; 500g Silver Spoon brand box contains 160 cubes
packaged (US)	16-oz. pkg. [454g] contains 96 cubes

→ Tate & Lyle sugar cubes are ³⁄₄ x ½ x ½ inches [18 x 13 x 13mm]; Silver Spoon cubes are ³⁄₄ x ⁹⁄₁₆ x ⁷⁄₁₆ inches [18 x 14 x 11mm].

⇨ For quick reference on granulated sugar, see the **WHITE GRANULATED SUGAR & BROWN SUGAR CHART** on page 228.

---

sugar, superfine, *see* SUGAR, WHITE

SUGARPASTE ICING [fondant, US]   ¼ cup [4 Tbsp.] = about 85g; 100g = 4½–5 Tbsp.

---

sun-dried tomatoes, *see* TOMATOES

SUNFLOWER SEEDS

1 Tbsp. = 8–9g;
½ cup = about 70g;
100g = about ³⁄₄ cup

SWEDE [rutabaga, US]

         ½" *cubes*   1 cup cubes, 1cm = about 120g;
100g = about ³⁄₄–1 cup cubes;
1 lb. cubes = about 3 ³⁄₄ cups
(more on swede, overleaf)

---

1 US cup = 16 Tbsp.   1 Tbsp. = 3 tsp.   (1 Irish or old English Tbsp. = 4 tsp.)

whole, $3\frac{1}{2}$" wide	1 unpeeled 9cm swede, about 600g = about 435g peeled [$1\frac{1}{4}$ lb. unpeeled to 1 lb. peeled]

sweetcorn, *see* **CORN**

---

sweet potato, *see* **POTATOES, SWEET**

---

sweets [candy, US], *see* **BLACKPOOL ROCK, CHOCOLATE**, etc.

---

taco chips, *see* **TORTILLA CHIPS**

TAHINI (sesame paste)	1 cup = 225g; 100g = $\frac{1}{2}$ cup minus 1 Tbsp.
in jar (UK)	340g jar = $1\frac{1}{2}$ cups, enough for 2 recipes hummus

---

TAMARIND	*dried & compressed*	50g = $1\frac{1}{2}$ x $2\frac{1}{2}$ x $\frac{3}{4}$" block [4 x 6.5 x 2cm]; 100g = 3 x $2\frac{1}{2}$ x $\frac{3}{4}$" block [7.5 x 6.5 x 2cm]

→ Tamarind can be used as a souring agent, or as part of a marinade.

→ To extract tamarind juice: soak a large piece dried tamarind [about 110g] in 1 cup boiling water [240ml] for 15–30 minutes, then mash with a fork or your fingers to make a pulpy sauce. Squeeze through muslin to extract as much juice as possible; discard the seeds & stalks, and reserve the juice.

28g = 1 oz   57g = 2 oz   85g = 3 oz   100g = 3½ oz   113g = 4 oz   142g = 5 oz

TAPIOCA		1 cup = about 150g;
		100g = about $2/3$ cup
	(UK)	500g bag contains $3\frac{1}{3}$ cups
	quick-cooking (US)	8-oz. pkg. [227g] = $1\frac{1}{2}$ cups (or about $3\frac{3}{4}$ cups cooked)

TARRAGON		
FRESH	*leaves*	1 Tbsp. fresh leaves = 1–1.5g;
		10g = about $1/2$ cup
	7" bushy sprigs [18cm]	1 bushy sprig, about 6g = about 4g leaves = about 3 Tbsp;
		2 bushy sprigs, about 15g = about 9g leaves = about $1/2$ cup
DRIED		2 Tbsp. dried* = about 3g;
		10g = about 6–7 Tbsp.

➔ *It's best to use spoon measures when measuring small amounts of dried herbs; 1 Tbsp. dried tarragon registered no weight at all on my digital scale whilst 2 Tbsp. registered 3g.

➔ With fresh herbs, the weight of one sprig to another, and the number of leaves from the sprigs, can vary considerably so use the weights above as a rough guide only.

TEA	*loose tea*	1 teaspoon = about 2g;
		$1/4$ cup [4 Tbsp.] = about 24g;
		10g = about 5 teaspoons

➔ To brew tea: Allow 1 scant tsp. loose tea per cup of water [240ml].

---

1 US cup = 16 Tbsp.   1 Tbsp. = 3 tsp.   (1 Irish or old English Tbsp. = 4 tsp.)

THYME

    FRESH   *leaves*   1 Tbsp. fresh leaves = about 2–3g; 10g leaves = about $4\frac{1}{2}$ Tbsp.

                    7" sprigs [18cm]   10 sprigs [about 10g] = about $3\frac{1}{2}$ Tbsp. picked leaves [about 8g]; 14–15 sprigs [about 15g] = about 5 Tbsp. picked leaves [about 11g]

    DRIED   *dried leaves*   1 Tbsp. dried = about 3g; $\frac{1}{4}$ cup [4 Tbsp.] = about 13g

                    ground (powdered)   1 Tbsp. powdered = about 4–5g

➔ With fresh herbs, the weight of one sprig to another, and the number of leaves from the sprigs, can vary considerably so use the weights above as a rough guide only.

---

tiger lily buds, *see* **GOLDEN NEEDLES**

---

tofu, *see* **BEAN CURD**

TOMATILLOS   *fresh (US)*   1 lb. = about 16 medium

TOMATOES, FRESH

    BRITISH   *chopped*   1 cup chopped = 160–170g; 100g chopped = $\frac{1}{2}$–$\frac{2}{3}$ cup

                    whole, 2" [5cm]   1 med.-small tomato = 65–90g = $\frac{1}{3}$–$\frac{1}{2}$ cup cored, chopped (incl. seeds & peels); 100g med.-small toms = about $\frac{1}{2}$ cup cored, chopped;

28g = 1 oz   57g = 2 oz   85g = 3 oz   100g = 3½ oz   113g = 4 oz   142g = 5 oz

blanched, cored, seeded	1 lb. = about 6 med.-small toms = about $2\frac{1}{2}$ cups cored, chopped 100g tom(s) = about $\frac{1}{3}$ cup blanched, cored, seeded; 6 med.-small toms [455g] = about $1\frac{2}{3}$–$1\frac{3}{4}$ cups blanched, cored, seeded [about 300g]
cherry tomatoes	15 cherry tomatoes = about 170g = 1 heaped cup; 100g = about 8–9 cherry toms
AMERICAN *whole*	1 lb. = 4 small or 3 medium or 2 large US toms

→ When I weighed them, 6 British medium-small tomatoes equalled 1 pound and 3 American medium-small tomatoes equalled 10 ounces — just over $\frac{1}{2}$ pound, but these amounts per pound differ from the US amounts given above (and the US amounts are the standard amounts per lb. given in many American cookery books), so I assume that either what Americans would call small, we would call medium or even medium-large, or else the American toms were more full of juice when weighed, or a bit of both.

TOMATOES, DRIED & SEMI-DRIED ('SUN-BLUSH')

sun-dried (packed in oil)	1 cup (drained) = about 110g; 100g (drained) = 1 cup minus $1\frac{1}{2}$ Tbsp.
sun-dried (packed dried)	1 cup = 60–70g; 100g = $1\frac{1}{2}$–$1\frac{2}{3}$ cups
'sun-blush' tomatoes	*(see note, overleaf)*

---

1 US cup = 16 Tbsp.   1 Tbsp. = 3 tsp.   (1 Irish or old English Tbsp. = 4 tsp.)

⇨Despite being called for in a number of recent British recipes, I've not seen 'sun-blush' tomatoes in British or American supermarkets. To make your own, see *Tomatoes, sun-blushed* on page 162 in the *Substitutes & Other Transformations* section.

TOMATOES, TINNED

BRITISH	*tinned, chopped*	1 cup = about 205–210g; 100g = about $\frac{1}{2}$ cup chopped; 400g tin chopped = $1\frac{3}{4}$–2 cups
	tinned, whole	400g tin whole = about 200g drained = 1–$1\frac{1}{4}$ cups drained
AMERICAN	*canned, whole*	10-oz. can [285g] = 1 cup; $14\frac{1}{2}$/16-oz. can [415/454g] = $1\frac{3}{4}$ to 2 cups
	canned, diced (chopped)	16-oz. can [454g] = 2 cups
	canned, diced or stewed	$14\frac{1}{2}$-oz. can [415g] = $1\frac{1}{2}$ cups

(Source for the American information: Ostmann & Baker.)

TOMATOES: PURÉES, PASTES, SAUCES

KETCHUP & TOMATO PASTE [double-concentrated tom. purée, UK]

	1 Tbsp. = 15g; 10g = 2 teaspoons
dbl-con. tomato purée (UK)	sold in 135g/200g tubes, and in 142g tins
tomato paste (US)	sold in 6-/12-oz. cans [170g/340g], and $4\frac{1}{2}$-oz. tubes [126g], containing about $\frac{1}{3}$ cup per tube
STRAINED TOMATOES *(UK)*	passata is sold in 560g/690g

28g = 1 oz   57g = 2 oz   85g = 3 oz   100g = 3½ oz   113g = 4 oz   142g = 5 oz

tomato puree, canned (US)	bottles, and in 500g boxes sold in 8-oz. [230g], 15-oz. [425g] and 28-/29-oz. [795/820g] cans
tomato sauce, canned (US)	same as for *tomato puree*, above

➜ Strained tomatoes include passata in England, and tomato puree & tomato sauce in the US — American tomato puree is slightly thicker than American tomato sauce (and they drop the accent in puree). In England, 'tomato purée' usually refers to double-concentrated tomato purée [tomato paste, US] and, when you hear 'tomato sauce', they often mean ketchup.

TORTILLA CHIPS   1 cup = about 28g = about 14 tortilla chips; 100g = about $3\frac{1}{2}$ cups chips

---

TORTILLAS

FLOUR	*regular-sized (UK)*	these are about 8" across [20.5cm]; a 320g packet contains 8
	regular-sized (US)	these are about $7\frac{1}{2}$" across [19cm]; an $11\frac{1}{2}$-oz. pkg. [325g] contains 10
	burrito-sized (US)	these are 9" across [23cm]; a 14-oz. pkg. [400g] contains 10
CORN TORTILLAS	*fresh (US)*	these are just $5\frac{1}{2}$" across [14cm]; a 6-oz. pkg. [170g] has 10, and a $27\frac{1}{2}$-oz. pkg. [780g] has 30

TUNA   *tinned (UK)*   1 cup tinned = about 150g; *(more on tuna, overleaf)*

---

1 US cup = 16 Tbsp.   1 Tbsp. = 3 tsp.   (1 Irish or old English Tbsp. = 4 tsp.)

		100g tinned = about $2/3$ cup;
		200g tin = about 140g drained = about 1 cup minus 1 Tbsp.
	canned (US)	6-oz. can [170g] = about $2/3$ cup;
		9-oz. can [255g] = 1 cup;
		12-oz. can [340g] = $1\frac{1}{4}$ cups

turkey, see **MEAT**

TURMERIC

FRESH	*finely sliced*	$\frac{1}{2}$ cup finely sliced = about 45g;
		50g sliced = a $\frac{1}{2}$ cup plus 1 Tbsp.
	finely chopped	$2/3$ cup finely chopped = about 45g;
		50g chopped = about $3/4$ cup
	peeled to unpeeled	60g unpeeled = about 45g peeled;
		100g unpeeled = about 75g peeled
DRIED	*ground*	1 Tbsp. = about 7g

→ If a recipe calls for fresh turmeric and you have none, it's probably best to wait till you can get the fresh turmeric rather than substituting with ground turmeric.

TURNIPS	$\frac{1}{2}$*" cubes [1cm]*	1 very full cup = 115–120g;
		100g cubes = $3/4$–1 scant cup;
		1 med. turnip, cubed = 1–$1\frac{1}{3}$ cups
	whole, 3" x $1\frac{1}{2}$"	1 medium [7.5 x 4cm] = 130–170g;
		1 lb. = about 3 medium

See also **SWEDE**.

28g = 1 oz   57g = 2 oz   85g = 3 oz   100g = 3½ oz   113g = 4 oz   142g = 5 oz

LIST OF INGREDIENTS *Page 139*

vanilla, see *Vanilla* on page 162 in the *Substitutes & Other Transformations* section.

---

vanilla wafers, *see* **BISCUITS; vanilla wafer crust,** *see* **BISCUIT BASE**

WALNUTS	*chopped*	1 cup chopped = 105–130g;
		100g chopped = $^3/_4$–1 cup
	walnut halves	1 cup = 135–145g;
		100g halves = about $^2/_3$–$^3/_4$ cup
	in shell	1 lb. in shell = $1^1/_2$–2 cups walnuts;
		100g in shell = $^1/_3$–$^1/_2$ cup walnuts

WATER CHESTNUTS

	fresh or tinned	100g = about $^2/_3$–$^3/_4$ cup;
		1 lb. = 3–$3^1/_2$ cups
FRESH	*peeled, whole*	4 large = about 65–85g;
		1 cup = about 125g;
		100g = about $^3/_4$–1 cup
TINNED	*peeled, whole*	9 small-to-medium = about $^1/_2$ cup;
		1 cup = about 150g;
		100g = about $^2/_3$ cup

WATERCRESS	*bunch (UK)*	1 average bunch = about 95g
	chopped leaves & stalks	1 cup = about 50g

WHEATGERM		1 Tbsp. = about 7g;
		$^1/_2$ cup = about 55g;
		100g = 1 cup minus $1^1/_2$ Tbsp.

---

1 US cup = 16 Tbsp.   1 Tbsp. = 3 tsp.   (1 Irish or old English Tbsp. = 4 tsp.)

On the left, one cup dried wheat grains and the resulting cooked volume (about 2 cups). On the right, one cup dried spelt grains and the resulting cooked volume (about $2\tfrac{1}{4}$ cups).

WHEAT GRAINS & SPELT GRAINS

dried	1 cup dried grains = 155–170g; 100g dried = about $\tfrac{1}{2}$–$\tfrac{2}{3}$ cup
soaked and cooked	1 cup cooked grains = 135–155g; 100g cooked = about $\tfrac{2}{3}$–$\tfrac{3}{4}$ cup
dried-to-cooked	1 cup dried = about $1\tfrac{1}{2}$–$1\tfrac{3}{4}$ cups soaked = about 2–$2\tfrac{1}{4}$ cups cooked; 100g dried = about 130–150g soaked = about 175–190g cooked; 160–170g dried = about 220–235g soaked = about 300g cooked

---

28g = 1 oz   57g = 2 oz   85g = 3 oz   100g = 3½ oz   113g = 4 oz   142g = 5 oz

LIST OF INGREDIENTS *Page 141*

→ Wheat grains are called wheat berries in the US, and farro in Italy.

→ 1 cup dried wheat grains, soaked and then cooked, will fill about four 200g-sized cream cheese containers (soak the grains overnight, then boil till chewy — takes just a half-hour or so). You can then freeze the wheat grains for using later in recipes, e.g., granary bread; Seeded Soda Bread (page 166); Moosewood's 'Perfect Protein Salad'; rolled cabbage leaves with mushrooms, wheat grains and cheese; etc. If you're cooking for a vegetarian, they add a nice chewy texture to vegetarian dishes.

---

wild rice, *see* **RICE, WILD**

YEAST

FRESH		1 teaspoon fresh = 5g;
		1 scant Tbsp. fresh = 15g
	compressed yeast (US)	1 cake compressed fresh yeast = 17g [0.6 oz.] or about 1 Tbsp.
DRIED	*dried active*	1 teaspoon dried = 3g
		1 Tbsp. dried = 9g;
	packaged (UK & US)	one 7g sachet dried yeast [$\frac{1}{4}$-oz. envelope] contains about $2\frac{1}{4}$ teaspoons

→ Fresh yeast can be very hard to find in the US. In the UK, it is sold in some health food shops and some bakeries. Fresh yeast can be frozen, and it defrosts quickly.

→ If your dried yeast is past its 'best before' date, don't despair — it should still rise your dough, only more slowly.   *(more overleaf)*

---

1 US cup = 16 Tbsp.   1 Tbsp. = 3 tsp.   (1 Irish or old English Tbsp. = 4 tsp.)

When using yeast past its 'best before' date and making bread by hand, leave the dough plenty of time to rise (even overnight if the yeast is fairly old). However, if using a breadmaker, use yeast within its BBE date as breadmakers run on automatic timed settings and old yeast won't have enough time to rise properly.

➡ One packet active dried yeast is equivalent to 1 Tbsp. fresh.

⇨ For additional equivalents and information, see *Yeast* on page 163 in the *Substitutes & Other Transformations* section.

YOGURT, UNFLAVOURED [natural yogurt, UK; plain yogurt, US]

		1 Tbsp. = 13–14g
		1 cup = about 215g;
		100g = a ½ cup minus ½ Tbsp.
BRITISH		sold in 500ml pots [2¼ US cups]
		and in 200ml pots [1 scant US cup]
AMERICAN	*fat-free yogurt*	sold in 8-oz. cartons [230g], about
		1 cup; 24-oz. cartons [680g], about
		3 cups; and 32-oz. round tubs
		[900g], about 4¼ cups

➡ For measuring fromage frais and quark (the cheese), use the above yogurt equivalents.

➡ In both the UK and US, it's now often hard to find yogurts that are *not* the reduced-fat variety, so check to make sure you're buying the sort you want.

---

zucchini, *see* **COURGETTES**

28g = 1 oz   57g = 2 oz   85g = 3 oz   100g = 3½ oz   113g = 4 oz   142g = 5 oz

SUBSTITUTES

SUBSTITUTES & OTHER TRANSFORMATIONS

AGAR AGAR (or simply agar) is a setting agent made from dried seaweed and can withstand simmering and even boiling, unlike gelatine whose setting properties are diminished with too much heat. It sets fairly quickly at room temperature. Two tablespoons agar flakes are equivalent to 2 teaspoons powdered agar, which are equivalent to 2 teaspoons powdered gelatine.

→ To make a soft jelly [jello, US] from agar agar flakes:

- Pour 3 cups liquid [700ml] into a saucepan.
  This can be a mixture of juices and/or diluted squash or cordial, and can include wine (mulled wine and cranberry juice are nice), or a shot of liqueur, if you like.
- Sprinkle over it 2 slightly-rounded Tbsp. agar agar flakes.
  Let stand about 10–15 minutes.
- Place the pan over medium heat and bring to a gentle simmer.
  Let simmer about 10 minutes, until all the flakes have dissolved.
- Strain the mixture, then pour into ramekins or small dishes.
  This soft jelly will, in time, 'weep' its liquid; it also collapses easily when you spoon into it, so individual dishes are better suited than a large bowl.

→ Directions for a very firm jelly that won't weep: use 3 slightly rounded Tbsp. agar flakes in the recipe above but, be warned, it'll be so firm you could just about sculpt it.

→ To set 1 British pint [2½ cups]: use 2 Tbsp. agar flakes or 2 tsp. powdered agar for a fairly firm jelly.

---

1 US cup = 16 Tbsp.   1 Tbsp. = 3 tsp.   (1 Irish or old English Tbsp. = 4 tsp.)

BAKER'S CHOCOLATE SQUARES

➔ To substitute for 1½ squares [42g / 1½ oz.] semisweet chocolate (aka dark chocolate):

use:	• 1 square unsweetened chocolate [28g / 1oz.] plus 4 tsp. sugar [15g / ½ oz.]
or use:	• 3 Tbsp. cocoa powder [~20g / ¾ oz.] plus 1 Tbsp. butter [15g / ½ oz.] plus 4 tsp. sugar [15g / ½ oz.]
or use:	• 3 Tbsp. carob powder [~20g / ¾ oz.] plus 1 Tbsp. butter [15g / ½ oz.] plus 4 tsp. sugar [15g / ½ oz.] plus 2 Tbsp. water [30ml]

➔ To substitute for 1 square [28g / 1oz.] unsweetened chocolate (aka bitter chocolate):

use:	• 1 square semisweet (dark) chocolate [28g / 1oz.], and omit 1 Tbsp. sugar [13g / ½ oz.] from the recipe
or use:	• 3 Tbsp. cocoa powder [~20g / ¾ oz.] plus 1 Tbsp. butter [15g / ½ oz.]
or use:	• 3 Tbsp. carob powder [~20g / ¾ oz.] plus 1 Tbsp. butter [15g / ½ oz.] plus 2 Tbsp. water [30ml]

BAKING POWDER

➔ To substitute for 1 teaspoon baking powder:

combine:	• ¼ tsp. bicarbonate of soda [baking soda, US]
with:	• ½ tsp. cream of tartar

➔ Baking soda and cream of tartar make a gluten-free baking powder.

28g = 1 oz   57g = 2 oz   85g = 3 oz   100g = 3½ oz   113g = 4 oz   142g = 5 oz

SUBSTITUTES & OTHER TRANSFORMATIONS   *Page 145*

TO TEST FOR POTENCY OF HOMEMADE BAKING POWDER

Some books say not to store homemade baking powder as it doesn't keep well but when I tested my months-old homemade baking powder, it fizzed up just fine. To test baking powder for potency, do the following: in $\frac{1}{4}$ cup hot water, dissolve 1 teaspoon homemade baking powder. If it doesn't foam and bubble within a few seconds, replace it with some freshly-made baking powder.

➔ Other substitutes for 1 teaspoon baking powder:

combine: • $\frac{1}{4}$ tsp. bicarbonate of soda [baking soda, US]
with _one_* of the following:
  • at least $\frac{1}{2}$ cup of sour milk, buttermilk or yogurt [120ml];
or with: • $\frac{1}{2}$ cup applesauce, mashed bananas or tart jam [120ml];
or with: • $\frac{1}{2}$ Tbsp. vinegar or lemon juice, plus enough milk to make $\frac{1}{2}$ cup [120ml]
or with: • $\frac{1}{4}$–$\frac{1}{2}$ cup molasses [60–120ml]
or with: • 2 oz. chocolate [60g]

*Depending upon what you're using as your substitute, you'll need to adjust other recipe ingredients to allow for extra liquid, etc.

(Source: *The Kitchen Companion* by Polly Clingerman)

BROAD BEANS

The number of broad beans in one pod, and the sizes of those broad beans varies greatly, so the conversion formulas that follow are, at best, approximate.   *(more on broad beans, overleaf)*

---

1 US cup = 16 Tbsp.   1 Tbsp. = 3 tsp.   (1 Irish or old English Tbsp. = 4 tsp.)

➔ Conversion formulas by weight:

FROM WHOLE PODS,
WHAT WEIGHT OF BEANS CAN I EXPECT?

- **weight of pods x 0.33 = weight of shelled beans** — Multiply the weight of the whole pods by 0.33; this should give you the approximate weight of the shelled broad beans.

FROM WHOLE PODS,
WHAT WEIGHT OF *PEELED* BEANS CAN I EXPECT?

- **weight of pods x 0.25 = weight of shelled & peeled beans** — Multiply the weight of the whole pods by 0.25; this should give you the approximate weight of the shelled and peeled broad beans.

MY RECIPE CALLS FOR BROAD BEANS —
WHAT WEIGHT OF WHOLE PODS SHOULD I START WITH?

- **weight of shelled beans ÷ 0.33 = weight of pods you'd have needed to start with** — Divide the weight of the shelled beans called for in your recipe by 0.33; this should give you the approximate weight of the pods needed to yield this amount of beans.

MY RECIPE CALLS FOR *PEELED* BROAD BEANS —
WHAT WEIGHT OF WHOLE PODS SHOULD I START WITH?

- **weight of shelled & peeled beans ÷ 0.25 = weight of pods you'd have needed to start with** — Divide the weight of the shelled & peeled beans called for in your recipe by 0.25; this should give you the approximate weight of the pods needed to yield this amount of peeled broad beans.

28g = 1 oz   57g = 2 oz   85g = 3 oz   100g = 3½ oz   113g = 4 oz   142g = 5 oz

BEANS, DRIED

The formulas for converting weights, below, are fairly accurate for most types of dried beans, e.g., azuki, cannelini, haricot and kidney beans, but for soya beans use 2.4 rather than 2.2, and for chickpeas, use 2.

→ Conversion formulas by weight:

FROM DRIED BEANS,
WHAT WEIGHT OF COOKED BEANS CAN I EXPECT?

- **dried beans x 2.2 = cooked weight**
  Multiply the weight of your dried beans by 2.2 to give you the approximate cooked weight (or by 2.4 for soya beans, or by 2 for chickpeas).

MY RECIPE CALLS FOR COOKED BEANS (OR TINNED OR SOAKED) — WHAT WEIGHT OF DRIED BEANS SHOULD I START WITH?

- **cooked beans ÷ 2.2 = dried weight**
  Divide the weight of the cooked beans by 2.2 to give you the approximate weight of dried beans you'd have had to start with (or by 2.4 for soya beans, or by 2 for chickpeas).

The formulas for converting volume, below, are as accurate as I could make them but overall they varied from x 2 (azuki) to x 2.5 (kidney beans, chickpeas) to x 2.5–3 (cannelini, haricot and soya beans).

→ Conversion formulas by volume (cups):

FROM DRIED BEANS,
WHAT AMOUNT OF COOKED BEANS CAN I EXPECT?

by cups • **dried beans x 2.75 = number of cooked cups**
For cannelini, haricot and soya beans, multiply the number of cups of dried beans by 2.75 to give you the approximate number of cooked cups, but for

---

1 US cup = 16 Tbsp.   1 Tbsp. = 3 tsp.   (1 Irish or old English Tbsp. = 4 tsp.)

kidney beans & chickpeas, multiply by 2.5, and for azuki, multiply x 2.

MY RECIPE CALLS FOR COOKED BEANS (OR TINNED OR SOAKED) — WHAT AMOUNT OF DRIED BEANS SHOULD I START WITH?

by cups
- **cooked beans ÷ 2.75 = number of cups of dried beans** — For cannelini, haricot and soya beans, divide the number of cups of cooked beans by 2.75 to give you the approximate number of cups of dried beans you'd have had to start with, but for kidney beans & chickpeas, divide by 2.5, and for azuki, divide x 2.

➔ Tinned beans and beans cooked from dried are about the same weight and volume to one another so can use these interchangeably. To figure out how much tinned to use instead of dried, refer to the calculations above for cooked and dried. For example, if a recipe calls for 6 ounces dried, check the weight calculations, above: 6 oz. x 2.2 = about 13 ounces, so use 13 ounces drained tinned beans, but omit the soaking and cooking of the beans in the recipe — the tinned beans will only require warming up in the recipe.

BUTTERMILK

The main difference between buttermilk and skimmed milk is buttermilk is sour. 'Buttermilk' was the liquid that remained after milk was churned to butter (hence its name), and it soured naturally on the farm. Supermarkets sell 'cultured buttermilk' which is effectively soured skimmed milk.

➔ To substitute for buttermilk when cooking, you can use instead:

28g = 1 oz   57g = 2 oz   85g = 3 oz   100g = 3½ oz   113g = 4 oz   142g = 5 oz

- soured milk

    (That is, milk that's gone sour but not 'off' — soured milk simply smells sour; milk that's spoiled has a repellant smell.)

- fresh milk that you've 'soured' yourself

    (To do this, combine lemon juice with milk [1 Tbsp. lemon per cup / 240ml milk] and let it stand 5 minutes or so — if you've no lemon juice, use another acid, such as vinegar or wine.)

- plain unflavoured yogurt

CAROB

➔ To substitute for one 200g bar [7-oz.] sweetened carob:

combine:
- $1\frac{1}{3}$ cups carob powder [110-127g]

with:
- $\frac{1}{2}$ cup minus 1 Tbsp. butter [100g]
- $\frac{3}{4}$ cup plus 2 Tbsp. water [210ml]
- $\frac{1}{2}$ cup plus 1 Tbsp. sugar [115g]

➔ To substitute for one 200g bar *un*sweetened carob:

Do the same as above but omit the sugar.

CARROTS

➔ Conversion formulas by weight:

I'VE GOT WHOLE CARROTS —

WHAT WILL THEY WEIGH ONCE THEY'RE PEELED & TRIMMED?

- **weight of good-sized untrimmed carrots ÷ 1.2 = approximate weight of trimmed carrots** — Divide the weight of the untrimmed carrots by 1.2 for the approximate weight of the peeled & trimmed carrots.

(more on carrots, overleaf)

---

1 US cup = 16 Tbsp.   1 Tbsp. = 3 tsp.   (1 Irish or old English Tbsp. = 4 tsp.)

MY RECIPE CALLS FOR PEELED & TRIMMED CARROTS —
WHAT WEIGHT OF UNTRIMMED CARROTS SHOULD I START WITH?

- **weight of trimmed good-sized carrots x 1.2 = weight of untrimmed carrots** — Multiply the weight of the peeled & trimmed carrots by 1.2 for the approximate weight of the untrimmed & unpeeled carrots with which you'd have had to start.

➔ By 'trimmed', I mean between $1/4$–$1/2$ inch [6–13mm] trimmed from the tops. The above formulas are for good-sized carrots, about 6–7 inches long [15–18cm]; if using small carrots, reckon closer to 1.35 rather than 1.2 for your calculations.

CELERIAC

This is a gnarly root vegetable so the amount you'll have to peel will vary from one to another. The unpeeled celeriac ranged from 1.3–1.4 times the weight of the resulting peeled celeriac; I've given both figures below — take your pick, either way, you won't be far off.

➔ Conversion formulas by weight:

I'VE GOT A WHOLE CELERIAC —
WHAT WILL IT WEIGH ONCE IT'S PEELED?

- **weight of unpeeled celeriac ÷ 1.3 (or 1.4) = weight of peeled celeriac** — Divide the weight of the unpeeled celeriac by 1.3 (or 1.4) to give you the approximate weight of the peeled celeriac.

MY RECIPE CALLS FOR PEELED CELERIAC —
WHAT WEIGHT OF UNPEELED CELERIAC SHOULD I START WITH?

- **weight of peeled celeriac x 1.3 (or 1.4) = weight of unpeeled celeriac** — Multiply the weight of the

---

28g = 1 oz   57g = 2 oz   85g = 3 oz   100g = 3½ oz   113g = 4 oz   142g = 5 oz

peeled celeriac by 1.3 (or 1.4) to give you the approximate weight of the unpeeled celeriac with which you'd have had to start.

CHESTNUTS

→ Conversion formulas:

MY RECIPE CALLS FOR DRIED CHESTNUTS —
BUT I'VE GOT COOKED (OR TINNED); WHAT DO I DO?

- **weight/volume of dried chestnuts x 2 = weight/volume of cooked/tinned chestnuts**
  Multiply by 2 the weight or volume of the dried chestnuts called for in your recipe; this should give you the approximate weight/volume of the cooked (or tinned) chestnuts you should use, but be sure to omit the soaking/cooking steps in the recipe for the dried chestnuts — the cooked or tinned chestnuts should only require warming up in the recipe.

BUT I'VE GOT UNPEELED FRESH; WHAT DO I DO?

- **weight of dried chestnuts x 2.5 = weight of unpeeled fresh chestnuts**
  Multiply by 2.5 the weight of the dried chestnuts called for in your recipe; this should give you the approximate weight of the unpeeled fresh you'll need. Omit the chestnut-soaking/cooking steps in the recipe for the dried chestnuts. Instead, cook the fresh ones: cut slits in their flat sides, boil for 1–2 minutes, shell and skin them, then cook for 15–20 minutes and they should be ready to use in your recipe.

(more on chestnuts, overleaf)

---

1 US cup = 16 Tbsp.   1 Tbsp. = 3 tsp.   (1 Irish or old English Tbsp. = 4 tsp.)

MY RECIPE CALLS FOR PEELED FRESH CHESTNUTS
(OR COOKED OR TINNED) —
> BUT I'VE GOT DRIED; WHAT DO I DO?
>> • **weight/volume of peeled fresh (or cooked/tinned) ÷ 2 = weight/volume of dried**
>> Divide by 2 the weight/volume of the peeled fresh (or cooked or tinned) chestnuts called for in your recipe; this will give you the approximate weight/volume of dried to use. Then soak the dried chestnuts overnight and cook till tender, about an hour; they should now be ready to use in your recipe.
>
> BUT I'VE GOT UNPEELED FRESH; WHAT DO I DO?
>> • **weight of peeled fresh (or cooked/tinned) ÷ 0.8 = weight of unpeeled fresh**
>> Divide by 0.8 the weight of the peeled fresh (or cooked or tinned) chestnuts called for in your recipe, this will give you the approximate weight of unpeeled fresh to use. To prepare the fresh chestnuts, cut slits in their flat sides, boil for 1–2 minutes, and shell and skin them — and if your recipe calls for cooked rather than fresh chestnuts, then cook them for about 15–20 minutes, and then proceed with your recipe.

.MY RECIPE CALLS FOR *U*NPEELED FRESH CHESTNUTS —
> BUT I'VE GOT PEELED FRESH (OR COOKED OR TINNED); WHAT DO I DO?
>> • **weight of unpeeled fresh x 0.8 = peeled weight**
>> Multiply by 0.8 the weight of the unpeeled chestnuts called for in your recipe to give you the approximate weight of peeled chestnuts to use. Then omit the

---

28g = 1 oz 57g = 2 oz 85g = 3 oz 100g = 3½ oz 113g = 4 oz 142g = 5 oz

chestnut-peeling and skinning steps in the recipe (if using cooked/tinned chestnuts, omit the chestnut-cooking step as well).

BUT I'VE GOT DRIED; WHAT DO I DO?

- **weight of unpeeled fresh x 0.4 = dried weight**
  Multiply by 0.4 the weight of the unpeeled chestnuts called for in your recipe to give you the approximate weight of dried to use. Then soak the dried chestnuts overnight and cook till tender, about an hour. Omit the chestnut-peeling, skinning and cooking steps in your recipe — your cooked-from-dried chestnuts should only require warming up in the recipe.

---

chocolate & cocoa, *see* **BAKER'S CHOCOLATE SQUARES**

COCONUT CREAM AND COCONUT MILK

How to make your own coconut cream and coconut milk (though be warned, these won't be as thick as the canned varieties).

→ From grated fresh (or desiccated) coconut:
<u>To make coconut cream</u>, pour 1 cup boiling water over 1 cup grated coconut. Let it cool a bit, then squeeze out the coconut.
<u>To make a thick coconut milk</u>, do as above but use 2 cups boiling water to 1 cup shredded coconut.
<u>To make a thin coconut milk</u>, re-use the grated coconut which you used to make your coconut cream or thick coconut milk. Pour 2 cups boiling water over it. Let it cool a bit, then squeeze out the coconut.
(Source: *The Cook's Encyclopaedia* by Tom Stobart)

(more on coconut cream, overleaf)

---

1 US cup = 16 Tbsp.   1 Tbsp. = 3 tsp.   (1 Irish or old English Tbsp. = 4 tsp.)

→ From a 200g block of creamed coconut:
To make coconut cream, break up the block into a bowl.
Add 450ml boiling water [2 cups] and stir to dissolve
(the original instructions said 'warm' water but I'd use boiling).
Strain through a fine mesh strainer or muslin.
To make a thick coconut milk, do as above but add an extra 150ml [$^2/_3$ cup] warm water before straining.
(Source: KTC Edibles packet instructions)

Creamed coconut blocks are made from unsweetened, pure creamed coconut, which is compressed into hard blocks. The 200g blocks measure $4^3/_4$ x 1 x $2^1/_2$ inches [12 x 2.5 x 6.5cm] and although commonly sold in the UK, I've not seen them in the US.

CREAM For whipped cream, use a high-fat cream such as American heavy cream, British double cream, or 'whipping' cream.

→Conversion formulas:

MY RECIPE CALLS FOR WHIPPED CREAM —
I'VE GOT UNWHIPPED; HOW MUCH WILL I NEED TO WHIP?

- **volume of whipped ÷ 1.7 = unwhipped volume**
  Divide by 1.7 the volume of whipped cream called for in your recipe to give you the approximate volume of unwhipped you'll need to start with. For example, $1^3/_4$ cups whipped cream ÷ 1.7 = 1; this tells you that for $1^3/_4$ cups whipped cream, you'd have had to start with 1 cup unwhipped cream.

I'VE GOT CREAM — WHAT VOLUME WILL IT WHIP TO?

- **volume of unwhipped x 1.7 = whipped volume**
  Multiply the volume of cream you have by 1.7; this will

28g = 1 oz   57g = 2 oz   85g = 3 oz   100g = 3½ oz   113g = 4 oz   142g = 5 oz

give you the approximate whipped volume. For example,
1 cup unwhipped x 1.7 = $1^3/_4$ cups whipped.

FLOUR, SELF-RAISING

➔ To substitute for 1 cup self-raising flour [~130g]:

combine: • 1 cup minus 2 Tbsp. all-purpose flour [about 115g plain flour]

with: • $1^1/_2$ teaspoons baking powder and
• $1/_8$ teaspoon salt

or with: • 1 teaspoon baking powder, plus
• $1/_4$ teaspoon bicarbonate of soda [baking soda] and
• $1/_2$ teaspoon salt

➔ To substitute for 100g self-raising flour [~$3/_4$ cup]:

combine: • 90g plain flour [about $3/_4$ cup minus $1^1/_2$ Tbsp. all-purpose flour]

with: • $1^1/_4$ teaspoons baking powder and
• scant $1/_8$ teaspoon salt

or with: • $3/_4$ teaspoon baking powder, plus
• scant $1/_4$ teaspoon bicarbonate of soda [baking soda] and
• scant $1/_2$ teaspoon salt

➔ To substitute for $1/_2$ pound self-raising flour [227g, about $1^3/_4$ cups]:

combine: • 200g plain flour [about $1^1/_2$ cups all-purpose]

with: • $2^1/_2$ teaspoons baking powder and
• $1/_4$ teaspoon salt

---

1 US cup = 16 Tbsp.   1 Tbsp. = 3 tsp.   (1 Irish or old English Tbsp. = 4 tsp.)

PASTA & NOODLES

Packets of pasta & noodles often carry little or no instructions, and in the case of Oriental noodles, instructions may be confusingly translated, hence some more detailed instructions follow.

→ *ITALIAN PASTA & NOODLES*

- *How much pasta per person?*
  It depends upon people's appetites but for a main course, figure on about 4 oz. dried pasta per person [115g], and for a starter, about half that amount.

- *How much water in the pot?* *
  Advice varies. For 1 pound of pasta, I boil about 4 quarts water [~4L] in a very large lightweight pot. Most American books say to cook pasta in a lot of boiling water — about 7 quarts water per pound of pasta, while British books advise using about half that amount — 2–3 litres water [~2–3 quarts] per pound of pasta.

  * To save energy and time, first boil the water in an electric kettle (if you have one) — you'll need to boil more than one kettle-full, then pour each kettle-full into your pot, turn on the heat under it and once it's boiling away, add your pasta or noodles.

- *How long to cook?*
  For dried: 8–15 minutes; for fresh: 2–8 minutes.
  The length of time will depend upon the pasta's shape, size and thickness but in general, the times given above for dried and fresh pasta & noodles cover most types. To test it if it's done, remove a piece and bite it — if it's still too hard in the centre, then let the pasta carry on cooking, and test it again in a few minutes.

- *How much cooked pasta will I get from dried?*
  Reckon about 1 part dried to 2 parts cooked, whether going by

---

28g = 1 oz   57g = 2 oz   85g = 3 oz   100g = 3½ oz   113g = 4 oz   142g = 5 oz

weight or by volume. Two cups of dried penne [quills] expands to nearly 4 cups when cooked so double your dried volume (or weight) to give you your approximate cooked volume (or weight).

➔ *ORIENTAL NOODLES*
- RICE STICKS ($\frac{1}{4}$" WIDE RIBBON-TYPE NOODLES): *How to cook?*
  Half-fill a large pot with water — boiled first in an electric kettle, if you have one — and place on the hob. Add 1 tsp. salt and bring to a rolling boil, then add the dried rice noodles. Loosen them using chopsticks or a fork. Cook for $2\frac{1}{2}$–3 minutes. Tip into a sieve, rinse in cold running water, separating the noodles with your fingers to cool them quickly and thoroughly, then let drain.
  ➢ *How to reheat?*
  Boil a pot of water, plunge the cooked noodles into it and leave no more than 20 seconds. Drain into a sieve, shake off the water and add the noodles to your recipe.
- RICE VERMICELLI (FINE RICE NOODLES): *How to cook ?*
  Place in a deep bowl. Boil the kettle and leave it 5 minutes, then pour enough just-boiled water over the dried vermicelli to immerse them completely. Cover and let soak 6–8 minutes. Drain and refresh in cold water, as for the rice sticks, above, but spend about 2 minutes pulling them apart under cold running water.
  ➢Reheat as per instructions, above.
- FINE CHINESE EGG NOODLES: *How to cook ?*
  ⇨For dried egg noodles, cook as per the rice sticks, above. After draining, mix with a little oil, then set aside.
  ⇨For frozen (from fresh) egg noodles, boil the water as per the rice sticks, above, but when the water's at a rolling boil, add the block of frozen noodles — don't let them thaw first; cooking

---

1 US cup = 16 Tbsp.   1 Tbsp. = 3 tsp.   (1 Irish or old English Tbsp. = 4 tsp.)

thawed noodles produces a mass of inseparable mushy noodles. Using chopsticks, slowly loosen the noodles from the frozen block and continue to do this until all the noodles are floating free. Once they're all loose in the water, let them cook another $1-1\frac{1}{2}$ minutes, then strain and rinse as for the rice sticks, above.

➢ Reheat as above or, to reheat in a wok, heat 2 Tbsp. oil, add the cooked noodles, and stir-fry 2 minutes.

- UDON NOODLES, FRESH: *How to cook ?*
Put the fresh udon noodles in a pot of boiling water. Once it returns to the boil, cook for about 2 minutes, then drain.

(Sources for most of the above: Sri Owen, Deh-ta Hsiung.)

RICE

→ CONVERSION FORMULAS

These conversion formulas for uncooked-to-cooked rice (and vice versa) are based on rice cooked using the *absorption method*. This is the method whereby the rice fully absorbs the water in which it's cooked (it's also the way rice cookers cook rice). Use the formulas below as a rough guide only as results will vary — during tests, when cooked in a pan using the absorption method, 1 cup uncooked rice yielded between $3\frac{1}{4}-4\frac{1}{3}$ cups cooked, and once, over 5 cups cooked, but $3\frac{1}{2}-4$ cups was about average; if cooked in a rice cooker, $3\frac{1}{2}$ cups was the average. I have used cups but not weights, as the number of cups were more consistently in agreement than were the weights.

MY RECIPE CALLS FOR COOKED RICE —
HOW MANY CUPS OF UNCOOKED RICE SHOULD I START WITH?

- **cooked cups ÷ 3.5 = uncooked cups**

28g = 1 oz   57g = 2 oz   85g = 3 oz   100g = 3½ oz   113g = 4 oz   142g = 5 oz

Divide the number of cups of cooked rice called for in your recipe by 3.5; this should give you the approximate number of cups of uncooked rice with which you'll need to start.

I'VE GOT UNCOOKED RICE —
HOW MANY CUPS OF COOKED RICE WILL THIS MAKE?

- **uncooked cups x 3.5 = cooked cups**
  Multiply the number of cups of uncooked rice by 3.5; this should give you roughly the number of cooked cups.

→ COOKING METHODS

All the following rice-cooking methods work by steaming the rice in a pan on the hob [stovetop, US], i.e., the absorption method.

- <u>basmati rice</u> (Indian method) — this works for other long-grain rices, too

  Volume ratio: 1 part rice to 2 parts water.
  Amount to allow per person: $\frac{1}{3}$ cup dried rice [$5\frac{1}{3}$ level Tbsp.]

  ➢ *Wash it*: Place the rice in a bowl, fill with cold water, then pour off the water. Repeat 8–9 times, until the water runs clear.

  ➢ *Soak it*: Add fresh water to the bowl of washed rice, using 2 parts water to 1 part rice, and let soak 30 minutes. Don't discard the water after soaking as you'll be cooking with it.

  ➢ *Cook it*: Strain the soaking-water into a heavy-based pan, cover and bring to the boil. Add the soaked rice, stir and return to the boil. Reduce heat to low and simmer, partially covered, until most of the water is absorbed (about 10–15 minutes). Next, reduce heat to lowest level, cover tightly, and raise the pot from the heat — use a wok ring if you have one — and let it

---

1 US cup = 16 Tbsp.   1 Tbsp. = 3 tsp.   (1 Irish or old English Tbsp. = 4 tsp.)

steam like this for 10 minutes. Then turn off the heat. Let it rest, undisturbed, for 5 minutes before serving.

(Source for instructions: *Classic Indian Cooking* by J. Sahni.)

- brown rice

    Volume ratio: 2 parts rice to 3 parts water.

    Amount to allow per person: $1/4$ cup dried rice [4 level Tbsp.]

    ➢ Take a heavy-based pan, add the rice and water and cover (for 2 cups rice, add 3 cups water; for 1 cup rice, add $1\frac{1}{2}$ cups water, etc.). Bring to the boil, then reduce heat to low, uncover slightly (1 small vent), and simmer for about 25–30 minutes — mine usually takes 30 minutes exactly. You can stir once or twice during this time but replace the lid immediately afterwards to prevent the hot steam escaping. Once it's cooked, add salt and butter to taste, and serve.

    (Source: *The Enchanted Broccoli Forest* by M. Katzen.)

- short-grain rice (Japanese method)

    Volume ratio: 2 parts rice to 3 parts water.

    Amount to allow per person: $1/3$ cup dried rice [$5\frac{1}{3}$ level Tbsp.]

    ➢ *Wash it*: Wash the rice in several changes of cold water, swirling it to release the starch.

    ➢ *Drain it*: Pour into sieve and leave to drain for 30 minutes.

    ➢ *Cook it*: Take a heavy-based pan, add fresh water and the washed rice, using 3 parts water to 2 parts rice. Cover and bring to the boil, then reduce heat to its lowest setting and let it cook for 10 minutes. Remove from the heat and, keeping the lid on, let it steam, undisturbed, for a further 10 minutes. Remove the lid to stop the cooking, and serve.

28g = 1 oz   57g = 2 oz   85g = 3 oz   100g = 3½ oz   113g = 4 oz   142g = 5 oz

SUBSTITUTES & OTHER TRANSFORMATIONS *Page 161*

(Source for instructions: *Wagamama Cookbook* by H. Arnold.)

SHORTCRUST PASTRY [pie dough, US]

→ To make shortcrust pastry dough from scratch, use roughly half the weight of butter to flour. Richer crusts use more butter but rich pastry dough is also more difficult to handle.

- *for an 8" single-crust pie [20.5cm]:*
  use 8–9 oz. pastry dough [225–255g]
  To make this amount, combine 150g flour, 75g butter, $1/4$ tsp. salt and just enough cold water to bind (no more than 2–3 Tbsp.).
  If using cups, use about 1 cup plus 2 Tbsp. flour to $1/3$ cup butter.

- *for a 9" single-crust pie [23cm]:*
  use 12 oz. pastry dough [340g]
  To make this amount, combine 200g flour, 110g butter, $1/4$ tsp. salt and just enough cold water to bind (3–4 Tbsp.).
  If using cups, use about $1 1/2$ cups flour to $1/2$ cup butter.

SUGAR

A powdered substance such as icing sugar will vary in its weight-per-cup ratio due to things like how compacted it is, humidity in the air, etc, so the 1.15 figure below is an average — sometimes it was 1.1 or 1.2.

→ Conversion formulas for unsifted-to-sifted icing sugar
  (and vice versa):

MY RECIPE CALLS FOR SIFTED ICING SUGAR —
I'VE GOT UNSIFTED; HOW MUCH WILL I NEED TO SIFT?

- **sifted cups ÷ 1.15 = number of unsifted cups**
  Divide by 1.15 the number of cups of sifted sugar called for in your recipe to give you the approximate number of

---

1 US cup = 16 Tbsp.   1 Tbsp. = 3 tsp.   (1 Irish or old English Tbsp. = 4 tsp.)

unsifted cups to use (and sift). So for 1 cup sifted, start with about ³/₄ cup plus 2 Tbsp. unsifted.

I'VE GOT UNSIFTED ICING SUGAR —
HOW MANY CUPS SIFTED WILL IT MAKE?

- **unsifted cups x 1.15 = number of sifted cups**
  Multiply the number of cups of unsifted sugar you have by 1.15; this will give you the approximate number of sifted cups. For example, 1 cup unsifted x 1.15 = about 1 cup plus 2 Tbsp.

⇨ To see a quick-reference chart of volumes & weights of sifted and unsifted sugar, go to the Icing Sugar Chart on page 232.

TOMATOES, 'SUN-BLUSHED'

These are tomatoes that are partially dried and slow-cooked in an oven, rather than in the sun.

→ To make the equivalent of 10 oz. sun-blushed tomatoes [285g], buy 1 pound grape tomatoes and semi-dry them for about 1 hour in a preheated very slow (aka very low) oven — 120°C /GM½ / 250°F. If grape tomatoes are unavailable, use small cherry toms.

VANILLA

The amount of seeds you can scrape from a 1" section of a vanilla pod [vanilla bean, US] is equal in flavour to 1 tsp. vanilla essence. If substituting vanilla essence for vanilla seeds in a recipe, then to retain its greatest flavour, add the essence only when the food is cooling. For instance, if it says to bring cream and vanilla seeds to the boil, just bring the cream to the boil and add the essence after the cream is done cooking.

28g = 1 oz   57g = 2 oz   85g = 3 oz   100g = 3½ oz   113g = 4 oz   142g = 5 oz

YEAST

→ Fresh & dried yeast equivalents (in general):

FRESH		DRIED
for 17g fresh compressed	*substitute:*	7g active dry
[1 cake / 1 Tbsp.]		[1 pkg. / $2\frac{1}{4}$ tsp.]

→ Bread dough & yeast

For bread doughs with 2 risings over a period of 3 hours (or so), you can substitute the following:

FRESH		DRIED
for 1 oz. fresh yeast	*substitute:*	$\frac{1}{3}$ oz. dried
[28g / a scant 2 Tbsp.]		[9.5g / $2\frac{1}{3}$ tsp.]

➤ How much dried yeast to use in bread dough:

DRIED YEAST		FLOUR
7g dried yeast	*is enough to rise*	565g flour
[1 sachet]		[4–$4\frac{1}{2}$ cups]

So reckon on $\frac{1}{4}$ sachet per cup of flour, or about $\frac{1}{4}$ tsp. dried yeast per 100g of flour.

(Source for Bread dough and yeasts: Elizabeth David)

---

1 US cup = 16 Tbsp.   1 Tbsp. = 3 tsp.   (1 Irish or old English Tbsp. = 4 tsp.)

28g = 1 oz   57g = 2 oz   85g = 3 oz   100g = 3½ oz   113g = 4 oz   142g = 5 oz

RECIPES

RECIPES

RECIPE LIST

Seeded soda bread	166
Pancakes (crêpes)	170
Gluten-free pancakes	172
Chilli con carne	172
Ersatz enchilada	173
Mayonnaise	174
Waldorf salad	175
Potato latkes (potato pancakes)	176
Meatloaf	177
Stock jelly/jello	179
Sweet jelly/jello	180
Sweet jelly/jello made with Vege-gel	181
Peanut butter patties	181
Rice Krispies Treats	184

Seeded soda bread — MAKES 1 LARGE LOAF (4 QUARTERS)

Soda bread goes in the oven as soon as it's shaped and ready — no waiting for dough to rise, as soda bread contains no yeast. Instead it uses bicarbonate of soda which, when combined with an acid ingredient such as buttermilk, soured milk, or milk with lemon juice, will produce carbon dioxide which expands and rises the dough.

It's a great way to use up milk ($1\frac{1}{4}$ UK pints!) and if the milk is on the cusp or soured, use it (but not if it's gone off). This recipe is based on the one in Darina Allen's *Ballymaloe Cookery Course* book (which is in turn based on Myrtle Allen's recipe), but I've added seeds and cooked wheat grains to mine. It's excellent toasted, and freezes well, too.

Ingredients	
– 600g wholemeal flour [$4\frac{1}{4}$ cups]	*handful each of:*
– 600g white bread flour [$4\frac{1}{4}$ cups]	– pumpkin seeds
– 2 tsp. salt	– sunflower seeds
– 2 tsp. bicarbonate of soda	– sesame seeds
– 2 handfuls of cooked wheat grains (see p.141)	– linseeds
– 700–800ml buttermilk or soured milk, or milk with 4 Tbsp. lemon juice added [about $1\frac{1}{4}$ UK pints]	– poppy seeds

Procedure Preheat the oven to 230°C [210°C if fan-assisted / GM8 / 450°F].

Sprinkle cornmeal or polenta over a large baking sheet to thinly cover; this is to keep the loaf from sticking.

Lightly flour a work surface.

The raw soda bread with its deep cuts, on the polenta-covered baking sheet, ready for the oven.

The resulting baked soda bread — see how the bread swelled up around its gashes.

In a very large bowl — mine is 13" across [33cm], combine the flours, salt, bicarbonate of soda, cooked wheat grains and the seeds.

(By the way, the wheat grains and seeds are optional: you may add all, a few, or none. I keep batches of cooked wheat grains ready to use in the freezer, in those 200g cream cheese containers, and 1 container holds the right amount for 1 recipe soda bread.)

Make a well in the centre of the bowl and pour in the liquid. The original recipe called for buttermilk but I'd have to make a trip to a supermarket for this so I use soured milk, or fresh milk with lemon juice instead.

Mix in the liquid until it's all incorporated into the flour — use a dough scraper, pan scraper, or just your hand. Keep one hand clean and free to turn the bowl whilst you work, and to answer the phone or door, if needed.

Once the dough is ready, that is, soft but not too wet and sticky, flour your hands and form the dough into a ball, then place the ball of dough on the floured work surface. Shape it into a large circle and pat it down to about 2" high [5cm].

Lift the large circle of dough onto the prepared baking sheet and, using a knife, cut a deep cross into it — as it bakes, the dough will swell along these deep cuts, and provide guidelines for cutting the baked bread into quarters. Next, in each quarter of the bread, make a deep cut so that in the end, you're left with a sort of union jack design (see photo). These deep cuts are, I believe, to ensure these quarters bake through to their centres but they're also, as Darina Allen says, 'to let the fairies out'.

Bake 15–20 minutes in the preheated 230ºC oven, then reduce heat to 200ºC [180ºC if fan-assisted / GM6 / 400ºF] and bake a further 20–25 minutes. (If your oven isn't fan-assisted, then rotate the bread round when you change the temperature, to ensure it bakes evenly front and back.)

Remove the bread from the oven — I let mine sit 5 minutes or so on the baking sheet before removing it to a wire rack to cool. If your bread has stuck to your baking sheet, then let it sit longer, until the moisture from the bread's heat loosens it (and it will); then slide a spatula beneath it to loosen it, and lift onto a wire rack.

Once it's cooled, cut it into quarters and wrap each quarter in cling film. Put any you won't be using in the next few days into the freezer.

Seeded soda bread is great toasted but those little slices at the end get lost in a toaster so use a mini toaster oven instead, if you have one. And if you've leftover bits to use up, whizz them into crumbs and use for making meatloaf (page 177), or in place of matzoh meal in latkes (page 176).

Pancakes (crêpes)   MAKES 11 PANCAKES, 6–6½" WIDE [15–16 CM]

In the mid '90s around Shrove Tuesday, I bought a de Buyer pancake pan (crêpe pan), which I've used ever since but when trying to buy one recently, could only find teflon pancake pans — teflon's fine for some things, but for pancake-making, nothing beats a seasoned steel pan.

Pancakes are not difficult to make, yet it took moving to England for me to finally attempt them, and many other Americans, including accomplished cooks, have not made them, which is a shame as they're so versatile, and such a handy stand-by when cooking for people who are not well and may have lost interest in food.

Ingredients
– 3 eggs – a good pinch of salt – ¾ cup plus 2 Tbsp. plain flour [115g]   (*can also use gluten-free flour — see below*) – 1¼ cups milk (or soured milk) [½ UK pint / 300ml] – 2 Tbsp. butter [28g]

Procedure   In a large bowl, preferably one with a spout, whisk the eggs with the salt and then add the flour, ¼ cup or so at a time until all is smooth. Pour in the milk, whisk it in, and leave the whisk in the bowl.

                     Melt the butter in the pancake pan, then pour it into the batter and whisk to combine. Doing it this way greases the pan, ready for cooking the pancakes, and also helps to keep the pan seasoned.

➢ *Stovetop set up*: In a 7" de Buyer pancake pan [18cm], 4 Tbsp. batter is the right amount to use so I put a $\frac{1}{4}$ cup measure on a board next to the pan and pour the batter into that, ready for pouring into the pan. I also set out a plate for stacking the pancakes, along with some 8" baking parchment circles [20cm] which I use to separate every 4 or so pancakes — if for immediate use, you'll not need the parchment circles but if freezing the pancakes or using later in the week, the circles help keep the pancakes from sticking together.

Heat the pan until hot, pour in $\frac{1}{4}$ cup batter and tilt the pan to swirl the batter round till it covers the base of the pan. Cook over medium heat till the base of the pancake is set — usually 1 minute or less — then use a spatula to flip the pancake and cook the other side. (Once I've flipped the pancake, I whisk the batter again and pour out another $\frac{1}{4}$ cupful, ready for the next pancake.) Stack them on a plate as they're cooked.

Pancakes freeze fine; to use from frozen, let them defrost, then proceed as you would with ones from the fridge. A single pancake heats in about 10 seconds in the microwave.

There are endless sorts of fillings you can make for savoury pancakes: mushrooms & cream; creamed spinach with Asian spices; scrambled eggs & cheese; chilli con carne; etc. For an ersatz enchilada made with pancakes, see page 173.

And in addition to the traditional melted butter, lemon juice & sugar, there are endless other sweet options — just use your imagination!

For gluten-free pancakes: Replace the plain flour with gluten-free flour(s), such as those below, but remember to whisk each time before you pour the batter.
- $\frac{1}{4}$ cup gluten-free plain flour
- $\frac{1}{4}$ cup potato flour
- $\frac{1}{4}$ cup plus 2 Tbsp. rice flour

Chilli con carne — SERVES 4–6

Chilli is such an easy dish to make and such lively flavours, friends always welcome it but, if you're on your own, freeze the leftovers in individual portions. Then, a month or so later when you're peckish and sifting through the freezer, you'll be happy to find them there.

This recipe is based on the 'Chilli Beef with Beans' recipe in Craig Claiborne's *A Kitchen Primer*, with just minor changes.

Ingredients	

– 2 Tbsp. butter [28g]
 – 2 medium onions, chopped
 – 1–2 cloves garlic, minced
 – 1½ lb. minced beef [680g]
 – 1½ tsp. kosher salt
 – ground black pepper, to taste
 – 1 Tbsp. chilli powder
 – 1 tsp. cumin seeds
	then add:
	 – ½ tsp. sugar (opt.)
	 – 400g tin Italian peeled
	   (or chopped) tomatoes
	
	 and lastly add:
	 – 420g tin kidney beans
	   [1½–1⅔ cup drained]

Procedure In a large frying pan with high sides, melt the butter. Then add the onion and garlic and cook, stirring, till onions are transluscent.

Add the mince (ground beef) along with the remaining ingredients in the left-hand column. Break up the meat with the side of a spoon and cook about 10 minutes.

Add the tomatoes (and sugar, if you think it needs it) and simmer, covered, for about 20 minutes.

Then add the drained kidney beans, cover again, and simmer till beans are heated through, about 5 minutes.

Serve with a green salad and French bread or . . .

For an ersatz enchilada: fill and roll some pancakes (page 170) with chilli con carne, lay the rolled pancakes in an ovenproof dish, top with some tomato sauce and shredded cheese, and heat in a 160°C oven [140°C if fan-assisted / GM3 / 325°F] till warmed through and the cheese has melted, 20–30 minutes or so.

Mayonnaise — MAKES ABOUT 2 CUPS

This double recipe of mayonnaise, based on Rose Elliot's 'Blender Mayonnaise' recipe in *The Bean Book*, can also be made by hand though I find it firms up better if made in a food processor, and even better if her recipe is doubled, as this one is, and then made in the food processor. But feel free to cut this recipe in half, back to its original volume, if you prefer.

Ingredients *and* Procedure

Blend 1 minute in blender or food processor (or whisk by hand):
- 2 eggs
- 4 tsp. wine vinegar
- 4 tsp. lemon juice
- $\frac{1}{2}$ tsp. sea salt (or kosher)
- $\frac{1}{2}$ tsp. dry mustard
- $\frac{1}{2}$ tsp. black pepper

Set the blender or food processor to high speed (or whisk quickly) whilst slowly pouring in, drop by drop at first, then more steadily as it thickens:
- 14 fl. oz. oil [400ml] — I use olive oil

If too thick, add a little boiling water to thin it.

The original recipe says it keeps very well for up to a fortnight in the fridge but mine keeps well for much longer — a good month and more, but I use fresh free-range eggs from the egg stall on my local market so perhaps the fresh eggs help.

Waldorf salad   SERVES 4–6

This is such a refreshing salad — apples, celery, walnuts — and an easy way to liven up an otherwise lacklustre menu.

Ingredients *and* Procedure
Core and cut up into a large bowl: – 3 dessert apples
Sprinkle over them, to keep them from going brown: – fresh lemon juice
Add, and toss to combine: – 1 cup cut-up celery [about 130g or about 2 ribs] – $1/2$ cup chopped walnuts or pecans [110–120g] – about $1/2$ cup mayonnaise [120ml] – a tablespoon or so of honey, if the apples are too tart [opt.]
Serve on lettuce leaves.

Potato latkes (potato pancakes) — SERVES 8

When visiting my friend Seth one lunchtime, he took out a grater and, as we talked, began grating potatoes. Then followed the enchanting smell of frying latkes. Taste and smell are strong memory triggers, and I always think of that impromptu latke lunch when I make these. Never had them before? What's keeping you?

Ingredients *and* Procedure

Place the following ingredients in a colander set over a bowl and squeeze out the liquid as they drain.
- 5–6 potatoes, coarsely grated [about 950g]
- 1 medium onion, coarsely grated or chopped [about 150g]

Discard the liquid from the bowl but leave the potato starch left in the bottom of the bowl. Add to the bowl and mix to combine:
- 2 small eggs or 1 large, beaten
- 3 Tbsp. matzoh meal (or fine cracker or soda bread crumbs)
- 1 tsp. kosher salt
- $\frac{1}{4}$ tsp. pepper
- the drained potato & onion mixture

Heat in a frying pan till very hot:
- about $\frac{1}{2}$" olive oil [13mm] (can be reused — see page 88)

Drop the latkes into the hot oil, about a tablespoon at a time. Cook till browned — mine take 2–3 minutes/side — then flip, flattening them a bit, and cook the other side. Drain on paper towels. They're delicious served with applesauce.

Based on a recipe from Seth Dunn of Northampton, Massachusetts.

Meatloaf   SERVES 6

Meatloaf, gravy and mashed potatoes — the perfect meal to warm you through after a rainy, wintery day. If you've never made it before, don't worry, this recipe's easy, plus it uses up leftover bread or breadcrumbs and, if planning meals in advance, can be frozen uncooked or cooked.

Whilst it's baking is the perfect time to make up a gravy and mash to go with it. Any leftovers can be made into your own individual 'TV dinners' of mash, meatloaf and gravy, and popped into the freezer.

for making the meatloaf mixture

Mix together in a large bowl:
– 2–3 beaten eggs
– $1/3$ cup ketchup [5 Tbsp.]
– heaped $1/3$ cup chopped onion [about 50g, or $1/2$ small onion]
– $1/3$ cup chopped green bell pepper [about 35g, or $1/5$ pepper]
– 1 tsp. kosher salt
– 2 Tbsp. prepared mustard

Then add and combine:
– $1 1/2$ cups fine soft breadcrumbs [75–90g], or 1 cup dried crumbs
– $1/2$ cup milk [120ml]

And lastly, add and thoroughly combine (it's ok to use your hands):
– $1 1/2$ lb. minced beef [680g] (or a beef/pork or beef/lamb mixture)

Optional:
– 2 peeled hard-boiled eggs for inside the loaf

Procedure	Preheat oven to 175°C [155°C if fan-assisted / GM4 / 350°F]. Have a baking pan or ovenproof dish ready for the meatloaf.

Prepare the meatloaf mixture. If you've odd bits of other ingredients to use up, such as mushrooms and parsley, just chop and add them.

Place in the baking dish and form into a loaf.

Optional: If you wish to add the hard-boiled eggs, then create a rut running down the centre of the loaf. Place the peeled eggs lengthwise in the rut, and cover over with the rest of the meatloaf.

for the top of the meatloaf
– about 4 rashers streaky or back bacon *Or:* – ketchup

Lay the bacon slices over the top of the meatloaf or else drizzle the top with ketchup.

Bake, uncovered, for 1 hour or until the centre is cooked. If using streaky bacon on top, you may want to place the meatloaf under a hot grill for 5 minutes or so at the end to help crisp up the bacon, if necessary.

Pour off any fat that's collected in the dish and let rest about 20 minutes before slicing.

Cooking for one in a mini-oven: Prepare the meatloaf mixture, divide it in half and shape into 2 mini-meatloaves. Put one mini-meatloaf in a small ovenproof dish. Lay 2 bacon rashers on top, or drizzle with ketchup. Set the dish in a rimmed tray to catch any liquids that may bubble over whilst it cooks. Place in a cold mini-oven. Set the temperature to 130°C [275°F] and bake 30 minutes. Rotate the meatloaf round so it cooks evenly front and back, and raise the temp to 160°C [325°F]. Bake a further 20 minutes. Remove from the oven and let it rest a good 10 minutes or so before slicing.

With the other mini-meatloaf, you can either freeze it raw, ready to be defrosted and cooked another day, or cook it now and freeze it, ready to be defrosted, reheated and eaten.

Original recipe based on John Ryel's meatloaf recipe, but it's been round the block a few times since then.

Stock jelly/jello — MAKES 1 PINT

This gelatine-based dish made with broth or stock is one I originally concocted for my overweight cat. I hadn't been over-feeding him — he gained his weight through sauntering into neighbours' homes, hoovering up their cat's food, then returning home for his tea. I'm now making a pint of stock jelly every other day for him, and I believe he's leaving the neighbours' cat food alone now.

For one serving, he gets 2 large dollops of the jelly, with a couple of spoonfuls of his shop-bought cat food mixed in, and a few dry biscuits on top. Now the neighbour's cat comes over here to eat his food!

But stock jelly needn't be limited to cats. A friend told me she used to mix a chilled can of Campbell's Soup Concentrated Consommé with cottage cheese for a refreshing summer snack. I've tried this with the stock jelly and guess what — it's actually quite nice. You could go on a diet along with your cat (but omit the dry cat biscuits from yours).

Ingredients
– 1 stock cube or bouillon cube (or 1 pint homemade stock) – 4 tsp. granulated gelatine for a British pint, or 3 tsp. for a US pint – optional: 1 tsp. Marmite

Procedure   If using a stock cube or bouillon cube, place the cube in a 1-pint heatproof measuring jug. Boil some water and pour to the 1-pint line on the jug [or 600ml for 1 British pint]. Add a spoonful of Marmite, if you like, as the cat certainly will, and stir till it's all dissolved. Pour the liquid — or 1 pint homemade stock, if using — into a pan and heat on the hob to just below boiling.

Sprinkle over the top 4 tsp. gelatine (or 3 tsp., if making 1 US pint) and let the gelatine melt into the hot liquid, then stir until it's all dissolved. Don't let it boil.

Pour into a heatproof bowl and chill until set.

For a sweet jelly/jello: In a heatproof measuring jug, pour in about $\frac{1}{2}$ cup squash or cordial [120ml], then fill with boiling water to the 1-pint line [600ml] — if making a US pint, then just use $6\frac{1}{2}$ Tbsp. syrup. Pour into a pan, heat to nearly boiling, then add the gelatine, as above. Pour into ramekins and chill to set.

For a jelly/jello using Vege-gel: In a pan, combine the squash/cordial and cold water (same amounts as above). Sprinkle 1 packet Vege-gel over the cold liquid, and stir thoroughly till completely dissolved. Heat till nearly boiling but don't let it boil. Pour into ramekins and chill — it sets very quickly.

Peanut butter patties   MAKES ABOUT 80 PATTIES

This recipe first appeared in *American Cooking in England* but as it's altered with use, a revised recipe appears below.

Peanut butter patties, a homemade version of Reese's Peanut Butter Cups, have become a standard sweet in my Christmas cookie parcels but I've had to double the recipe, and double it again, due to demand and also, due to wanting to have enough left for me! The recipe below is just doubled once from the original.

for making the insides of the patties
In a large bowl, cream together: – 240g softened butter [1 cup plus 1 Tbsp.]   (if the kitchen's cold, leave it near a radiator to soften) – 500g jar of peanut butter [$2\frac{1}{4}$ cups] *Sift onto it, then stir well to combine:* – 480g icing sugar [$3\frac{1}{3}$ cups confectioners' sugar] – 2 tsp. salt

Procedure	Combine the patty mixture, as above, then set it aside to chill a little (a chilled mixture won't stick to your hands as much when you roll the patties later). Line a baking sheet or tray with parchment or waxed paper.

Roll the chilled mixture into balls, then flatten into 1–2" wide patties [2.5–5cm], about $3/8$–$1/2$" thick [1 cm], and place on the lined baking sheet. Chill again for at least 1 hour.

Once chilled, they're ready for coating. You'll need to melt chocolate & butter, for which you'll want a double boiler, or a bowl set over hot water (though a double boiler's easier).

---

for coating the patties

In the top pan of a double boiler over simmering water, melt for your first coating:
– 900g milk chocolate & dark chocolate [2 lb.]
– 300g butter [$1\frac{1}{3}$ cups]

I usually do 2 coatings. For the 2nd, I melt:
– 900g dark chocolate (preferably 60% cocoa fat)
– 300g butter [$1\frac{1}{3}$ cups]

I used to use my bare hands to coat the patties but have found an easier way which is this: after the chocolate and butter have melted and then cooled ever-so-slightly, rest a patty on the flat of a pallette knife blade and slide it into the chocolate. Use a butter knife to flip it to coat the other side, then slide it back onto the pallette knife and then onto the parchment-lined baking sheet or a tray. Once all the patties are coated, set them somewhere cold to chill.

By the way, when I'm coating the patties, I put the top of the double boiler — the pan holding the melted chocolate — on a mat on the kitchen table. I then place a lid over the bottom pan of the double boiler — the pan holding the hot water— to trap the heat. If the chocolate starts to harden before I'm done coating the patties, I pop the chocolate pan back over the hot water pan and let the chocolate melt again.

When the first chocolate coating has hardened with the cold, they're ready for their second coating. Repeat as for the first coating and chill again. Once these are chilled, they're ready to be eaten. Keep them chilled from now on or the chocolate will go soft and messy.

I usually make these in the winter, when the garage can double as a cold pantry but in the summer, I have to make room in the fridge, which is not so convenient.

Note: In the past when I've made these, the coatings have sometimes been a bit thin and I've even treble-coated them. However, this winter was bitter cold and so was my kitchen, and the melted chocolate stayed fairly thick on the patties — 2 coatings made for quite thickly coated patties. So a cold kitchen may be a plus when coating these.

Based on a recipe from Leah Ryel of Hendersonville, North Carolina (whose recipe was based on one from the *Amish Way Cookbook*).

Rice Krispies Treats MAKES 24 SQUARES, 2" X 2" [5 X 5CM]

When I was young, breakfast cereal manufacturers concocted no end of recipes featuring their product — in a pie crust, as meatloaf filler, as an added texture to cookies or salads — and many of these recipes were fine but often, one could have used any number of things in place of their featured ingredient, such as the original ingredient *it* was replacing. But one recipe, developed in the 1930s, that makes the most of its featured breakfast cereal, and for which there are no substitutes, is Kellogg's Rice Krispies Treats. You can't beat them.

Ingredients *and* Procedure:

In a large pan, melt over low heat:
– ¼ cup butter [58g]

Add, and stir until melted:
– 285–300g white marshmallows, regular or miniature [10½ oz.] [one 300g bag]

Remove from heat. Then add, and stir until well-coated:
– 6 cups Kellogg's® Rice Krispies® cereal [140–145g]

Procedure   Butter the inside of a 13" x 9" x 2" pan [33 x 23 x 5cm]. Prepare the mixture, as above.

Using baking parchment or a used butter wrapper, press the mixture evenly into the prepared pan. Cut into squares when cool.

NOTE: Use fresh marshmallows for best results. Also, if using British miniature marshmallows, you'll need 1½ of the 200g bags.

WEIGHTS

MEASUREMENTS CHARTS, CONVERSIONS, &C.

Quick-reference charts & conversion formulas

This section includes measurement charts that increase incrementally, for quick and easy reference, and also conversion formulas, for when the amount you need to convert isn't in one of the Quick Reference Charts, or for when you need an exact conversion.

DRY WEIGHTS
  QUICK REFERENCE CHART — from $\frac{1}{4}$ oz. to $6\frac{3}{4}$ lb.................*186*
  CONVERSION FORMULAS — for converting exact weights............*189*

FLUID VOLUME (FL. OZ.) *191*

LINEAR MEASURES *203*

TEMPERATURES *209*

Dry Weights (Quick Reference)

The avoirdupois ounce equals 28.35 grams. In the table below, weights from 1/3 oz.–16 oz. are rounded up/down to the nearest 5g; 17–32 oz. are rounded to the nearest 10g; 33 oz. and over are rounded to the nearest 20g. For other weights and for exact conversions, see the *Dry Weights Conversion Formulas* on page 189.

Avoirdupois	Metric	Avoirdupois	Metric
1/4 oz.	*7g*	6 oz.	*170g*
1/3 oz.	*10g*	7 oz.	*200g*
1/2 oz.	*15g*	8 oz. [1/2 lb.]	*225g*
3/4 oz.	*20g*	9 oz.	*255g*
1 oz.	*30g*	10 oz.	*285g*
1 1/2 oz.	*40g*	10 1/2 oz.	*300g*
2 oz.	*55g*	11 oz.	*310g*
2 1/2 oz.	*70g*	11 1/2 oz.	*325g*
3 oz.	*85g*	12 oz. [3/4 lb.]	*340g*
3 1/2 oz.	*100g*	13 oz.	*370g*
4 oz. [1/4 lb.]	*115g*	14 oz.	*395g*
4 1/2 oz.	*125g*	15 oz.	*425g*
5 oz.	*140g*	16 oz. [1 lb.]	*455g*
5 1/2 oz.	*155g*	17 oz.	*480g*

Dry Weights (Quick Reference), cont.

Avoirdupois	Metric
18 oz.	510g
19 oz.	540g
20 oz. [1¼ lb.]	570g
21 oz.	600g
22 oz.	620g
23 oz.	650g
24 oz. [1½ lb.]	680g
25 oz.	710g
26 oz.	740g
27 oz.	770g
28 oz. [1¾ lb.]	790g
29 oz.	820g
30 oz.	850g

Avoirdupois	Metric
31 oz.	880g
32 oz. [2 lb.]	910g
33 oz.	940g
34 oz.	960g
35 oz.	1000g [1kg]
36 oz. [2¼ lb.]	1020g [1.02kg]
37 oz.	1040g
38 oz.	1080g
39 oz.	1100g [1.1kg]
40 oz. [2½ lb.]	1140g [1.14kg]
44 oz. [2¾ lb.]	1240g [1.24kg]
48 oz. [3 lb.]	1360g [1.36kg]
52 oz. [3¼ lb.]	1480g [1.48kg]

Dry Weights (Quick Reference), cont.

Avoirdupois	Metric	Avoirdupois	Metric
56 oz. [$3\frac{1}{2}$ lb.]	*1580g* [*1.58kg*]	84 oz. [$5\frac{1}{4}$ lb.]	*2380g* [*2.38kg*]
60 oz. [$3\frac{3}{4}$ lb.]	*1700g* [*1.7kg*]	88 oz. [$5\frac{1}{2}$ lb.]	*2500g* [*2.5kg*]
64 oz. [4 lb.]	*1820g* [*1.82kg*]	92 oz. [$5\frac{3}{4}$ lb.]	*2600g* [*2.6kg*]
68 oz. [$4\frac{1}{4}$ lb.]	*1920g* [*1.92kg*]	96 oz. [6 lb.]	*2720g* [*2.72kg*]
72 oz. [$4\frac{1}{2}$ lb.]	*2040g* [*2.04kg*]	100 oz. [$6\frac{1}{4}$ lb.]	*2840g* [*2.84kg*]
76 oz. [$4\frac{3}{4}$ lb.]	*2160g* [*2.16kg*]	104 oz. [$6\frac{1}{2}$ lb.]	*2940g* [*2.94kg*]
80 oz. [5 lb.]	*2260g* [*2.26kg*]	108 oz. [$6\frac{3}{4}$ lb.]	*3060g* [*3.06kg*]

Dry Weights Conversion Formulas

It's the metric system that's now used in Britain for weights, but not so long ago it was pounds and ounces and, with the exception of large commercial weights such as tons, and the fact that the American system has no stone, dry weights were the same for Britain and the US: 1 British lb. avoirdupois equalled 1 US lb. avoirdupois.

In the old British system, 1 stone = 14 pounds; 2 stones [28 lb.] = 1 quarter; 4 quarters [112 lb. or 8 st.] = 1 cwt (hundredweight); 20 cwt [2,240 lb.] = 1 'long' ton. Although American dictionaries list both the long and short tons, I had not heard of the long ton before moving to England.

The metric tonne = 1,000kg [2,204.6 lb.].
The British ton ('long' ton) = 20 cwt = 2,240 lb. [1016kg].
The American ton ('short' ton) = 2,000 lb. [907.2kg].

1 ounce = *28.35 grams = 2835 milligrams*
1 pound = 16 ounces = *454 grams = .454 kilograms*
1 kilogram = 1,000 grams = 1,000,000 milligrams

TO CONVERT *TO* METRIC:

From:	To:	Multiply by:
ounces (avoirdupois)	*grams*	28.349523
ounces (avoirdupois)	*kilograms*	0.0283
pounds (avoirdupois)	*grams*	453.59237
pounds (avoirdupois)	*kilograms*	0.45359237

TO CONVERT *FROM* METRIC:

From:	To:	Multiply by:
grams	ounces (avoirdupois)	0.035273962
grams	pounds (avoirdupois)	0.0022046
kilograms	ounces (avoirdupois)	35.335689
kilograms	pounds (avoirdupois)	2.2046

FL. OZ.

FL. OZ.

Fluid Volume

The British Imperial fluid ounce and the American fluid ounce are not exactly the same so this section is comprised of two parts: a *British Imperial Fluid Volume* chart and a *US Fluid Volume* chart, so be sure to refer to the right country's chart (although the slight difference isn't really noticeable until you get up into gallons). To convert larger volumes, see the *Fluid Volume Conversion Formulas* on page 199.

The metric system is now the primary system for most volume measures used in Britain, with a few exceptions such as returnable milk bottles.

FLUID VOLUME

> *QUICK REFERENCE CHART, BRITISH* — up to 1 Imperial gallon...*192*
> *QUICK REFERENCE CHART, AMERICAN* — up to 1 US gallon......*195*
> *CONVERSION FORMULAS* — for converting exact volumes...........*199*
> > *To convert from metric*..*200*
> > *To convert from British*...*201*
> > *To convert from American*...*201*
> > *Bonus: To convert UK petrol prices*...............................*202*

One British pint (20 fl. oz.) in a British pint bottle and one American pint (16 fl. oz.) in a British pint bottle.

British Imperial Fluid Volume (Quick Reference)

The British fluid ounce, based on the British Imperial system, equals 28.41 millilitres. The British pint contains 20 of these fluid ounces and, as there are 8 pints in a gallon, this makes the British gallon 160 fluid ounces — considerably larger than the US gallon.

In the chart below, volumes up to 20 fl. oz. are rounded up/down to the nearest 5 millilitres; 21–30 fl. oz. are rounded to the nearest 10ml; 31 fl. oz. and over are rounded to the nearest 50ml. For exact conversions, see the *Fluid Volume Conversion Formulas* on page 199.

Also, where you see an odd fluid ounce amount in the table below, for example 15$\frac{3}{4}$ fl. oz, this will be a conversion of a round-number millilitre amount, e.g., 450ml, 500ml.

The abbreviations below are: fl. oz. = British fluid ounce; bkfst. cup = breakfast cup; ml = millilitre (1/1000th of a litre).

British	*Metric*
1 fl. oz.	*30ml*
1$\frac{3}{4}$ fl. oz.	*50ml*
2 fl. oz.	*55ml*
3 fl. oz.	*85ml*
3$\frac{1}{2}$ fl. oz.	*100ml*
4 fl. oz.	*115ml*
5 fl. oz. [$\frac{1}{4}$ pint]	*140ml*
5$\frac{1}{4}$ fl. oz.	*150ml*

British	*Metric*
6 fl. oz.	*170ml*
7 fl. oz.	*200ml*
8 fl. oz.	*225ml*
8$\frac{3}{4}$ fl. oz.	*250ml*
9 fl. oz.	*255ml*
10 fl. oz. [$\frac{1}{2}$ pint / bkfst. cup]	*285ml*
10$\frac{1}{2}$ fl. oz.	*300ml*
11 fl. oz.	*315ml*

British Fluid Volume (Quick Reference), cont.

British	Metric
12 fl. oz.	340ml
12$\frac{1}{3}$ fl. oz.	350ml
13 fl. oz.	370ml
14 fl. oz.	400ml
15 fl. oz. [$\frac{3}{4}$ pint]	425ml
15$\frac{3}{4}$ fl. oz.	450ml
16 fl. oz.	455ml
17 fl. oz.	485ml
18 fl. oz.	510ml
19 fl. oz.	540ml
19$\frac{1}{3}$ fl. oz.	550ml

British	Metric
20 fl. oz. [1 pint]	570ml
21 fl. oz.	600ml
24$\frac{2}{3}$ fl. oz.	700ml
25 fl. oz. [1$\frac{1}{4}$ pints]	710ml
28 fl. oz.	800ml
30 fl. oz. [1$\frac{1}{2}$ pints]	850ml
31$\frac{2}{3}$ fl. oz.	900ml
35 fl. oz. [1$\frac{3}{4}$ pints]	1 litre
40 fl. oz. [2 pints]	1.15 litres
42 fl. oz.	1.2 litres
45 fl. oz. [2$\frac{1}{4}$ pints]	1.3 litres

British Fluid Volume (Quick Reference), cont.

British	Metric
50 fl. oz. [2½ pints]	1.4 litres
52¾ fl. oz.	1.5 litres
55 fl. oz. [2¾ pints]	1.55 litres
60 fl. oz. [3 pints]	1.7 litres
65 fl. oz.	1.85 litres
70 fl. oz. [3½ pints]	2 litres
75 fl. oz.	2.15 litres
80 fl. oz. [4 pint / ½ gallon]	2.25 litres

British	Metric
88 fl. oz.	2.5 litres
100 fl. oz. [5 pint]	2.85 litres
105½ fl. oz.	3 litres
120 fl. oz. [6 pint]	3.4 litres
123 fl. oz.	3.5 litres
140 fl. oz. [7 pint]	4 litres
158⅓ fl. oz.	4.5 litres
160 fl. oz. [8 pint / 1 gallon]	4.55 litres

US Fluid Volume (Quick Reference)

The American fluid ounce, based on the US Customary System, equals 29.57 millilitres. For American fluid volumes, 1 US cup = 8 fl. oz; 2 cups = 1 US pint [16 fl. oz.]; 2 pints = 1 US quart [32 fl. oz.]; 4 quarts = 1 US gallon [128 fl. oz.] — much less than the Imperial gallon.

The volumes in the chart below are rounded off, as they were in the *British Imperial Fluid Volume* chart (page 192). For exact conversions, see the *Fluid Volume Conversion Formulas* on page 199.

The abbreviations below are:
fl. oz. = US fluid ounce; Tbsp. = tablespoon; C = cup; pt. = US pint; qt. = US quart; ml = millilitre (1/1000th of a litre).

US volume measures	US fl. oz.	Metric
1 teaspoon	$1/6$ fl. oz.	*5ml*
1 Tbsp.	$1/2$ fl. oz.	*15ml*
2 Tbsp. [$1/8$ C]	1 fl. oz.	*30ml*
3 Tbsp.	$1 1/2$ fl. oz.	*45ml*
$3 1/2$ Tbsp.	$1 2/3$ fl. oz.	*50ml*
4 Tbsp. [$1/4$ C]	2 fl. oz.	*60ml*
5 Tbsp. [~$1/3$ C]	$2 1/2$ fl. oz.	*75ml*
6 Tbsp. [~$1/3$ C]	3 fl. oz.	*90ml*
$1/3$ C plus 1 Tbsp.	$3 1/3$ fl. oz.	*100ml*
8 Tbsp. [$1/2$ C]	4 fl. oz.	*120ml*
10 Tbsp. [~$2/3$ C]	5 fl. oz.	*150ml*

US Fluid Volume (Quick Reference), cont.

US volume measures	US fl. oz.	Metric
12 Tbsp. [³/₄ C]	6 fl. oz.	*175ml*
13⅓ Tbsp. [³/₄–1 C]	6¾ fl. oz.	*200ml*
	7 fl. oz.	*205ml*
1 cup [16 Tbsp.]	8 fl. oz.	*235ml*
1 cup plus 1 Tbsp.	8½ fl. oz.	*250ml*
	9 fl. oz.	*265ml*
1¼ cups	10 fl. oz.	*295ml*
	11 fl. oz.	*325ml*
1½ cups	12 fl. oz.	*355ml*
	13 fl. oz.	*385ml*
1¾ cups	14 fl. oz.	*415ml*
	15 fl. oz.	*445ml*
1 US pint [2 cups]	16 fl. oz.	*475ml*
2 cups & 2 Tbsp.	17 fl. oz.	*500ml*
2¼ cups	18 fl. oz.	*530ml*

US Fluid Volume (Quick Reference), cont.

US volume measures	US fl. oz.	Metric
	19 fl. oz.	*560ml*
$2\frac{1}{2}$ cups	20 fl. oz.	*590ml*
$2\frac{3}{4}$ cups	22 fl. oz.	*650ml*
3 cups ($1\frac{1}{2}$ pints)	24 fl. oz.	*710ml*
$3\frac{1}{4}$ cups	$25\frac{1}{3}$ fl. oz.	*750ml*
scant $3\frac{1}{2}$ cups	$27\frac{3}{4}$ fl. oz.	*820ml*
$3\frac{1}{2}$ cups plus 2 tsp.	$28\frac{3}{4}$ fl. oz.	*850ml*
4 C minus 2 Tbsp.	30 fl. oz.	*890ml*
4 C minus $1\frac{1}{2}$ Tbsp.	$30\frac{1}{2}$ fl. oz.	*900ml*
1 quart [4 cups / 2 pt.]	32 fl. oz.	*950ml*
4 cups & ~3 Tbsp.	$33\frac{3}{4}$ fl. oz.	*1 litre*
5 cups	40 fl. oz.	*1.2 litres*
$1\frac{1}{2}$ quarts [6 cups]	48 fl. oz.	*1.4 litres*
6 cups & 4 Tbsp.	50 fl. oz.	*1.5 litres*

US Fluid Volume (Quick Reference), cont.

US volume measures	US fl. oz.	Metric
7 cups	56 fl. oz.	1.65 litres
7½ cups	60 fl. oz.	1.75 litres
½ gallon [8 C / 2 qt.]	64 fl. oz.	1.9 litres
8½ C [2 qt. & ½ C]	68 fl. oz.	2 litres
9 cups	72 fl. oz.	2.1 litres
10 cups	80 fl. oz.	2.35 litres
3 quarts [12 C]	96 fl. oz.	2.85 litres
3 quarts & ¾ cup	102 fl. oz.	3 litres
3 quarts & 2¾ cups	118 fl. oz.	3.5 litres
1 gallon [4 qt. / 16 C]	128 fl. oz.	3.8 litres
1 gallon & 1 cup	136 fl. oz.	4 litres

Fluid Volume Conversion Formulas

A fluid ounce is a measure of *volume* rather than weight. One fluid ounce is equal to the amount that will fill 2 level tablespoons, and the weight of 2 tablespoons of one ingredient often differs from the weight of 2 tablespoons of another, for example, 2 Tbsp. of flour is much lighter than 2 Tbsp. of cream.

Teaspoons, tablespoons and cups; fluid pints, quarts and gallons; and millilitres, centilitres and litres are all measures of volume.

➔ **If a recipe calls for 15g, then weigh it;
if it calls for 15ml, measure it (1 level tablespoon = 15ml).**

The measures below are exact measures intended for calculating conversions — don't expect to measure to this exactness. For measuring volumes in a measuring jug, the closest you can hope to achieve is the nearest 10–20ml of your target volume, which is fine. For very small volumes, use teaspoons and tablespoons.

I've included US cups and quarts below but not British cups and quarts as these measures are no longer in common use in the UK, whereas they are in the US, but for the record, 10 fl. oz. = 1 British cup = half a British pint; and 40 fl. oz. = 1 British quart = 2 British pints = a quarter of an Imperial gallon.

1 British fl. oz. = *28.41 millilitres*
1 British pint = 20 British fl. oz. = *568ml*
1 British gallon = 8 British pints = 160 British fl. oz. = *4.54 L*

1 US fl. oz. = *29.57 millilitres*
1 US cup = 8 US fl. oz. = *237ml*
1 US fl. pint = 16 US fl. oz. = *473ml*
1 US fl. quart = 2 US fl. pints = 32 US fl. oz. = *946ml (0.946 L)*
1 US gallon = 4 US fl. quarts = 8 US fl. pints = 128 US fl. oz. = *3.78 L*

1 litre = 100 centilitres = 1,000 millilitres = **1.76 British pints =**
    2.11 US fl. pints = 1.05 US fl. quarts

The tables on the following pages give the convertion formulas for metric, British and American fluid volumes.

Fluid Volume Conversion Formulas, cont.
To Convert from Metric Volumes

From:	To:	Multiply by:
millilitres	**British fl. ounce**	0.03519609
millilitres	**British pint**	0.001759804
millilitres	US fl. ounce	0.03381497
millilitres	US pint	0.002113436
centilitres	**British fl. ounce**	0.3519609
centilitres	**British pint**	0.01759804
centilitres	US fl. ounce	0.3381497
centilitres	US pint	0.02113436
litres	**British fl. ounce**	35.19609
litres	**British pint**	1.759804
litres	**Imperial gallon**	0.2199755
litres	US fl. ounce	33.81497
litres	US cup	4.2268704
litres	US pint	2.1134352
litres	US quart	1.0567176
litres	US gallon	0.2641794

Fluid Volume Conversion Formulas, cont.

To Convert from British Imperial Volumes

From:	To:	Multiply by:
fl. ounce (British)	US fl. ounce	0.9607594
fl. ounce (British)	*millilitres*	28.41
fl. ounce (British)	*litres*	0.02841225
pint (British)	US cups	2.4019276
pint (British)	US pint	1.2009638
pint (British)	US quart	0.6004819
pint (British)	*millilitres*	568.2
pint (British)	*litres*	0.5682
gallon (Imperial)	US gallon	1.2009638
gallon (Imperial)	*litres*	4.546

To Convert from US Volumes

From:	To:	Multiply by:
fl. ounce (US)	**British fl. ounce**	1.040843
fl. ounce (US)	*millilitres*	29.57
fl. ounce (US)	*litres*	0.029572702
cup (US)	**British pint**	0.4163322
cup (US)	*millilitres*	236.56
pint (US)	**British pint**	0.8326645
pint (US)	*millilitres*	473.12
pint (US)	*litres*	0.47312
quart (US)	**British pint**	1.665329
quart (US)	*litres*	0.946326
gallon (US)	**Imperial gallon**	0.8326645
gallon (US)	*litres*	3.785306

Fluid Volume Conversion Formulas, cont.

Bonus calculation: petrol price conversions

What's petrol doing in a *Measurements for Cooking* book? I've included it in this section because half of the equation is already here, in the litres-to-US-gallons equation, so I thought it would be helpful to include the rest of the equation, for interest if nothing else.

First convert pence-per-litre to pence-per-US gallon:

divide the UK price of 1 litre of petrol by 0.2641794

so, for example, if 1 litre costs £1.30, then a volume equal to 1 US gallon would cost = £4.92.

Next convert the £ to US $ — you'll need the current exchange rate so check a newspaper or the Internet for that day's exchange rate and:

multiply the £ per US gallon (4.92 in the above example)
times the number of US dollars in one pound Sterling.

If there are $1.65 in £1, then in this example, multiply 4.92 x 1.65 and you get $8.12 per US gallon. So if the British price of petrol is £1.30/litre and the exchange rate is $1.65 to the pound, then we're paying the equivalent of $8.12 per US gallon.

LENGTH

Linear Measures

The metric lengths in the *Quick Reference Chart* are rounded up or down to the nearest millimeter (mm) for measures less than one inch; for longer lengths they're rounded to the nearest half-centimeter (0.5cm).

Britain now uses metric measures for length; Americans use feet and inches.

To calculate exact lengths or longer lengths, see the *Linear Measures Conversion Formulas* on page 207.

LINEAR MEASURES

   QUICK REFERENCE CHART — from $\frac{1}{16}$ in. to $3\frac{1}{4}$ ft. (1metre)........*204*

   CONVERSION FORMULAS — for converting exact lengths............*207*

Linear Measures Chart (Quick Reference)

Inches	Metric	Inches	Metric
$1/16$"	1.5mm	**2"**	5cm
$1/8$"	3mm	$2\frac{1}{4}$"	5.5cm
$1/4$"	6mm (~0.5cm)	$2\frac{1}{2}$"	6.5cm
$3/8$"	9mm (~1cm)	$2\frac{3}{4}$"	7cm
$1/2$"	13mm	**3"**	7.5cm
$5/8$"	16mm (~1.5cm)	$3\frac{1}{4}$"	8cm
$3/4$"	19mm (~2cm)	$3\frac{1}{2}$"	9cm
$7/8$"	22mm	$3\frac{3}{4}$"	9.5cm
1"	2.5cm	**4"**	10cm
$1\frac{1}{4}$"	3cm	$4\frac{1}{4}$"	11cm
$1\frac{1}{2}$"	4cm	$4\frac{1}{2}$"	11.5cm
$1\frac{3}{4}$"	4.5cm	$4\frac{3}{4}$"	12cm

Linear Measures (Quick Reference), cont.

Inches	*Metric*	Inches	*Metric*
5"	*12.5cm*	**8 1/2"**	*21.5cm*
5 1/4"	*13.5cm*	8 3/4"	*22cm*
5 1/2"	*14cm*	**9"**	*23cm*
5 3/4"	*14.5cm*	9 1/4"	*23.5cm*
6" (1/2 ft.)	*15cm*	9 1/2"	*24cm*
6 1/4"	*16cm*	9 3/4"	*25cm*
6 1/2"	*16.5cm*	**10"**	*25.5cm*
6 3/4"	*17cm*	10 1/4"	*26cm*
7"	*18cm*	10 1/2"	*26.5cm*
7 1/4"	*18.5cm*	10 3/4"	*27.5cm*
7 1/2"	*19cm*	**11"**	*28cm*
7 3/4"	*19.5cm*	11 1/4"	*28.5cm*
8"	*20.5cm*	11 1/2"	*29cm*
8 1/4"	*21cm*	11 3/4"	*30cm*

Linear Measures (Quick Reference), cont.

Inches	Metric	Inches	Metric
12" (1 foot)	30.5cm	**26"**	66cm
13"	33cm	**27"**	68.5cm
14"	35.5cm	**28"**	71cm
15"	38cm	**29"**	73.5cm
16"	40.5cm	**30"** ($2\frac{1}{2}$ ft.)	76cm
17"	43cm	**31"**	79cm
18" ($1\frac{1}{2}$ ft.)	45.5cm	**32"**	81cm
19"	48cm	**33"**	84cm
20"	51cm (~0.5m)	**34"**	86.5cm
21"	53.5cm	**35"**	89cm
22"	56cm	**36"** (1 yard / 3 ft.)	91.5cm
23"	58.5cm	**37"**	94cm
24" (2 feet)	61cm	**38"**	96.5
25"	63.5cm	**39"**	99cm
		$39\frac{1}{3}$" (~$3\frac{1}{4}$ feet)	100cm (1 metre)

Linear Measures Conversion Formulas[*]

1 inch = *2.54 centimetres*
1 foot = 12 inches = *30.48 centimetres*
1 yard = 3 feet = 36 inches = *91.44 centimetres or 0.9 metre*
1 mile = 1,760 yards = 5,280 feet = *1,609.34 metres or 1.6 kilometres*

1 millimetre = 0.1 centimetre
1 centimetre = 10 millimetres = 0.39 inch
1 metre = 100 centimetres = 1,000 millimetres = 0.001 kilometres
  = 39.37 inches (1 yard plus 3.37 inches)
1 kilometre = 1,000 metres = 0.62137 mile

TO CONVERT *TO* METRIC:

From:	To:	Multiply by:
inches	*centimetres*	2.54
feet	*centimetres*	30.4801
feet	*metres*	0.30466
feet	*kilometres*	0.00030466
yards	*metres*	0.914
miles	*kilometres*	1.60934

TO CONVERT *FROM* METRIC:

From:	To:	Multiply by:
centimetres	inches	0.39370079
centimetres	feet	0.0328
metres	feet	3.282
metres	yards	1.094
kilometres	feet	3,282
kilometres	miles	0.6213727

---

[*] There is no difference between British and American inches, feet and yards.

TEMPS

Temperatures

Whether Fahrenheit or Celsius, the temperatures we *know* are the ones we're familiar with. I grew up using Fahrenheit and now live in England where Celsius is used, so the Celsius air temperatures I *know* tend to be those between 0° and 20°C; temps higher than that I'm more familiar with in Fahrenheit, simply because they don't occur so often in England so I haven't developed a Celsius-number concept to relate to that level of warmth.

To find equivalent Fahrenheit and Celsius temperatures for air and oven, see the *Outdoors* and *Oven* charts, pages 210 & 211. For some food-safety and other cooking temperatures, see *Food & Cooking* on page 212.

TEMPERATURES

    OUTDOORS — Celsius and Fahrenheit air temperatures, and calculations for converting *210*

    OVEN — Celsius, Gas Mark and Fahrenheit oven temperatures *211*

    FOOD & COOKING — Some common cooking and food-safety temperatures *212*

Temperatures: Outdoors

Celsius	Fahrenheit
-20	-4
-15	5
-10	14
-5	23
0	32
5	41
10	50

Celsius	Fahrenheit
15	59
20	68
25	77
30	86
35	95
40	104
45	113

Three methods for converting temperatures — take your pick

If using a calculator:

To convert *Celsius* to Fahrenheit, multiply by 1.8; and then add 32.

To convert Fahrenheit to *Celsius*, subtract 32; and then divide by 1.8.

If using pencil & paper:

To convert *Celsius* to Fahrenheit, multiply by $9/5$; and then add 32.

To convert Fahrenheit to *Celsius*, subtract 32; and then multiply by $5/9$.

If using your head:

Zero degrees Celsius equals 32°F. Every 5°C is equal to 9°F, so 5°C equals 41°F [32 + 9]; 10°C equals 50°F [32 + 18]; 15°C equals 59°F [32 + 27], and so on. It works for minus-zero Celsius temperatures, too.

Temperatures: Oven

Celsius	Gas Mark	Fahrenheit	Descriptions
110	¼	225	very slow
120	½	250	very slow
135	1	275	very slow
150	2	300	slow
160	3	325	moderately slow
175	4	350	moderate
190	5	375	moderately hot
205	6	400	hot
220	7	425	very hot
230	8	450	very hot
245	9	475	very hot
260	10	500	extremely hot

To get your roughly equivalent Celsius oven temperature, divide your Fahrenheit oven temperature in half; to get your roughly equivalent Fahrenheit oven temperature, double your Celsius one. (The Celsius oven temperatures listed on this chart are approximately equal to their corresponding Fahrenheit oven temperatures.)

If you have a fan-assisted oven, you'll want to set it about 10–20°C lower than your recipe calls for, but check your oven manual first.

Temperatures: Food & Cooking

Food Safety Temperatures

for these foods:	*store at these temps:*
highly perishable foods e.g., raw meats (and for raw fish, preferably even colder)	**less than 5°C [41°F]** *this is the limit for cold food storage recommended by the Food Standards Agency*
perishable foods e.g., cooked meats & other cooked dishes, cooked rice & other cooked grains	**less than 8°C [46°F]** *this is the legal limit for cold food storage, cold enough so bacteria can't grow*
fresh eggs, and many fresh fruits & vegetables	**cool temperatures, dry environment, out of sunlight**
Stilton cheese and other cheeses which ripen at room temperature	**room temperature**

Storage temps cold enough so bacteria can't grow
For cold food storage: below 8°C [46°F] is the legal limit
(the Food Standards Agency recommends below 5°C [41°F]).
For freezing: best to freeze at below -18°C [0°F] as bacteria are dormant at this temperature.

How quickly to cool down cooked food
Cooked foods should be cooled to 10°C [50°F] within $1\frac{1}{2}$ hours. There is leeway here — I often leave mine to cool in the garage overnight —but if you work in the food industry, best to stick to the $1\frac{1}{2}$ hour rule, then you *know* it's safe.

Temperatures: Food & Cooking, cont.

Food Safety Temperatures, *cont.*

Temps at which food-poisoning bacteria multiply most swiftly

Food-poisoning bacteria multiply fastest at 35–45°C [95–113°F], roughly body temperature, so avoid leaving food out for too long on too warm a day.

Hot enough to kill bacteria: above 63°C [145°F]

Or else cook the food until its centre reaches one of these temperatures, and cook for the corresponding length of time:

when its centre reaches 65°C [149°F], cook for 30 minutes; or
when its centre reaches 70°C [158°F], cook for 2 minutes; or
when its centre reaches 75°C [167°F], cook for 30 seconds.

Temperatures: Food & Cooking, cont.

Oven Temperatures for Baking

biscuits [cookies, US]: most baked at moderate to moderately hot: 175–190°C [GM4–5/350–375°F]

- chocolate chip cookies: moderately hot for 8–10 minutes: 190°C [GM5/375°F]
- shortbread biscuits: moderate for 20–25 minutes: 175°C [GM4/350°F]

breads, soda: very hot for first 15–20 minutes: 230°C [GM8/450°F], then hot for remaining 20–25 minutes: 200°C [GM6/400°F]

- scones [rolled biscuits, US]: very hot for 10–15 minutes: 220°C [GM7/425°F] — scones are basically soda bread dough patted out to about $1/2$–1 inch thick [1.3–2.5cm]

breads, yeast: very hot: around 230°C [GM8/450°F] for 25–35 minutes

- pizzas: very hot: 240–250°C [GM9/475°F] for 10–12 minutes

cakes: most baked at moderate: 175°C [GM4/350°F]

- brownies: moderate for 20–30 minutes
- cake in 2 sandwich tins [round cake pans, US]: depending on recipe and size of tins, bake at moderate for 20–25 minutes for smaller tins, and 25–40 minutes for 8–9" tins [20–23cm]
- cake in 1 rectangular tin: moderate for 40–45 minutes

chicken, roast: moderately hot to hot: around 190–200°C [GM5–6/375–400°F], at 20 minutes per pound [450g], till internal temperature of breast reaches 80°C [175°F]

Temperatures: Food & Cooking, cont.

Oven Temperatures for Baking, cont.

custards in bain marie [water bath, US]: moderately slow: around 160°C [GM3/325°F]

- in 1-litre baking dish [1-qt.] in bain marie: moderately slow for about 45 minutes
- in ramekins [custard cups] in bain marie: moderately slow for 20–30 minutes

meat dishes (but not roasts or joints of meat): most baked at moderately low to moderate: 160–175°C [GM3–4/325–350°F]

- shepherd's pie (lamb & gravy base with mashed potato topping): at 175°C [GM4/350°F] for about 30 minutes
- meatloaf: at 175°C [GM4/350°F] for about 1 hour

meringues: low — around 120°C [GM$^1/_2$/250°F] for around an hour, or until dried

pies, sweet: very hot for first 10 minutes: 220°C [GM7/425°F], then low–moderate for remaining time: 150–175°C [GM2–4/300–350°F]

- unfilled pastry cases [pie shells]:
  very hot: 220°C [GM7/425°F] for 10–20 minutes, depending on the type of pastry
- fruit pies (including apple), and most filled pies:
  very hot for first 10 minutes: 220°C [GM7/425°F],
  then moderate for the remaining time — 30–40 minutes, in the case of fruit pies: 175°C [GM4/350°F]
- pumpkin pie:
  very hot for first 10 minutes: 220°C [GM7/425°F],
  then low for last 45 minutes or so: 150°C [GM2/300°F]

Temperatures: Food & Cooking, *cont.*

Oven Temperatures for Baking, *cont.*

potatoes, baked: hot: 200°C [GM6/400°F], for $1\frac{1}{4}$–$1\frac{1}{2}$ hours, depending on size of potato

Deep-frying Temperatures

For most foods: heat oil to 185°C [365°F] before adding the food (memory tip for Fahrenheit: 365 = the number of days in a year)
- <u>chips</u> [french fries, US]: first fry in 150°C [300°F] oil for 5–8 minutes, till soft but still pale, then drain, and refry later in 200°C [400°F] oil for 2–3 minutes, till crisp

Reheating Instructions

To reheat large amounts of mashed potato or other mashed veg: place a covered ovenproof dish of mashed potato or veg, in a bain marie and heat till warmed through in a 160°C [GM3/325°F] oven

To reheat deep-fried foods: spread on racks and heat till warmed through, uncovered, in a very slow oven: 120°C [GM$\frac{1}{2}$/250°F]

BUTTER : FLOUR : SUGAR

Food staples: Butter, Flour, Sugar
quick reference charts

This section includes quick-reference charts for butter, flour and sugar. The measures in these charts increase incrementally, for quick and easy reference without having to calculate.

BUTTER CHART

QUICK REFERENCE CHART — butter volumes, rounded off, for 5g up to 500g *219*

FLOUR CHART

QUICK REFERENCE CHART — volumes for both plain flour [all-purpose flour] and strong flour [bread flour], rounded off, for 5g up to 1kg *222*

SUGAR CHARTS

QUICK REFERENCE CHART, WHITE GRANULATED SUGAR & BROWN SUGAR — volumes rounded off, for 5g up to 600g *228*

QUICK REFERENCE CHART, ICING [CONFECTIONERS'] SUGAR — volumes for both unsifted and sifted icing sugar, rounded off, for 5g up to 1kg *231*

Some food staples and their calories

How many calories in these food staples? Pictured are half-cup measures [8 Tbsp.] and tablespoon measures of butter, flour and sugar.

Butter: *a level tablespoon butter weighs about 15g and contains about 100 calories; a level half-cup [1 stick] weighs about 115g and contains about 815 calories. Other fats and oils are similarly high in calories.*

Plain flour [all-purpose flour, US]: *a level tablespoon plain flour weighs about 8–9g and contains about 26 calories; a level half-cup weighs about 70g and contains about 210 calories.*

Sugar: *a level tablespoon granulated sugar weighs about 12–13g and contains about 47 calories; a level half-cup weighs about 100g and contains about 370 calories.*

Butter Chart (Quick Reference)

In the UK, butter typically comes in a single 250g block [9 oz.]. In the US, a pound of butter comes in four 'sticks' (sometimes called 'cubes'), individually-wrapped and usually marked with lines showing where to cut for tablespoon measures. Some British butter wrappers are printed with lines showing where to cut for 50g of butter.

The weight-to-volume equivalents below are correct to within a few grams. The teaspoons, tablespoons and cups used in the butter chart are 5ml teaspoons, 15ml tablespoons and American 8-fl.-oz. cups [240ml], all measured level, not rounded. The dessertspoon, a British measure, is equal to two teaspoons.

One level $\frac{1}{4}$ cup of butter [$\frac{1}{2}$ stick / 60g] contains 408 calories [kcal], so about 100 calories per level tablespoon [15g]. (For American cups and other US volumes, see page 244.)

metric weight [avoirdupois oz.]	teaspoons, Tablespoons, cups	other volume equivalents
5g [~$\frac{1}{5}$ oz.]	1 tsp.	$\frac{1}{2}$ dessertspoon
10g [~$\frac{1}{3}$ oz.]	2 tsp.	1 dessertspoon
15g [~$\frac{1}{2}$ oz.]	1 Tbsp.	3 tsp; $\frac{1}{8}$ stick
20g [~$\frac{3}{4}$ oz.]	1$\frac{1}{2}$ Tbsp.	
30g [~1 oz.]	2 Tbsp.	$\frac{1}{4}$ stick
40g [~1$\frac{1}{2}$ oz.]	3 Tbsp.	
50g [~1$\frac{3}{4}$ oz.]	3$\frac{1}{2}$ Tbsp.	

Butter Chart, continued

metric weight [avoirdupois oz.]	teaspoons, Tablespoons, cups	other volume equivalents
60g [~2 oz.]	¼ cup	4 Tbsp; ½ stick
70g [~2½ oz.]	⅓ cup *minus* 1 tsp.	5 Tbsp; ~⅔ stick
75g [~2⅔ oz.]	⅓ cup	5⅓ Tbsp; ~¾ stick
85g [3 oz.]	⅓ cup *plus* 2 tsp.	6 Tbsp; ¾ stick
100g [3½ oz.]	½ cup *minus* 1 Tbsp.	7 Tbsp; 1 stick *minus* 1 Tbsp.
110g [scant 4 oz.]	½ cup *minus* ¼ Tbsp.	7¾ Tbsp; ~1 stick
115 [~4 oz.]	½ cup	8 Tbsp; 1 stick
125g [~4½ oz.]	½ cup *plus* 1 Tbsp. [1⅛ sticks]	9 Tbsp.
130g [~4½ oz.]	½ cup *plus* 1 Tbsp.	9 Tbsp; 1⅛ sticks
140g [~5 oz.]	⅔ cup *minus* 2 tsp.	10 Tbsp; 1¼ sticks
150g [~5⅓ oz.]	⅔ cup	10⅔ Tbsp; ~1¼ sticks
160g [~5⅔ oz.]	¾ cup *minus* 2 tsp.	~1½ sticks
170g [6 oz.]	¾ cup	12 Tbsp; 1½ sticks
175g [~6 oz.]	¾ cup *plus* 1 tsp.	~1½ sticks
180g [~6⅓ oz.]	¾ cup *plus* 2 tsp.	~1½ sticks
190g [~6¾ oz.]	¾ cup *plus* 1⅓ Tbsp.	1½ sticks *plus* 1⅓ Tbsp.

Butter Chart, continued

metric weight [avoirdupois oz.]	cups [sticks]
200g [~7 oz.]	$3/4$ cup *plus* 2 Tbsp. [$1^3/_4$ sticks]
225g [~8 oz.]	**1 cup** [2 sticks]; also 16 Tbsp.
250g [~9 oz.]	1 cup *plus* 2 Tbsp. [$2^1/_4$ sticks]
275g [~$9^3/_4$ oz.]	$1^1/_4$ cups *minus* 2 tsp. [~$2^1/_2$ sticks]
285g [~10 oz.]	**$1^1/_4$ cups** [$2^1/_2$ sticks]
300g [~$10^1/_2$ oz.]	**$1^1/_3$ cups** [~$2^3/_4$ sticks]
325g [~$11^1/_2$ oz.]	$1^1/_2$ cups *minus* 1 Tbsp. [$2^3/_4$ –3 sticks]
340g [12 oz.]	**$1^1/_2$ cups** [3 sticks]
350g [$12^1/_3$ oz.]	$1^1/_2$ cups *plus* 2 tsp. [~3 sticks]
375g [$13^1/_4$ oz.]	$1^3/_4$ cups [$3^1/_2$ sticks] *minus* $1^1/_2$ Tbsp.
400g [~14 oz.]	**$1^3/_4$ cups** [$3^1/_2$ sticks]
425g [15 oz.]	2 cups [4 sticks] *minus* 2 Tbsp.
450g [~1 lb.]	about 2 cups [~4 sticks]
454g [1 lb.]	**2 cups** [4 sticks]
475g [~17 oz.]	2 cups [4 sticks] *plus* $1^1/_2$ Tbsp.
500g [~18 oz.]	$2^1/_4$ cups *minus* 2 tsp. [~$4^1/_2$ sticks]

Flour Chart (Quick Reference)

The same volume of flour can vary in weight based on a variety of things such as moisture in the air, how settled it is in the cup you're using, the type of flour you're measuring, etc., so view the volumes given in the chart that follows as approximate equivalents to the corresponding weights of flour.

From a number of weighings of cupfuls of strong flour (bread flour), and cupfuls of plain flour, I took the average weight from each type of flour and used this as the basis for the volume equivalents in the chart below. One cup of strong flour averaged out to 140g [~5 oz.], and 1 cup of plain flour averaged out to 132g [~$4\frac{2}{3}$ oz.], but bear in mind there were weighings above and below these averages so view the volumes below as a guide.

British plain flour is milled from a 'softer' wheat (i.e., one with less gluten) than American all-purpose flour. Volumes for all-purpose flour should lie somewhere in between those given in the PLAIN FLOUR and STRONG FLOUR columns, but for weights up to 1 lb., use either column.

If using self-raising flour, look in the PLAIN FLOUR column for your equivalents.

The teaspoons, tablespoons and cups used in the following chart are 5ml teaspoons, 15ml tablespoons and American 8-fl.-oz. cups [240ml], all measured level, not rounded.
The dessertspoon is a British measure, equal to two teaspoons.

One level $\frac{1}{4}$ cup of all-purpose flour [about 35g] contains about 105 calories [kcal], so 26 calories per level tablespoon. (For American cups and other US volumes, see page 244.)

metric weight [avoirdupois oz.]	PLAIN FLOUR teaspoons, Tablespoons, cups	STRONG FLOUR (bread flour) teaspoons, Tablespoons, cups
2.75–3g	1 tsp.	1 tsp.
5g	1¾ tsp.	1¾ tsp.
5.5–6g	1 dessertsp. [2 tsp.]	1 dessertsp. [2 tsp.]
8.5g [~⅓ oz.]	1 Tbsp. [3 tsp.]	1 Tbsp. [3 tsp.]
10g [~⅓ oz.]	3½ tsp.	3½ tsp.
15g [~½ oz.]	1¾ Tbsp.	1¾ Tbsp.
17g [½–⅔ oz.]	2 Tbsp. [6 tsp.]	2 Tbsp. [6 tsp.]
20g [~⅔ oz.]	2⅓ Tbsp.	2¼ Tbsp.
25g [1 scant oz.]	3 Tbsp.	2¾ Tbsp.
30g [~1 oz.]	3⅔ Tbsp.	scant 3½ Tbsp.
35g (~1¼ oz.)	4¼ Tbsp. [~¼ cup]	**4 Tbsp. [¼ cup]**
40g [~1½ oz.]	4¾ Tbsp. [heaping ¼ cup]	4½ Tbsp. [heaping ¼ cup]
45g [~1⅔ oz.]	5½ Tbsp. [~⅓ cup]	5 Tbsp. [~⅓ cup]
50g [~1¾ oz.]	6 Tbsp. [heaping ⅓ cup]	5¾ Tbsp. [heaping ⅓ cup]
60g [~2 oz.]	7¼ Tbsp. [scant ½ cup]	6¾ Tbsp. [⅓–½ cup]
70g [~2½ oz.]	½ cup *plus* ½ Tbsp. [8½ Tbsp.]	½ cup [8 Tbsp.]

metric weight [avoirdupois oz.]	**PLAIN FLOUR** teaspoons, Tablespoons, cups	**STRONG FLOUR** (bread flour) teaspoons, Tablespoons, cups
75g [~2²/₃ oz.]	½ cup *plus* 1 Tbsp. [9 Tbsp.]	½ cup *plus* ½ Tbsp. [8½ Tbsp.]
80g [~2¾ oz.]	⅔ cup *minus* 1 Tbsp. [9²/₃ Tbsp.]	½ cup *plus* 1 Tbsp. [9 Tbsp.]
90g [~3 oz.]	**⅔ cup** [10²/₃ Tbsp.]	about ⅔ cup [about 10²/₃ Tbsp.]
100g [~3½ oz.]	**¾ cup** [12 Tbsp.]	¾ cup *minus* ½ Tbsp. [11½ Tbsp.]
110g [~4 oz.]	¾ cup *plus* 1½ Tbsp. [13½ Tbsp.]	¾ cup *plus* ½ Tbsp. [12½ Tbsp.]
115g [4 oz.]	¾ cup *plus* 2 Tbsp. [14 Tbsp.]	¾ cup *plus* 1 Tbsp. [13 Tbsp.]
120g [~4¼ oz.]	1 cup *minus* 1½ Tbsp. [14½ Tbsp.]	¾ cup *plus* 2 Tbsp. [14 Tbsp.]
125g [~4½ oz.]	1 cup *minus* 1 Tbsp. [15 Tbsp.]	¾ cup *plus* 2 Tbsp. [14 Tbsp.]
130g [~4½ oz.]	**1 cup** [16 Tbsp.]	1 cup *minus* 1 Tbsp. [15 Tbsp.]
135g [~4¾ oz.]	**1 cup** [16 Tbsp.]	scant 1 cup [scant 16 Tbsp.]
140g [~5 oz.]	1 cup *plus* 1 Tbsp.	**1 cup** [16 Tbsp.]
150g [~5¼ oz.]	1 cup *plus* 2 Tbsp.	about 1 cup

metric weight [avoirdupois oz.]	**PLAIN FLOUR** teaspoons, Tablespoons, cups	**STRONG FLOUR** (bread flour) teaspoons, Tablespoons, cups
160g [~5²/₃ oz.]	scant 1¼ cups	1 cup *plus* 2 Tbsp.
170g [~6 oz.]	**1¼ cups**	scant 1¼ cups
175g [~6 oz.]	**1⅓ cups**	1¼ cups
180g [~6⅓ oz.]	**1⅓ cups**	about 1¼ cups
190g [~6¾ oz.]	1½ cups *minus* 1 Tbsp.	**1⅓ cups**
200g [7 oz.]	**1½ cups**	1½ cups *minus* 1 Tbsp.
210g [~7⅓ oz.]	about 1½ cups	**1½ cups**
220g [~7¾ oz.]	**1⅔ cups**	about 1½ cups
225g [~8 oz.]	about 1¾ cups	about 1⅔ cups
230g [~8 oz.]	**1¾ cups**	**1⅔ cups**
240g [~8½ oz.]	about 1¾ cups	about 1¾ cups
250g [~8¾ oz.]	1¾ cups *plus* 2 Tbsp.	about 1¾ cups
260g [~9 oz.]	**2 cups**	2 cups *minus* 2 Tbsp.
270g [~9½ oz.]	**2 cups**	scant 2 cups
275g [~9¾ oz.]	about 2 cups	**2 cups**
280g [~10 oz.]	2 cups *plus* 2 Tbsp.	**2 cups**

metric weight [avoirdupois oz.]	PLAIN FLOUR teaspoons, Tablespoons, cups	STRONG FLOUR (bread flour) teaspoons, Tablespoons, cups
290g [~10¼ oz.]	2 cups *plus* 3 Tbsp.	**2 cups**
300g [~10½ oz.]	about 2¼ cups	2 *cups* plus 2 Tbsp.
320g [~11¼ oz.]	2½ cups *minus* 1 Tbsp.	about 2¼ cups
325g [~11½ oz.]	scant 2½ cups	**2⅓ cups**
340g [12 oz.]	about 2½ cups	scant 2½ cups
350g [~12⅓ oz.]	**2⅔ cups**	**2½ cups**
360g [~12⅔ oz.]	about 2¾ cups	about 2½ cups
375g [~13¼ oz.]	2¾ cups *plus* 1½ Tbsp.	**2⅔ cups**
380g [~13⅓ oz.]	3 cups *minus* 2 Tbsp.	about 2¾ cups
400g [14 oz.]	**3 cups**	2¾–3 cups
420g [~14¾ oz.]	scant 3¼ cups	**3 cups**
425g [15 oz.]	about 3¼ cups	**3 cups**
440g [~15½ oz.]	**3⅓ cups**	3–3¼ cups
454g [16 oz; 1 lb.]	scant 3½ cups	about 3¼ cups
460g [~16¼ oz.]	**3½ cups**	**3¼ cups**
475g [16¾ oz.]	about 3½ cups	**3⅓ cups**
480g [~17 oz.]	**3⅔ cups**	3⅓–3½ cups

metric weight [avoirdupois oz.]	PLAIN FLOUR teaspoons, Tablespoons, cups	STRONG FLOUR (bread flour) teaspoons, Tablespoons, cups
500g [~$17^2/_3$ oz.]	**$3^3/_4$ cups**	$3^1/_2$–$3^2/_3$ cups
550g [~$19^1/_3$ oz.]	scant $4^1/_4$ cups	scant 4 cups
565g [~$1^1/_4$ lb.]	**$4^1/_4$ cups**	**4 cups**
600g [~21 oz.]	**$4^1/_2$ cups**	**$4^1/_4$ cups**
650g [~23 oz.]	about 5 cups	**$4^2/_3$ cups**
680g [$1^1/_2$ lb.]	scant $5^1/_4$ cups	$4^3/_4$–5 cups
700g [~25 oz.]	**$5^1/_3$ cups**	**5 cups**
750g [~26 oz.]	**$5^2/_3$ cups**	**$5^1/_3$ cups**
800g [$1^3/_4$ lb.]	**6 cups**	**$5^3/_4$ cups**
850g [~30 oz.]	$6^1/_3$–$6^1/_2$ cups	**6 cups**
900g [~2 lb.]	$6^3/_4$–7 cups	$6^1/_3$–$6^1/_2$ cups
950g [~34 oz.]	7–$7^1/_4$ cups	**$6^3/_4$ cups**
1kg [~35 oz.]	$7^1/_2$–$7^2/_3$ cups	7–$7^1/_4$ cups

Sugar Charts

White Granulated Sugar & Brown Sugar Chart (Quick Reference)

The chart that follows is correct for both regular granulated sugar and packed cups of brown sugar.

A half cup of granulated sugar or packed brown sugar weighs about the same — roughly 100g [$3\frac{1}{2}$ oz.] — but a half cup of caster sugar weighs about 90g [~3 oz.] so for caster sugar, it's best to calculate yourself rather than trying to use this chart or you may find your dishes coming out too sweet.

In the UK, caster sugar is widely used. In the US, however, the use of caster sugar, called superfine sugar there, is limited pretty much to recipes that require a quick-dissolving sugar crystal like meringues or cocktail drinks, so many American kitchens don't stock it. Caster and granulated sugar can be used interchangeably, the main difference being caster sugar's fine crystals dissolve more quickly, and there's a slight difference between the volume-to-weight of the two, mentioned above.

The weight-to-volume equivalents below are correct to within a few grams. The teaspoons, tablespoons and cups used in the sugar chart are 5ml teaspoons, 15ml tablespoons and American 8-fl.-oz. cups [240ml]. All are measured level, not rounded, and for brown sugar, it's packed cups. The dessertspoon, a British measure, is equal to two teaspoons.

One level $\frac{1}{4}$ cup of white granulated sugar [about 50g] contains about 192 calories [kcal], so 48 calories per level tablespoon. Brown sugar contains about 210 calories [kcal] per $\frac{1}{4}$ cup, so 52 calories per level tablespoon. (For American cups and other US volumes, see page 244.)

White Granulated Sugar & Brown Sugar Chart

metric weight [avoirdupois oz.]	teaspoons, Tablespoons, cups
4g [$1/7$ oz.]	1 tsp.
5g [$1/5$–$1/6$ oz.]	$1\frac{1}{4}$ tsp.
8g [$1/3$–$1/4$ oz.]	1 dessertspoon [2 tsp.]
10g [~$1/3$ oz.]	$2\frac{1}{2}$ tsp.
15g [~$1/2$ oz.]	2 dessertspoons [4 tsp.]
20g [~$3/4$ oz.]	1 Tbsp. *plus* 2 tsp.
30g [~1 oz.]	$2\frac{1}{2}$ Tbsp.
40g [~$1\frac{1}{2}$ oz.]	$3\frac{1}{4}$ Tbsp.
50g [~$1\frac{3}{4}$ oz.]	**$1/4$ cup** [4 Tbsp.]
60g [~2 oz.]	5 Tbsp. [$1/3$ cup *minus* 1 tsp.]
70g [~$2\frac{1}{2}$ oz.]	$5\frac{2}{3}$ Tbsp. [$1/3$ cup *plus* 1 tsp.]
75g [~$2\frac{2}{3}$ oz.]	6 Tbsp. [$1/3$ cup *plus* 2 tsp.]
85g [3 oz.]	7 Tbsp. [$1/2$ cup *minus* 1 Tbsp.]
100g [$3\frac{1}{2}$ oz.]	**$1/2$ cup** [8 Tbsp.]
110g [scant 4 oz.]	$1/2$ cup *plus* 1 Tbsp.
115 [~4 oz.]	$1/2$ cup *plus* $1\frac{1}{4}$ Tbsp.
125g [~$4\frac{1}{2}$ oz.]	$2/3$ cup *minus* 2 tsp.
130g [~$4\frac{1}{2}$ oz.]	about $2/3$ cup
140g [~5 oz.]	$3/4$ cup *minus* 2 tsp.
150g [~$5\frac{1}{3}$ oz.]	**$3/4$ cup** [12 Tbsp.]
160g [~$5\frac{2}{3}$ oz.]	$3/4$ cup *plus* 1 Tbsp.

White Granulated Sugar & Brown Sugar Chart, continued

metric weight [avoirdupois oz.]	teaspoons, Tablespoons, cups
170g [6 oz.]	¾ cup *plus* 1½ Tbsp.
175g [~6 oz.]	¾ cup *plus* 2 Tbsp.
180g [~6⅓ oz.]	1 cup *minus* 1½ Tbsp.
190g [~6¾ oz.]	1 cup *minus* ½ Tbsp.
200g [~7 oz.]	**1 cup** [16 Tbsp.]
225g [~8 oz.]	1 cup *plus* 2 Tbsp.
250g [~9 oz.]	**1¼ cups** [20 Tbsp.]
275g [~9¾ oz.]	1½ cups *minus* 2 Tbsp.
285g [~10 oz.]	1½ cups *minus* 1 Tbsp.
300g [~10½ oz.]	**1½ cups** [24 Tbsp.]
325g [~11½ oz.]	1½ cups *plus* 2 Tbsp.
340g [12 oz.]	1¾ cups *minus* ½ Tbsp.
350g [12⅓ oz.]	**1¾ cups** [28 Tbsp.]
375g [13¼ oz.]	2 cups *minus* 2 Tbsp.
400g [~14 oz.]	**2 cups** [32 Tbsp.]
425g [15 oz.]	2 cups *plus* 2 Tbsp.
450g [~1 lb.]	**2¼ cups** [36 Tbsp.]
454g [1 lb.]	2¼ cups *plus* ½ Tbsp.
500g [~18 oz.]	**2½ cups** [40 Tbsp.]
550g [~19 oz.]	**2¾ cups** [44 Tbsp.]
600g [~21 oz.]	**3 cups** [48 Tbsp.]

Icing Sugar Chart (Quick Reference)

Icing sugar, called confectioners' sugar or powdered sugar in the US, is granulated sugar that's been finely ground to a powder and, just like other powders, icing sugar can vary in weight from one cupful to another due to things like humidity in the air or unsifted icing sugar clumping up.

It also follows that the weight of 1 cup unsifted and 1 cup sifted icing sugar will differ because sifting incorporates air into the sugar, so a cup of sifted sugar will be lighter. One cup unsifted yields about $1\frac{1}{8}$ to $1\frac{1}{4}$ cups sifted, so be sure you know whether your recipe wants unsifted or sifted icing sugar, as using cupfuls of the wrong one can noticeably affect a recipe's sweetness.

In the chart that follows, the unsifted icing sugar column is based on an average of 140g [~5 oz.] to the level cupful, and the sifted icing sugar column is based on an average of 115g [4 oz.] to the level cupful, but bear in mind there were weighings above and below these averages — one cup unsifted weighed 128, another cup unsifted weighed 150g — so view the volumes below as simply a guide rather than a constant.

The teaspoons, tablespoons and cups used in the following chart are 5ml teaspoons, 15ml tablespoons and American 8-fl.-oz. cups [240ml], all measured level, not rounded. The dessertspoon, a British measure, is equal to two teaspoons.

One level $\frac{1}{4}$ cup of sifted icing sugar [about 30g] contains about 120 calories [kcal], so 30 calories per level tablespoon sifted (or about 34 calories per level tablespoon *un*sifted).

metric weight [avoirdupois oz.]	UNSIFTED ICING SUGAR teaspoons, Tablespoons, cups	SIFTED ICING SUGAR teaspoons, Tablespoons, cups
5g [~1/5 oz.]	1 3/4 tsp.	2 tsp.
8.5g [~1/3 oz.]	1 Tbsp. [3 tsp.]	3 1/2 tsp.
10g [~1/3 oz.]	3 1/2 tsp.	4 tsp.
15g [~1/2 oz.]	1 3/4 Tbsp.	2 Tbsp. [6 tsp.]
17g [1/2–2/3 oz.]	2 Tbsp. [6 tsp.]	2 1/3 Tbsp.
20g [~2/3 oz.]	2 1/4 Tbsp.	2 3/4 Tbsp.
25g [1 scant oz.]	2 3/4 Tbsp.	3 1/2 Tbsp.
30g [~1 oz.]	3 1/2 Tbsp.	**4 Tbsp. [1/4 cup]**
35g (~1 1/4 oz.)	**4 Tbsp. [1/4 cup]**	4 3/4 Tbsp. [1/4 cup *plus* 3/4 Tbsp.]
40g [~1 1/2 oz.]	4 1/2 Tbsp. [1/4 cup *plus* 1/2 Tbsp.]	5 1/2 Tbsp. [about 1/3 cup]
45g [~1 2/3 oz.]	5 Tbsp.	6 Tbsp. [1/3 cup *plus* 2 tsp.]
50g [~1 3/4 oz.]	5 3/4 Tbsp. [heaping 1/3 cup]	6 3/4 Tbsp. [1/3–1/2 cup]
60g [~2 oz.]	6 3/4 Tbsp. [1/3–1/2 cup]	**1/2 cup [8 Tbsp.]**
70g [~2 1/2 oz.]	**1/2 cup [8 Tbsp.]**	1/2 cup *plus* 1 1/2 Tbsp. [9 1/2 Tbsp.]

metric weight [avoirdupois oz.]	UNSIFTED ICING SUGAR teaspoons, Tablespoons, cups	SIFTED ICING SUGAR teaspoons, Tablespoons, cups
75g [~2²/₃ oz.]	½ cup *plus* ½ Tbsp. [8½ Tbsp.]	½ cup *plus* 1 Tbsp. [9 Tbsp.]
80g [~2¾ oz.]	½ cup *plus* 1 Tbsp. [9 Tbsp.]	about ⅔ cup
85g [3 oz.]	½ cup *plus* 1⅔ Tbsp.	**¾ cup** [12 Tbsp.]
90g [~3 oz.]	about ⅔ cup [about 10⅔ Tbsp.]	scant ¾ cup [11 Tbsp.]
100g [~3½ oz.]	¾ cup *minus* ½ Tbsp. [11½ Tbsp.]	¾ cup *plus* 1½ Tbsp. [13½ Tbsp.]
105g [~3½ oz.]	**¾ cup** [12 Tbsp.]	¾ cup *plus* 2½ Tbsp. [14½ Tbsp.]
110g [~4 oz.]	¾ cup *plus* ½ Tbsp. [12½ Tbsp.]	1 cup *minus* 1 Tbsp. [15 Tbsp.]
115g [4 oz.]	¾ cup *plus* 1 Tbsp. [13 Tbsp.]	**1 cup** [16 Tbsp]
120g [~4¼ oz.]	¾ cup *plus* 2 Tbsp. [14 Tbsp.]	**1 cup** [16 Tbsp]
125g [~4½ oz.]	¾ cup *plus* 2 Tbsp. [14 Tbsp.]	1 cup *plus* 1 Tbsp.
130g [~4½ oz.]	1 cup *minus* 1 Tbsp. [15 Tbsp.]	1 cup *plus* 1½ Tbsp.

metric weight [avoirdupois oz.]	**UNSIFTED ICING SUGAR** teaspoons, Tablespoons, cups	**SIFTED ICING SUGAR** teaspoons, Tablespoons, cups
135g [~4¾ oz.]	scant 1 cup	1 cup *plus* 2½ Tbsp.
140g [~5 oz.]	**1 cup [16 Tbsp.]**	1 cup *plus* 3 Tbsp.
150g [~5¼ oz.]	about 1 cup	**1¼ cups**
160g [~5⅔ oz.]	1 cup plus 2 Tbsp.	**1⅓ cups**
170g [~6 oz.]	scant 1¼ cups	scant 1½ cups
175g [~6 oz.]	**1¼ cups**	**1½ cups**
180g [~6⅓ oz.]	about 1¼ cups	**1½ cups**
190g [~6¾ oz.]	**1⅓ cups**	**1⅔ cups**
200g [7 oz.]	1½ cups *minus* 1 Tbsp.	**1¾ cups**
210g [~7⅓ oz.]	**1½ cups**	**1¾ cups**
220g [~7¾ oz.]	about 1½ cups	1¾ cups *plus* 2 Tbsp.
225g [~8 oz.]	about 1⅔ cups	2 cups *minus* 1 Tbsp.
230g [~8 oz.]	**1⅔ cups**	**2 cups**
240g [~8½ oz.]	about 1¾ cups	**2 cups**
245g [~8¾ oz.]	**1¾ cups**	2 cups *plus* 2 Tbsp.
250g [~8¾ oz.]	about 1¾ cups	2 cups *plus* 2 Tbsp.

metric weight [avoirdupois oz.]	UNSIFTED ICING SUGAR teaspoons, Tablespoons, cups	SIFTED ICING SUGAR teaspoons, Tablespoons, cups
260g [~9 oz.]	2 cups *minus* 2 Tbsp.	2¼ cups
270g [~9½ oz.]	scant 2 cups	2⅓ cups
275g [~9¾ oz.]	**2 cups**	2⅓ cups
280g [~10 oz.]	**2 cups**	2⅓ cups
290g [~10¼ oz.]	**2 cups**	2½ cups
300g [~10½ oz.]	2 cups *plus* 2 Tbsp.	2½ cups
320g [~11¼ oz.]	about 2¼ cups	2¾ cups
325g [~11½ oz.]	**2⅓ cups**	2¾ cups
340g [12 oz.]	scant 2½ cups	scant 3 cups
350g [~12⅓ oz.]	**2½ cups**	3 cups
360g [~12⅔ oz.]	about 2½ cups	**3 cups**
375g [~13¼ oz.]	**2⅔ cups**	3¼ cups
380g [~13⅓ oz.]	about 2¾ cups	3¼ cups
400g [14 oz.]	2¾–3 cups	scant 3½ cups
420g [~14¾ oz.]	**3 cups**	about 3½ cups
425g [15 oz.]	**3 cups**	3⅔ cups
440g [~15½ oz.]	3–3¼ cups	3¾ cups
454g [16 oz; 1 lb.]	about 3¼ cups	scant 4 cups

metric weight [avoirdupois oz.]	UNSIFTED ICING SUGAR teaspoons, Tablespoons, cups	SIFTED ICING SUGAR teaspoons, Tablespoons, cups
460g [~16¼ oz.]	3¼ cups	about 4 cups
475g [16¾ oz.]	3⅓ cups	4 cups
480g [~17 oz.]	3⅓–3½ cups	4 cups
500g [~17⅔ oz.]	3½–3⅔ cups	4¼ cups
550g [~19⅓ oz.]	scant 4 cups	4¾ cups
565g [~1¼ lb.]	4 cups	about 4¾ cups
600g [~21 oz.]	4¼ cups	5 cups
650g [~23 oz.]	4⅔ cups	5½ cups
680g [1½ lb.]	4¾–5 cups	about 5¾ cups
700g [~25 oz.]	5 cups	6 cups
750g [~26 oz.]	5⅓ cups	about 6½ cups
800g [1¾ lb.]	5¾ cups	about 6¾ cups
850g [~30 oz.]	6 cups	7¼ cups
900g [~2 lb.]	6⅓–6½ cups	7⅔ cups
950g [~34 oz.]	6¾ cups	8 cups
1kg [~35 oz.]	7–7¼ cups	8½ cups

EGGS : MILK : CREAM

Food staples: Eggs, Milk, Cream
British v American

This section includes charts comparing EU (including British) and American egg sizes, and charts comparing fat contents of British and American milks and creams.

EGGS

EU SIZES (ALSO OLD EEC SIZES) — for current British egg sizes, look in the EU egg chart; for old British egg sizes (the 0–7 size), look in the old EEC egg chart.. 238

AMERICAN SIZES 239

MILK

FAT PERCENTAGE CHART — for comparing fat contents of British and American milks 240

CREAM

FAT PERCENTAGE CHART — for comparing fat contents of British and American creams 241

EU (including British) Egg Sizes

European egg sizes are based on a weight per egg. When an American recipe calls for an egg and doesn't specify a size, use an egg weighing about 2 ounces (a Medium egg based on the current EU egg sizes).

Current EU Egg Sizes (from January, 1998)

Small	Medium	Large	XL or Very Large
under 53 grams	*53-63 grams*	*63-73 grams*	*73g and above*
under 1.87 ounces	1.87-2.22 ounces	2.22-2.57 ounces	2.57 oz. and above

Egg weights courtesy the Ministry of Agriculture, Fisheries and Food (now called DEFRA: Dept. for the Environment, Fisheries and Rural Affairs).

Old EEC Egg Sizes (prior to January, 1998)

7	6	5	4	3	2	1	0
under 45g	*45-50 grams*	*50-55 grams*	*55-60 grams*	*60-65 grams*	*65-70 grams*	*70-75 grams*	*over 75g*
~1.57 oz.	~1.68 oz.	~1.85 oz.	~2 oz.	~2.2 oz.	~2.38 oz.	~2.5 oz.	~2.65 oz.

Egg weights courtesy the British Egg Information Service.

American Egg Sizess

American egg sizes are based on a minimum weight per dozen eggs as set by the US Department of Agriculture. The weights below were calculated based on the weight per dozen.

American Egg Sizes					
Small	Medium	Large	Extra large	Jumbo	
~43-50g/ egg	~50-57g/ egg	~57-64g/ egg	~64-71g/ egg	~71g/egg and above	
1.5-2.0 oz./egg	1.75-2.0 oz./egg	2-2.25 oz./egg	2.25-2.5 oz./egg	2.5 oz./egg and above	
at least 18 oz./ dozen	at least 21 oz./ dozen	at least 24 oz./ dozen	at least 27 oz./ dozen	at least 30 oz./ dozen	

Milk chart

% Fat	British milk	American milk
0.5	⇐ Skimmed Milk: 0.1% avg. fat (max: 0.3%)	↑ Skim or Nonfat Milk: ↓ *less than* 0.5% fat
1.0		⇐ 1% Milk ↑ Lowfat Milk: 0.5–2% fat ↓
1.5	Semi-skimmed milk[*] ⇐ (aka *half-fat milk*): 1.6% avg. fat content (min: 1.5%; max: 1.8%)	
2.0		⇐ 2% Milk
2.5		
3.0		
3.5		⇐ Whole Milk: *at least* 3.5% fat (though this amount may vary from state to state in the US)
4.0	↑Whole Milk: 3.8–3.9% avg. fat (min: 3.5; max: 4.2%)[**] ↓	
4.5	↑ Channel Is. Milk (aka *Breakfast Milk*): 4.8–5.1% avg. fat (min. 4% fat) ↓	
5.0		

---

[*] 1% and 2% milks have recently been appearing in British supermarkets.
[**] *Full cream milk* used to just refer to Channel Islands milk but now has come to mean any whole milk.

Cream chart

% Fat	British creams	American creams
10	Half cream: ⇐ 12–13% avg. fat Half-fat crème fraîche: ⇐ 15% avg. fat	↑ Half & Half: 10.5–11.7% avg. fat (min: 10.5%; max: 18%) ↓
20	⇐ Single cream & Soured cream: 19% avg. fat for single cream (min. 18% fat)	↑Sour cream: *at least* 18% 　　↑ Light or coffee cream: 18–30% ↓
30	↑ Crème fraîche: ↓ 30–35% fat	↑ Light whipping cream: ↓ 30-36% fat
40	Whipping cream: ⇐ 39% avg. fat content (min. 35% fat)	↑ Heavy whipping or ↓ heavy cream: 36–40%
50	⇐ Double cream: 48% fat	
	↑ Clotted cream: ↓ 55%–63.5% avg. fat	

US MEASURES

American sizes: cups and cans

This section includes a chart of common American measures, such as the $1/4$ cup, $1/3$ cup, etc., and their equivalent volumes, plus a chart of American can sizes, and their equivalent volumes.

AMERICAN COOKING EQUIVALENTS

    COOKING EQUIVALENTS CHART — showing equivalent volumes for standard American cooking measures, such as the cup, US liquid pint, US liquid quart, etc. *244*

AMERICAN CAN SIZES

    CAN SIZES CHART — showing equivalent volumes for American can sizes, listed by their can number *246*

American Cooking Equivalents

This is a quick-reference chart of American cooking measures. In the US, teaspoons, tablespoons and cups are always measured level unless otherwise stated. The spoon and cup measures in the chart below are all level measures. In the UK, teaspoons and tablespoons traditionally meant *rounded* or *heaped* spoonfuls but more recent British cookery books have been calling for level spoonfuls, so be sure to check which to use. Two level spoonfuls are roughly equivalent to one rounded spoonful. See also *Imperial vs. US Customary* on page 9.

US measure	**British measure**	US fl. oz.	*Metric*	Also equal to these US measures
teaspoon	**1 tsp.**		*5ml*	60 drops; $\frac{1}{3}$ Tbsp.
	dessert-spoon	$\frac{1}{3}$ fl. oz.	*10ml*	2 tsp. (the US has no dessertspoon measure)
Tablespoon	**1 Tbsp.**	$\frac{1}{2}$ fl. oz.	*15ml*	3 teaspoons
fluid ounce		1 fl. oz.	*30ml*	2 Tbsp.
$\frac{1}{4}$ cup		2 fl. oz.	*59ml*	4 Tbsp; $\frac{1}{2}$ US gill
$\frac{1}{3}$ cup		$2\frac{2}{3}$ fl. oz.	*79ml*	$5\frac{1}{3}$ Tbsp.
$\frac{1}{2}$ cup	**$\frac{1}{5}$ UK pint**	4 fl. oz.	*118ml*	8 Tbsp; 1 US gill*
$\frac{2}{3}$ cup	**1 UK gill***	$5\frac{1}{3}$ fl. oz.	*158ml*	$10\frac{2}{3}$ Tbsp.

---

* The American gill is 4 US fl. oz. The British gill is 5 Imp. fl. oz. ($\frac{1}{4}$ Imp. pint) but in the north and west of England it is 10 Imp. fl. oz. ($\frac{1}{2}$ Imp. pint). The gill is rarely used nowadays in either the US or the UK.

AMERICAN COOKING EQUIVALENTS, cont.

US measure	British measure	US fl. oz.	Metric	Also equal to these US measures
¾ cup		6 fl. oz.	*177ml*	12 Tbsp.
	teacup	about 7 fl. oz.	*200ml*	1 scant cup; 14 Tbsp.
1 cup**		8 fl. oz.	*237ml*	½ US pint; 16 Tbsp; 2 US gills
	breakfast cup; ½ UK pint	10 fl. oz.	*284ml*	1¼ cups; 20 Tbsp. (the US has no breakfast cup measure)
1 US pint	**about ⁴/₅ UK pint**	16 fl. oz.	*473ml*	2 cups; ½ US quart
1 US quart	**33⅓ UK fl. oz.**	32 fl. oz.	*946ml*	4 cups; 2 US pints; ¼ US gallon
½ US gallon	**66⅔ UK fl. oz.**	64 fl. oz.	*1.89L*	2 US quarts; 4 US pints
1 US gallon	**133 UK fl. oz.**	128 fl. oz.	*3.78L*	4 US quarts; 8 US pints

tsp. = teaspoon; Tbsp. = tablespoon; *ml = millilitre*; *L = litre*

** The British standard cup is 10 fl. oz. but cup measures sold in British cookery shops tend to be American cup measures (8 fl. oz.). At any rate, British cooks tend to measure by weight rather than volume.

American Can Sizes

You may come across an old recipe calling for a particular sized can, and there is much scope for confusion with American can sizes. For example, there's a No. 3, No. 3 squat and No. 3 cylinder, and each No. 3 can holds a different amount, plus the No. 3 cylinder is listed as holding about 51 oz. avoirdupois or 46 fl. oz.

In the table below, I've limited the can sizes to those you're most likely to come across, and have given their approximate avoirdupois weight except for the No. 3 cylinder can, for which most reference books give just a volume so for this, I've also given a volume (fluid ounces).

Can size	Estimated weight (or volume)	US cups (approx. no.)	Number of servings
7/8	4 oz. [115g]	1/2 cup	1
1/2	8 oz. [225g]	1 cup	2
1 ('Picnic')	10 1/2–12 oz. [300–340g]	1 1/4–1 1/3 cups	2–3
300	14–16 oz. [400–455g]	1 3/4 cups	3–4
303	15 1/2–17 oz. [440–480g]	2 cups	4
2	20 oz. [565g]	2 1/2 cups	5
2 1/2	27–29 oz. [765–820g]	3 1/2 cups	7
3 (cylinder)	46 fl. oz. [1.3L]	5 3/4 cups	10–12
10	6 1/2–7 1/4 lb. [3–3.3kg]	12–13 cups	25

MEASURING TOOLS & DEFINITIONS, PAN SIZES, &C.

BAR MEASURES (*see also* **WINEGLASS**)

BRITISH	*single measure*	25ml [1 Tbsp. plus 2 tsp.]
	double measure	50ml [3 Tbsp. plus 1 tsp.]
AMERICAN	*barspoon*	½ level teaspoon
	shot glass, also *pony*	1 fluid ounce [30ml or 2 Tbsp.]
	jigger	1½ fluid ounces [45ml or 3 Tbsp.]
	double jigger	This is a two-sided measure with a single measure on one end, flip it over and you've a larger measure on the other end. What the two measures are, though, varies: Hoffritz make a 1 & 2 fl. oz. double jigger; Pedrini make a ¾ & 1¼ fl. oz. double jigger; Franmara make a 1 & 1¼ fl. oz. double jigger.

---

barspoon, *see* **BAR MEASURES**

---

breakfast cup, *see* **CUP MEASURES**

CUP MEASURES (& OTHER FL. OZ. COOKING MEASURES)

Note: Canadians measure by volume, using the American cup, but before they went metric, their pints and gallons were the Imperial-sized ones, not the American-sized ones.

The Australian cup is 250ml, or 1 American cup plus 1 Tablespoon.

CUP MEASURES (& OTHER FL. OZ. MEASURES), *continued*
AMERICAN

1 US gill (rarely used now)	4 US fl. oz. [118ml]; ½ US cup
1 US cup	8 US fl. oz. [237ml]; ½ US liquid pint
1 US liquid pint*	16 US fl. oz. [473ml]; 2 US cups [~¾ UK pint]
1 US liquid quart*	32 US fl. oz. [946ml]; 4 US cups [~1½ UK pints]
1 US gallon	128 US fl. oz. [3.785L]; 4 US fluid quarts [133 Imp. fl. oz.; ~6⅔ UK pints]

BRITISH

Note: The British usually weigh ingredients rather than use cups, and many cooks here may not be familiar with the standard British cup so I list these just in case your British recipe calls for them.

1 standard Imperial cup	10 Imp. fl. oz. [284ml]; ½ UK pint [1¼ US cups]
1 breakfast cup	same as *standard Imperial cup*
1 teacup (as a measure)	about 7 Imp. fl. oz. [200ml; a scant US cup]
1 gill — two sizes:	in the south of England: 1 gill = 5 Imp. fl. oz. [142ml]; ¼ UK pint [~⅔ US cup] in the north or west of England: 1 gill = 10 Imp. fl. oz. [284ml]; ½ UK pint [1¼ US cups]

---

* American liquid pints and quarts are different to their dry pints and quarts. See **DRY PINTS & QUARTS (AMERICAN)**, page 249.

CUP MEASURES (& OTHER FL. OZ. MEASURES), continued
BRITISH, cont.

	1 Imperial pint	20 Imp. fl. oz.
		[568ml; about 19 US fl. oz.]
1 Imp. quart (rarely used now)		40 Imp. fl. oz.
		[1.136L; about 38 US fl. oz.]
	1 Imp. gallon	160 Imp. fl. oz.
		[4.545L; about 153 US fl. oz.]

DASH
If liquid, a dash is a few drops. If dry, a dash is a small amount, and just how small varies according to the source but overall, figure on somewhere between $\frac{1}{16}$ and $\frac{1}{8}$ teaspoon. Technically, it's just a smidge larger than a pinch (see **PINCH**) but really, the two are interchangeable.

DRY PINTS & QUARTS (US)
Note: American fluid pints & quarts, and American dry pints & quarts are not the same. Dry pints & quarts are used to measure things like cherries, blueberries, etc. (For US Fluid pints & quarts, see page 248.)

1 US dry pint	18.6 US fl. oz. [551ml];
	33.6 cubic inches
1 US dry quart	37.2 US fl. oz. [1.1L];
	67.2 cubic inches

DRY PINTS & QUARTS (BRITISH)
There is no difference between British fluid and British dry pints & quarts. One British pint equals 20 Imp. fluid ounces [570ml]; one British quart equals 40 Imp. fluid ounces [1.14L], though in England you don't tend to hear of quarts these days.

gill, *see* CUP MEASURES (& OTHER FL. OZ. COOKING MEASURES)

jigger, *see* BAR MEASURES

minutes, *see* TIME

PANS SIZES FOR BAKING

To avoid confusion, I've listed all pan sizes first in inches, then in metric, so if the pan's original measures had been in metric, you may see things like $1\frac{1}{4}$" [3cm] and other times $1\frac{1}{4}$" [3.5cm]. This is because $1\frac{1}{4}$ inches was the closest equivalent to both 3cm and 3.5cm.

ROUND CAKE PANS (TINS)

    sandwich tins (UK)   6" x $1-1\frac{1}{2}$" deep [15 x 2.5–4cm];
    7" x $1-1\frac{1}{2}$" deep [18 x 2.5–4cm];
    8" x $1-1\frac{1}{2}$" deep [20 x 2.5–4cm];
    9" x $1-1\frac{1}{2}$" deep [23 x 2.5–4cm]

    round cake pans (US)   9" x $1\frac{1}{2}$" deep [23 x 4cm];
    8" x $1\frac{1}{2}$" deep [20.5 x 4cm]
    (other sizes: 10"-wide [25.5cm] round pans, and 1"-deep [2.5cm] round pans)

➔ The 7" tin is the size used for most sponge cakes and sponge sandwiches (a sponge sandwich is a sponge cake with jam and/or cream sandwiched between the layers, hence sandwich tin).

➔ The 9" round pan is the standard American size, used for 2-layer birthday cakes. When filled to the 1" [2.5cm] mark, a 9" pan holds 4 cups batter [950ml; about $1\frac{1}{2}$ UK pints].

PANS SIZES FOR BAKING, *continued*

→ When baking, fill cake pans at least half full but not more than two-thirds full; loaf and tube pans may be filled higher.

→ *Substituting square for round pans*: If your recipe calls for a square pan and you wish to use a round pan instead, use a round pan that's an inch [2.5cm] wider than the square pan called for in your recipe. For example, use a 9" round pan instead of an 8" square pan.

RECTANGULAR AND SQUARE PANS
See note above, *Substituting square for round pans*.

rectangular tins (UK)	11" x 7" x $1\frac{1}{4}$" [28 x 18 x 3.5cm]; 12" x 8" x $1\frac{1}{4}$" [30 x 20 x 3cm]; 12" x 9" x $1\frac{1}{2}$" [30 x 23 x 4cm]
rectangular pans (US)	12–13" x 9" x 2" [30–33 x 23 x 5cm]

→ When filled to the $1\frac{1}{4}$" [3cm] mark, a 13" x 9" x 2" pan holds 8 cups [1.9L; about $3\frac{1}{4}$ UK pints]. (There are other rectangular US sizes as well but the above size is the most common.)

baking trays (UK)	Swiss-roll [jelly-roll] tin: 12–13" x 9" x $\frac{3}{4}$" [30–33 x 23 x 2cm]
(US)	Jelly-roll pan: 15–$15\frac{1}{2}$" x 10–$10\frac{1}{2}$" x $\frac{3}{4}$" [38–39 x 25.5–26.5 x 2cm]
baking sheets (UK)	12" x 12" [30 x 30cm] is common; 14" x 11" [35.5 x 28cm]; 16" x 14" [40.5 x 35.5cm]
Cookie sheets (US)	15" x 10" [38 x 25.5cm], often with $\frac{3}{4}$" [2cm] sides

PANS SIZES FOR BAKING, *continued*

→ Americans tend to call both baking sheets and baking trays 'cookie sheets' (technically, a 'tray' has short sides and a 'sheet' is flat).

→ American baking trays whose sides have lips extending out to $17\frac{1}{2}$" [44cm] or more may not fit in your British oven.

square 1-piece tins (UK) $7\frac{1}{2}$–8" square x $1\frac{1}{2}$" deep [19 x 19 x 4cm] (other sizes: a deep 6"-square [15cm] tin; plus various sized loose-based square tins — see *loose-based tins*, below)

square pans (US)   8" x 8" x $1\frac{1}{2}$–2" [20.5 x 20.5 x 4–5cm]; 9" x 9" x $1\frac{1}{2}$–2" [23 x 23 x 4–5cm]

REMOVABLE-BOTTOMED PANS (LOOSE-BASED TINS)

These pans have a base sitting loosely in the bottom, kept in place by the weight of the batter (a little of which sometimes seeps out). They're widely used in the UK and often called for in British recipes, but are not common in the US — in fact, the 'Equipment' section of my *Fannie Farmer Cookbook* says '[pans with] removable bottoms are not necessary'. They come in both round and square pans, and both deep and shallow.

loose-based tins (UK)   widths: 7, 8 and 9" [18, 20, 23cm]; depths: $1\frac{1}{2}$–4" [4–10cm] (other widths are available)

PANS SIZES FOR BAKING, *continued*

SPRING-CLIP TINS (SPRINGFORM PANS)

Spring-clip tins have a hinge on the sides that, when opened, expands the sides by about $1/2$ inch [1cm], releasing the base. They usually come with three removable bases: one flat, one fluted and one fluted with tube, and are used for tortes and cheesecakes and any cakes difficult to unmould.

spring-clip tins (UK)	widths: $7^1/_2$, 8 and 9" [19, 20 and 24cm]; sides: about $2-2^3/_4$" [5–7cm]
springform pans (US)	typical width: $9-9^1/_2$" [23–24cm]; sides: about $2^1/_2-3$" [6.5–7.5cm] (other widths available: from 8–12" [20.5–30cm])

→ The $9-9^1/_2$" springform pan holds about 3 quarts batter [2.8L; ~5 UK pints].

LOAF PANS (LOAF TINS)

2-pound loaf pan (loaf tin)	9" x 5" x 3" [23 x 12.5 x 7.5cm]
1-pound loaf pan (loaf tin)	8" x 4" x 2" [20.5 x 10 x 5cm]
$1^1/_2$-quart loaf pan (US)	roughly $8^1/_2$" x $4^1/_2$" x $2^1/_2$" [21.5 x 11.5 x 6.5cm]

→ 2-lb. loaf pans are used for yeast breads and are considered the standard size for loaf pans. Other 2-lb. loaf pan sizes include $9^1/_4$" x $5^1/_4$" x $2^3/_4$" and $9^1/_2$" x $5^1/_2$" x 3" [23.5 x 13.5 x 7cm and 24 x 14 x 7.5cm].

→ 1-lb. loaf pans and $1^1/_2$-quart loaf pans are the sizes typically used for 'quick breads', i.e., breads using baking powder rather than yeast,

PANS SIZES FOR BAKING, *continued*

    LOAF PANS (LOAF TINS), *cont.*

    such as banana bread, pumpkin bread, etc. Other 1-lb. loaf pan sizes: $7\frac{3}{4}$" x $3\frac{3}{4}$" x $2\frac{1}{2}$" and $7\frac{3}{4}$" x 4" x $2\frac{1}{4}$" and $6\frac{1}{2}$" x $4\frac{1}{4}$" x3" [19.5 x 9.5 x 6.5cm, 19.5 x 10 x 5.5cm and 17 x 11 x 8cm].

➔ When filled to the 2" [5cm] mark, a $1\frac{1}{2}$-quart loaf pan holds 4 cups batter [950ml; ~$1\frac{1}{2}$ UK pints].

    PIE PANS (PIE PLATES)

shallow pie pans (US)	9" x $1\frac{1}{4}$–$1\frac{1}{2}$" [23 x 3–4cm]; 8" x $1\frac{1}{4}$" [20 x 3cm]
deep pie dishes (UK)	$6\frac{1}{2}$" [16.5cm] is a 1-serving size; larger sizes range from $9\frac{3}{4}$–12" wide [25–30cm]
(US)	9–11" wide x 2" deep [23–28 x 5cm]
flan dishes [quiche pans] (UK)	11" wide [28cm]; $9\frac{1}{4}$" wide [23.5cm] (other sizes: 6" wide [15cm] and $4\frac{1}{2}$" wide [11.5cm])
quiche pans (US)	10" wide [25.5cm] is the typical size (other sizes: 8–12" [20.5–30cm], and 1–2" [2.5–5cm] deep)

➔ Most fruit pies use a wide shallow pie pan or pie plate, or a fluted quiche pan (also called flan dish in England).

➔ Meat pies use a deep pie dish, though these vessels can also be used for a deep fruit pie.

PINCH

A pinch is a small amount, about $\frac{1}{16}$ teaspoon. It refers to the amount you can pinch between your thumb and index finger but as I'm able to 'pinch' nearly $\frac{1}{4}$ teaspoon salt between mine, I'd say to pinch just a small amount whenever a recipe calls for a pinch, rather than pinching as much as you can fit between your thumb and forefinger.

pint & quart, dry (American), *see*
    DRY PINTS & QUARTS (AMERICAN)

pint & quart, fluid, *see*
    CUP MEASURES (& OTHER LIQUID MEASURES)

seconds, *see* **TIME**

sherry glass, *see* **WINEGLASS**

SPOON MEASURES

Americans measure their spoons level, not rounded. Many contemporary British cookery books also call for level spoon measures, unless otherwise indicated. Irish and traditional British cookery books usually use rounded spoon measures, unless otherwise stated.

Some of the older British cookery books also called for 20ml tablespoons but the contemporary ones tend to call for 15ml tablespoons, and the tablespoons sold in the cookery shops in England all tend to be 15ml tablespoons.

A rounded spoonful holds as much above as below the line of the spoon, so 1 rounded spoonful = 2 level spoonfuls.

SALTSPOON	*British*	1 level saltspoon = 2.5ml [$\frac{1}{2}$ tsp.]
TEASPOON	*US & UK*	1 level teaspoon = 5ml [$\frac{1}{3}$ Tbsp; $\frac{1}{2}$ dessertspoon]
DESSERTSPOON	*British*	1 level dessertspoon = 10ml [2 tsp.]
TABLESPOON	*US & UK*	1 level tablespoon = 15ml [3 tsp; $\frac{1}{2}$ fl.oz.]
	Irish (& British traditional)	1 level Irish tablespoon = about 20ml [4 tsp; $\frac{2}{3}$ fl.oz.]
	Australian	same as *Irish tablespoon*, above

---

tablespoon & teaspoon, *see* SPOON MEASURES

---

teacup, *see* CUP MEASURES (& OTHER LIQUID MEASURES)

TIME

When flipping through my mother's 'GE Log Book 1955' the other day — this is a book in which she kept her recipes, I came across a recipe that said to let dumplings cook 10–20". Based on how they were being cooked, I knew it wouldn't be minutes, but needed to confirm, so in case you ever come across these abbreviations in recipes, here are the answers. (The same symbols are used for the minutes and seconds in geometry, too.)

	minute	the symbol for minute is '
	second	the symbol for second is "

WINEGLASS, SHERRY GLASS (as a measure)

wineglass   1 wineglass = $\frac{1}{2}$ cup [120ml; 4 fl. oz.]
However, most wineglasses these days hold much more than 4 ounces so don't assume the wineglass you're drinking from is a 4-ounce glass. A British half-pint glass is equal to $2\frac{1}{2}$ of these 4-ounce wineglasses.

wineglass, small   1 small wineglass = scant $\frac{1}{2}$ cup [100ml; $3\frac{1}{2}$ fl. oz.]

sherry glass   1 sherry glass = $\frac{1}{4}$ cup [60ml; 2 fl. oz.]

BIBLIOGRAPHY

A number of sources were used as references for this book but the most helpful food-measurement sources included Ostmann & Baker's *The Recipe Writer's Handbook*, Rombauer & Becker's *Joy of Cooking*, Polly Clingerman's *The Kitchen Companion* and Sharon Herbst's *Food Lover's Companion*. And on the non-cookery side, *The American Heritage Dictionary* was a real asset for its thorough lists of and explanations of weights and measures.

BOOKS

Allen, Darina *Ballymaloe Cookery Course* Kyle Cathie Limited 2001

Allen, Myrtle *The Ballymaloe Cookbook* Gill and Macmillan 1987

Arnold, Hugo *The Wagamama Cookbook* Kyle Cathie Limited 2004

Beard, James *Beard on Bread* Alfred A Knopf 1993

_____ *James Beard's Theory and Practice of Good Cooking* Wings Books 1977

Bharadwaj, Monisha *The Indian Kitchen* Kyle Cathie Limited 1998

Bissel, Frances *Book of Vegetarian Cookery* Chatto & Windus Limited 1994

C, Mini *Healthy Dairy-free Eating* Kyle Cathie Limited 2009

Campbell, Susan *The Cook's Companion* Chancellor Press 1985

Claiborne, Craig *A Kitchen Primer* Penguin Books 1973

_____ *Craig Claiborne's Gourmet Diet* Times Books 1980

Clingerman, Polly *The Kitchen Companion* The American Cooking Guild 1994

Complete Guide to Food and Cooking Meredith Corporation (Better Homes and Gardens® Books) 1991

David, Elizabeth *English Bread & Yeast Cookery* Biscuit Books, Inc. 1994

Economist Measurement Guide & Reckoner Economist Newspaper 1975

Elliot, Rose *The Bean Book* Thorsons 1994

Fannie Farmer's Classic American Cookbook Papermac 1982

Gayler, Paul *A Passion for Potatoes* Kyle Cathie Limited 2001

Goodman, H. W. and Morse, B. *Just What the Doctor Ordered* Wings Books 1995

Hammond, Barbara *Cooking Explained* Longman Group Limited 1974

Herbst, Sharon Tyler *Food Lover's Companion* Barron's Educational Series, Inc. 2001

Hsiung, Deh-ta *The Chinese Kitchen* Kyle Cathie Limited 1999

Jaffrey, Madhur *World of The East Vegetarian Cooking* Alfred A. Knopf 1981

Jones, Delora *American Cooking in England* Glencoe House Publications 1998

Katzen, Mollie *The Enchanted Broccoli Forest* Ten Speed Press 1982

Kuo, Irene *The Key to Chinese Cooking* Alfred A. Knopf 1977

Leith, Prue *The Cook's Handbook* Windward 1981

London, Sheryl & Mel *Creative Cooking with Grains and Pasta* Rodale Press 1982

Mariani, John F. *The Encyclopedia of American Food and Drink* Lebhar-Friedman Books 1999

McEvedy, Allegra *The Colour Cookbook* Kyle Cathie Limited 2006

Mendel, Janet *Cooking from the Heart of Spain: Food of La Mancha* Frances Lincoln Publishers 2008

Moosewood Collective, The *Sundays at Moosewood* Simon and Schuster 1990

Morris, William, ed. *The American Heritage Dictionary of the English Language* The American Heritage Publishing Co., Inc. and Houghton Mifflin Company 1969

Mr Boston Official Bartender's Guide Warner Books 1988

New Cookery Encyclopedia, The Leopard Books (Good Housekeeping) 1995

Ostmann, B.G. and Baker, J.L. *The Recipe Writer's Handbook* John Wiley & Sons, Inc. 2001

Owen, Sri *Noodles* Quadrille Publishing Limited 2000

Rombauer, I. and Becker, M. *Joy of Cooking* Bobbs-Merrill 1979

Sahni, Julie *Classic Indian Cooking* William Morrow and Company, Inc. 1980

Stobart, Tom *The Cook's Encyclopaedia* Papermac 1982

Sunset Books *Fish & Shellfish* Lane Publishing Company 1989

"Taste Test . . . Liquid Chicken Stock" *Times Magazine*, 8 November 2008, p. 98

Williams, Chuck *The Williams-Sonoma Cookbook and Guide to Kitchenware* Random House 1986

INTERNET

Oxford English Dictionary on the Internet

Vegetarian Society web: www.vegsoc.org (agar agar)

www.icecreamsaver.com/service (ice cream)

www.dairyreporter.com January 2003 (ice cream)

Contact Details for Glencoe House Publications

189 Anglesey Road
Burton upon Trent
Staffordshire
DE14 3NS

01283 533106

comments, corrections, queries re: *Measurements for Cooking* to:
m4c@glencoehouse.co.uk

order requests to:
orders@glencoehouse.co.uk

all other queries and comments to:
enquiries@glencoehouse.co.uk

www.glencoehouse.co.uk

INDEX

Aduki Beans, 24
Agar Agar, 143
   jelly directions, 143
Alfalfa Sprouts, 17
all-purpose flour. *See Plain Flour*
Allspice, 17
Almonds, 17
Amaranth, 17
   cooked from uncooked, 18
American
   can sizes, 246
   cooking measures chart, 244
   fluid measures, 248
Americanizing Measures, 14, 16
Anchovies, 18
Anglicising Measures, 15, 16
Apples, 18
Apricots, 19
Arame Seaweed, 121
Artichokes, 19
Asparagus, 20
Aubergine, 20
Avocados, 21
Bacon, 21
Baked Beans, 25
   difference between British and American, 25
Baker's Chocolate Squares, 49, 144
Baking Powder, 22
   gluten-free, 144
   substitutions for, 144, 145
   testing for potency, 145
baking soda. *See Bicarbonate of Soda*
Bamboo Shoots, 22
Bananas, 23
Bar Measures
   barspoon, 247
   double, 247
   jigger, 247
   pony, 247
   sherry glass, 257
   shot glass, 247
   single, 247
   wineglass, 257
barley. *See Pearl Barley*
Base Megenep, 23
Basil, 23
Basmati Rice, 113
   conversion formulas, 158
   uncooked to cooked, 113
Bay Leaves, 23
Beancurd, 23
   dried, 24
beans. *See Aduki Beans, Dried Beans, etc.*
Beansprouts, 24
Beef, 80
Beer, 32
Beetroot [Beets,US], 32
berries. *See Blackberries, Blackcurrants, etc.*
Bicarbonate of Soda, 32
Biscuit Base, 32
Biscuits [cookies, US], 33
Black Chickpeas, Split, 76
Blackberries, 33
Blackcurrants, 34
Blackcurrants & Redcurrants, 34
Black-eyed Beans/peas, 25
Blackpool Rock, 34
Blueberries, 34

bok choy. *See Pak Choi*
Boston beans. *See Haricot Beans*
bouillon. *See Stocks, Broths,
   Bouillons, Consommés*
Bouquet Garni, 70
bows (pasta). *See Farfalle*
Bran, 34
Brazil Nuts, 35
Bread, 35
   soda bread, 166
bread flour. *See Strong Flour*
Breadcrumbs
   dried, 35
   fresh, 36
Breakfast Cereals, 42
   Cornflakes, 42
   Malt Bites (Chex), 42
   Rice Krispies, 42
   rolled oats, 88
Breakfast Cup, 248
Brewer's Yeast, 36
British Imperial Measurements, 9
British Measures, 248
Broad Beans, 26
   conversion formulas, 145
   unshelled to shelled, 26, 146
Broccoli, 36
broths. *See Stocks, Broths, Bouillons,
   Consommés*
Brown Rice, 114
   conversion formulas, 158
   uncooked to cooked, 114
Brown Sugar, 128
   calories of, 228
   sugar chart (quick-reference), 228
Brussels Sprouts, 36
Buckwheat Groats, 37
Bulgur, 37
Butter, 37
   butter chart (quick-reference), 219

Butter, *cont.*
   calories of, 218, 219
Buttermilk, 38, 148
   powder, 38
   to reconstitute, 38
   substitutions for, 148
Butternut Squash, 110
Button Mushrooms, 85
   fresh, 84
   tinned or bottled, 85
Cabbage, 38
Cake, 39
Cake Flour, 62
Calories of
   butter, 106, 218, 219
   flour, 218, 222
   marshmallows, 80
   popcorn, 105
   sugar, brown, 228
   sugar, granulated, 218, 228
   sugar, icing [confectioners', US],
      231
Can Sizes, American, 246
Canadian Measures, 247
candied peel. *See Mixed Peel*
candy. *See Blackpool Rock,
   Chocolate, etc.*
Candy Canes, 34
Cannellini Beans, 26
   dried to cooked, 27
Canteloupe, 81
Capers, 39
Caraway Seeds, 39
Carob, 149
   substitution for chocolate, 144
   substitutions, 149
Carrageen Seaweed, 121
Carrots, 39, 149
   unpeeled to peeled, 149
Cashews, 40

Cassia, 50
Caster Sugar, 130
Cauliflower, 40
Celeriac, 41, 150
   unpeeled to peeled, 150
Celery, 41
Celery Seeds, Salt & Flakes, 41
Celsius. *See Temperatures*
centimetres. *See Linear Measures*
Channa Dal (split black chickpeas),
   75, 76
Chard, 42
Cheese, 42
   blue cheese, 42
   Cheddar, 42
   cottage cheese, 44
   cream cheese, 44
   feta, 42
   hard cheeses, 43
   mozzarella, 43
   paneer, 43
   Parmesan, 43
   ricotta, 44
   soft cheeses, 44
   Swiss cheese, 43
Cherries, 44
Chestnuts, 45
   conversion formulas, 151
   dried to cooked, 45
   unpeeled to peeled, 46
Chicken, 108
   chicken stock, 127
   ordering chicken breast, 108
chickpea flour. *See Gram Flour*
Chickpeas, 46
   dried to cooked, 47
Chilli & Chillies
   chilli flakes, 48
   chilli powder, 48
   chillies, 47

Chilli con Carne, 172
Chinese Egg Noodles
   dried: how to cook, 157
   fresh to cooked, 86
Chinese Mushrooms
   dried, 85
   straw mushrooms, 85
Chives, 48
Chocolate, 48
   Baker's chocolate squares, 49, 144
      substitutions for, 144
   Cadbury Flake, 49
   chocolate chips, 49
   cocoa powder, 51
   peanut butter patties, 181
Chorizo, 49
chutney. *See Preserves*
cilantro. *See Coriander Leaves*
Cinnamon, 50
citrons. *See Mixed Peel*
Clams, 50
Clementines, 51
cloud ears. *See Wood Ears*
Cloves, 50
Cockles, 51
Cocktail Cherries, 45
Cocoa Powder, 51
Coconut, 51
   coconut cream, 52, 153
   coconut milk, 52, 153
   creamed coconut blocks, 154
   desiccated (dried), 51
   making coconut cream/milk from
      creamed coconut blocks, 154
      desiccated (dried), 153
      fresh, grated, 153
Cod, Dry Salt, 61
Coffee, 52
   amount to brew, 52
Condensed Milk, 82

Condensed Milk, *cont.*
   sweetened, 82
consommé. *See Stocks, Broths, Bouillons, Consommés*
Contact details, 262
Conversion Formulas
   dry weights, 189
   fluid volume, 199
      British Imperial, 201
      metric, 200
      US, 201
   linear, 207
   temperatures, 210
cookie crust. *See Biscuit Base*
cookies. *See Biscuits*
Coriander Leaves, 52
Coriander Seeds, 53
Corn, 53
Cornflakes, 42
Cornflour [cornstarch, US], 54
   substituting for, 54
Cornish Game Hen, 54
Cornmeal, 54
Cottage Cheese
   with stock jelly/jello, 180
Courgettes, 54
Couscous, 55
Crabmeat, 55
Crackers & Crumbs, 55
Cranberries, 56
Cranberry Juice, 56
Cream, 56. *See also Cream Chart, Fat Content*
   conversion formulas, 154
   double, UK, 56
      unwhipped to whipped, 56
   half & half, US, 57
   heavy, US, 57
   light, US, 57
   single, UK, 56

Cream, *cont.*
   sour, US, 57
   unwhipped to whipped, 154
   whipped from unwhipped, 154
Cream Chart, Fat Content, 241
Cream of Tartar, 57
Crêpes, 170
Crisco, 38
Croûtons, 57
Cucumbers, 58
Cumin, 58
Cups
   American/Canadian cup, 244, 248
   Australian cup, 247
   breakfast cup, 248
   British Imperial cup, 248
   converting to, 14, 16
   cup measures, 247
Currants, Dried, 58
Custard & Custard Powder, 58
   vanilla pudding, 59
daikon. *See Mooli*
Dash, 249
Dates, 59
Deep-frying
   reheating deep-fried foods, 216
   reusing olive oil, 88
   temperatures, 216
Dessertspoon, 256
Digestives, 33
   digestive crumbs, 55
Dill Seeds & Weed, 60
dough. *See Pastry*
dressing (stuffing). *See Stuffing*
Dried Beans, 28
   conversion formulas, 147
   dried to cooked, 28, 147
   using tinned instead of home-cooked beans, 148
Dried Milk, 81

Dried Milk, *cont.*
   to reconstitute, 82
dried plums. *Come on now, you know they're called 'prunes'. See Prunes*
Dried Tomatoes, 135
Dry Weights
   conversion formulas, 189
   quick reference charts, 186
Edamame, 31
Egg Noodles
   Chinese, dried
      how to cook, 157
   Chinese, fresh
      fresh to cooked, 86
      dried, 86
eggplant. *See Aubergine*
Eggs, 60
   British/EU, 60
   different US & UK weights, 61
   egg sizes, 238, 239
      American, 239
      EU & British, 238
      old EEC sizes, 238
   retrieving a bit of shell, 61
   to tell if it's rotten, 61
   US, 60
   whites, 60
   yolks, 60
Enchilada, Ersatz, 173
Evaporated Milk, 82
Fahrenheit. *See Temperatures*
Farfalle Pasta (bows), 96
farro. *See Wheat Grains*
fat. *See Butter, Lard, Suet, Shortening*
fava beans. *See Broad Beans*
Fennel Seeds, 61
Fenugreek Leaves, 61
Figs, 61
Filo/phyllo Pastry, 96, 97
fish. *See Anchovies, etc.*

Fish, 61
Flat Mushrooms, 84
flaxseeds. *See Linseeds*
Flour, 62
   cake flour, 62
   calories of, 218
   flour chart (quick-reference), 222
   gram flour [chickpea flour], 63
   in general, 62
   plain flour [all-purpose, US], 63
      calories of, 222
   potato flour, 64
   rice flour, 64
   rye flour, 64
   self-raising flour, 63
   substitutions for, 155
   strong flour [bread flour], 63
   tapioca flour, 64
   wholemeal flour [wholewheat, US], 64
Fluid Volume, 191
   American, 248
   British, 248
   conversion formulas, 199
      British Imperial, 201
      metric, 200
      US, 201
   fluid ounces, 9
   quick reference charts
      British Imperial, 192
      US, 195
Food Staples. *See also Quick Reference Charts for Butter, Flour, Sugar, Icing Sugar*
   cream, fat content, 241
   egg sizes, 238, 239
   milk, fat content, 240
French Beans, 28
Fromage frais, 142
fruit. *See Apples, etc.*

Fungus, Dried, 85. *See also Shiitake, Wood Ears, Chinese Mushrooms*
Fusilli Pasta (spirals), 95
Galangal, 65
Gallon
   British Imperial, 11, 249
   US, 11, 248
garbanzo beans. *See Chickpeas*
Garlic, 65
   garlic powder, 65
      equivalents for, 65
      unpeeled to peeled, 65
Gas Mark, 211
Gelatine, 65. *See also Jelly/jello*
   American, 66
   British, 65
   different measures for US & UK, 66
   leaf [sheets], 66
   stock jelly/jello, 179
   Vege-gel, 66
Gill
   British, 248
   US, 248
Ginger
   dried, 66
      ginger powder, equivalents for, 67
   fresh, 67
   pickled, candied, 68
Glacé Cherries, 45
Gluten-free Baking Powder, 144
Glycerine, Liquid, 68
Golden Needles, 68
Golden Syrup, 68
Gooseberries, 68
Graham Crackers, 33
   graham cracker crumbs, 55
   graham cracker crust [under Biscuit Base], 33

grains. *See Amaranth, etc.*
Gram Flour [chickpea flour], 63
Granulated Sugar, 130
   calories of, 218, 228
   sugar chart (quick-reference), 228
Grapefruit, 69
   juiced, 69
   tinned/canned, 69
   zest, 69
Grapes, 69
great northern beans. *See Haricot Beans*
Green Beans, 28
Green Lentils, 75
green onions. *See Spring Onions*
Green Split Peas, 75
Ham, 21
Haricot Beans, 29
   dried to cooked, 29
Hazelnuts, 69
Hemp Seeds, 69
Herbs, 70. *See also Mint, Parsley, etc.*
   bouquet garni, 70
   dried, 70
   equivalents of dried to fresh, 70
   fresh, 70
Honey, 70
Horseradish, 71
   equivalents of bottled to fresh, 71
Hot dogs, 71
Hundredweight, 189
Ice, 72
Ice Cream, 71
   shrinking US container, 72
Icing Sugar [confectioners', US], 129
   calories of, 231
   conversion formulas, 161
   sifted from unsifted, 129, 161
   sugar chart (quick-reference), 231

Icing Sugar, *cont.*
  unsifted to sifted, 129, 162
Icing, Sugarpaste [fondant, US], 131
inches. *See Linear Measures*
jam. *See Preserves*
jelly (preserves). *See Preserves*
Jelly/jello, 72, 143
  how to make from agar agar, 143
  jello powder (US), 72
  jelly cubes (UK), 72
  stock jelly/jello recipe, 179
  Vege-gel recipe, 181
Juniper Berries, 73
Kale, 73
kasha. *See Buckwheat Groats*
Ketchup, 136
Kidney Beans, 29
  dried to cooked, 30
Kilometres, 207
Kombu Seaweed, 121
Lard, 37
Lasagne, 73
  'no pre-cook' variety, 73
Leeks, 73
Lemongrass, 74
Lemons, 74
  juiced, 74
  preserved, 74
  zest, 74
Lentils & Split Peas, 75
  dried to cooked, 75
Lettuce, 76
  Cos [romaine, US], 77
  flat [Boston, US], 76
  iceberg, 77
  little Gem, 77
licorice. *See Liquorice*
Lima Beans, 30
Limes, 77
  juiced, 77

Limes, *cont.*
  zest, 77
Linear Measures, 204, 207
  conversion formulas, 207
  quick reference chart, 204
Linseeds, 77
Liquorice Root, 77
Livers, Chicken, 108
Lobster, 77
long-grain rice. *See also Basmati Rice*
Long-grain Rice, 114, 115
  conversion formulas, 158
  uncooked to cooked, 114
Longlife Milk, 82
  storage of, 82
Lotus Root, Dried, 78
lox. *See Salmon, Smoked*
Lychee Nuts, 78
Macaroni, 96
Mace, 78
Malt Bites (Chex), 42
Mange Tout & Sugar Snap Peas, 78
Mangoes, 78
Maraschino Cherries, 45
Marjoram, 79
marmalade. *See Preserves*
Marshmallows, 79
  British coloured, 80
  British vs American size, 80
  calories of, 80
  Rice Krispies Treats, 184
Marzipan (rolled icing), 80
Matzoh Crackers, 55
Mayonnaise, 80, 174
Measurements
  American cooking measures chart, 244
  British Imperial, 9
    gallon, 249
    pints & quarts, 10, 249

Measurements, *cont.*
  Canadian measures, 247
  conversion formulas. *See*
    Conversion Formulas
  cup measures, 247
    American/Canadian, 248
    Australian, 247
    British, 248
  cups
    American/Canadian, 244
    quick reference charts. *See Quick*
     Reference Charts
  spoon measures, 255
  US Customary, 9
    American fluid measures, 248
    gallon, 248
    pints & quarts, dry, 10, 249
    pints & quarts, fluid, 10, 248
Meat, 80
Meatloaf, 177
Melon, 81
  canteloupe, 81
Metrication
  Metrication Law, 7
  the 500g pound, 8
Miles, 207
Milk Chart, Fat Content, 240
Milk, Types of. *See also Milk Chart,*
  Fat Content
  buttermilk, 148
  canned & 'longlife', 82
    storage of, 82
  condensed, 82
    sweetened, 82
  dried, 81
    to reconstitute, 82
  evaporated, 82
  fresh, 81
  soured milk, 149
Millet Grains & Flakes, 82

Mincemeat, 82
Mint Leaves, 83
  dried, 83
  fresh, 70, 83
Minutes, symbol for, 256
Miso (soya bean paste), 83
Mixed Peel, 83
mo er. See Wood Ears
Molasses Sugar, 128
Mooli [daikon, US], 111
Moong Dal (split mung beans), 76
mostaccioli. *See Penne*
Muesli, 83
Mung Beans, 75
  split, 76
Muscovado Sugar, 128
Mushrooms
  dried, 85
  fresh, 84
  tinned or bottled, 85
Mussels, 85
  quantity per person, 85
Mustard
  dried (powdered), 86
  prepared (wet), 86
  seeds, 86
navy beans. *See Haricot Beans*
Nectarines, 86
Noodles, 86, 156, 157
  dried, 86
    Chinese egg noodles
      to cook, 157
    egg noodles (medium), 86
    pappardelle, 87
    rice sticks (wide), 87
      to cook, 157
      to reheat, 157
    rice vermicelli (fine), 87
      to cook, 157
    spaghetti, 87

Noodles, *cont.*
   fresh, 86
      Chinese egg noodles, 86
      fresh to cooked, 86
      Shanghai noodles, 87
   pad Thai (Thai noodle dish), 87
   sen mee (rice vermicelli), 87
   udon, fresh, 86, 158
Nori Seaweed, 121
Nutmeg, 87
nuts. *See Almonds, etc.*
oatbran. *See Bran*
Oats & Oatmeal, 88
   oatmeal
      British & US definitions of, 88
      coarse [steel-cut oats, US], 88
      medium, 88
      pinhead, 88
      rolled oats (old-fashioned oats), 88
      steel-cut oats, 88
Oils, 88
Okra, 88
Olive Oil
   reusing in deep-frying, 88
Olives, 90
   black (ripe), 90
   green, 90, 91
Onions, 91, 92
   cocktail (baby onions), 92
   dehydrated onion, equivalents for, 92
   onion powder, 92
      equivalents for, 92
   pickling (small boiling onions), 92
Orange Juice Concentrate, 92
Oranges, 92, 93
   juice, 93
   zest, 92, 93
Oregano, Dried & Powdered, 93
ounce, fluid. *See Fluid Volume*

ounces, Avoirdupois. *See Dry Weights*
Oysters, 93
Pad Thai, 87
Pak Choi, 94
Pan Sizes, Baking, 250
   baking sheets, 251
   baking trays, 251
   cookie sheets, 251
   flan dishes, 254
   how much to fill, 251
   loaf pans, 253
   pie pans, 254
   quiche pans, 254
   rectangular pans, 251
   removable-bottomed pans, 252
   round cake pans, 250
   round pans, substituting, 251
   sandwich tins, 250
   spring-clip tins, 253
   square pans, 251, 252
   square pans, substituting, 251
Pancakes
   crêpes, 170
   gluten-free crêpes, 172
   potato latkes, 176
Paneer, 43
Papayas
   crystallised chunks, 94
   fresh, 94
Pappardelle (noodles), 87
Paprika, 94
Parsley, 94
   dried, 94
   fresh, 94
Parsnips, 94
   time spent in storage, 95
   unpeeled to peeled, 95
Passata, 136
pasta. *See also Lasagne, etc.*
Pasta, 156

Pasta, *cont.*
   amount from dried, 156
   amount per person, 156
   energy-saving method, 156
   how long to cook?, 156
   how much water in the pot?, 156
Pasta, Types of, 95
   farfalle (bows), 96
   fusilli (spirals), 95
   macaroni, 96
   penne (quills), 96
   shells, 96
Pastry
   filo/phyllo, 96, 97
   puff, 97
   shortcrust [pie dough, US], 97, 161
     making from scratch, 161
     ready-made pastry blocks (UK), 97
     ready-made pie shells (US), 97
   strudel, 98
pastry dough. *See Pastry*
pastry flour. *See Cake Flour*
pea beans. *See Haricot Beans*
Peaches, 98
   canned, 98
   fresh, 98
Peanut Butter, 98
   peanut butter patties, 181
Peanuts, 98
Pearl Barley, 99
Pears, 99
   canned, 99
   dried, 99
   fresh, 99
Peas, 99
   canned, 99
   dried, 100
   fresh & frozen, 99

Pecans, 100
Penne Pasta (quills), 96
Peppercorns, 100, 101
   green, 101
   ground black, 100
   Szechuan, 101
   whole black, 100
Pepperoni, 101
Peppers, Sweet [bell peppers, US], 100. *See also Pimientos*
   fresh, 100
   roasted, in a jar, 101
Pesto, 101
Petrol Price Conversions, 202
pickled vegetables. *See Preserved Chinese Vegetables*
Pickles, 101
pie dough. *See Pastry, Shortcrust*
Pie Shells, American Ready-made, 97
pimentón. See Paprika
Pimientos, 101
Pinch, 249, 255
Pine Nuts, 102
Pineapple, 102
   fresh, 102
   tinned/canned, 102
Pinhead Oatmeal, 88
Pint, Dry
   British Imperial, 10, 249
   US, 10, 249
Pint, Fluid
   British Imperial, 10, 249
   US, 10, 248
Pinto Beans, 30
Plain Flour [all-purpose, US], 63
Plums, 103
   canned (US), 103
   damson, 103
   greengage, 103
   large (US), 103

Plums, *cont.*
 opal, 103
 Victoria, 103
polenta. *See Cornmeal*
Pomegranates, 105
Pony measure, 247
Popcorn, 105
 calories of butter, 106
 calories of popcorn, 105
 unpopped to popped, 105
Poppy Seeds, 106
Pork
 bacon, 21
 ham, 21
Portobello Mushrooms, 84
Potato Flour, 64
Potato Latkes (pancakes), 176
Potatoes, 106, 107
 dried flakes, 107
 sweet potatoes, 107
 whole
  American, 107
  British, 107
Poultry, 108
 chicken & turkey, 108
 Cornish game hen, 54
 prawns [shrimp, US]. *See Shrimps & Prawns*
Preserved Chinese Vegetables, 108
Preserves, 109
Prosciutto, 22
Prunes, 109
 with-pits to pitted, 109
Puff Pastry, 97
Pumpkin Seeds, 109
Pumpkins & Winter Squash, 110
 butternut, 110
 canned puree (US), 110
 pumpkin, 110
  unpeeled to peeled, 110

Puy Lentils [French lentils, US], 75
Quark (cheese), 142
Quart, Dry
 British Imperial, 249
 US, 249
Quart, Fluid
 British Imperial, 249
 US, 248
Quick Reference Charts
 American cooking measures, 244
 butter, 219
 dry weights, 186
 flour, 222
 fluid volume
  British Imperial, 192
  US, 195
 linear measures, 204
 sugar
  icing [confectioners', US], 231
  white & brown, 228
 temperatures, 209
  outdoors, 210
  oven, 211
quills. *See Penne*
Quinoa Grains & Flakes, 110
Radishes, 111
 Chinese, 111
 mooli [daikon, US], 111
Raising Agents. *See also Yeast*
 baking powder, 22
 bicarbonate of soda, 32
Raisins, 111
Raspberries, 111
Recipes
 chilli con carne, 172
 ersatz enchilada, 173
 mayonnaise, 174
 meatloaf, 177
 pancakes
  crêpes, 170

Recipes, *cont.*
  pancakes, *cont.*
    gluten-free crêpes, 172
    potato latkes, 176
    peanut butter patties, 181
    recipe list, 165
    Rice Krispies Treats, 184
    soda bread, 166
    stock jelly/jello, 179
    stock, chicken, 127
    Waldorf salad, 175
Red Lentils, 75
red pepper flakes. *See Chilli Flakes*
Refried Beans, 31
Reheating
  deep-fried foods, 216
  mashed potato, 216
Rhubarb, 111, 113
Rice. *See also Rice Flakes, Rice Flour, etc.*
  basmati, 113
    uncooked to cooked, 113
  brown, 114
    uncooked to cooked, 114
  conversion formulas, 158, 159
  cooking methods, 159
  long-grain, 114, 115
    uncooked to cooked, 114
  short-grain, 115
    uncooked to cooked, 115
  wild rice (not a rice), 116
Rice Flakes, 116
Rice Flour, 64
Rice Krispies, 42
  Rice Krispies Treats, 184
Rice Sticks (wide rice noodles)
  dried, 87
  how to cook from dried, 157
  how to reheat, 157
Rice Vermicelli (fine noodles), 87

Rice Vermicelli, *cont.*
  dried, 87
  how to cook from dried, 157
Rolled Oats, 88
Rosehips, 117
Rosemary, 116
  dried, 116
  fresh, 116
Roux, 117
rutabaga. *See Swede*
Rye Flour, 64
Saffron, 118
Sage, 118
  dried, 118
  fresh, 118
Salad, Waldorf, 175
Salmon, 118, 119
  smoked, 119
  tinned/canned, 118
Salt, 119
  coarse, 119
  fine, 119
  kosher, 119
  recommended daily limit, 119
Saltine Crackers, 55
Saltspoon, 256
Sardines, Tinned/canned, 119
Satsumas, 51
Sausages, 120. *See also Chorizo, Pepperoni*
  British fresh, 120
scallions. *See Spring Onions*
Scallops, 120
Seaweed, 121
Seconds, symbol for, 256
seeds. *See Cumin, Dill, etc.*
Self-raising Flour, 63
Sesame Paste (tahini), 132
Sesame Seeds, 122
Shallots, 122

Shanghai Noodles, Fresh, 87
Shells (pasta), 96
Sherry Glass, 257
Shiitake Mushrooms, Dried, 85
Shortbread, 33
Shortcrust Pastry [pie dough, US], 97, 161
    making from scratch, 161
    ready-made pastry blocks (UK), 97
    ready-made pie shells (US), 97
Shortening, 38
Short-grain Rice, 115
    conversion formulas, 158
    uncooked to cooked, 115
Shrimps & Prawns, 123
    American shrimp counts, 123, 124
    dried shrimps [miniature shrimp, US], 123
    prawns [shrimp, US], 123
        raw to cooked, 123
    US vs UK terminology, 124
snow peas. *See Mange Tout*
Soda Bread, 166
Soup
    condensed, canned, 124
    stock cubes, bouillon cubes & granules, 127
    stocks & broths, ready-made, 126
Soured Milk, 149
    pancakes, 170
    soda bread, 166
    to sour fresh milk, 149
Soya Beans
    dried, 31
        dried to cooked, 31
    edamame (fresh), 31
Soya Custard, 58
Spaghetti, Dried, 87
Spelt Grains, 140

Spelt Grains, *cont.*
    dried to cooked, 140
    spices. *See Allspice, etc.*
Spinach, 125
    fresh, 125
    frozen, 125
    tinned/canned, 125
spirals (pasta). *See Fusilli*
Split Kala Channa (black chickpeas), 75
split peas. *See Lentils & Split Peas*
Spoon Measures, 255
Spring Onions, 126
sprouts. *See Alfalfa Sprouts, etc.*
Squash, Summer, 126
squash, winter. *See Pumpkins & Winter Squash*
Steel-cut Oats, 88
Stocks, Broths, Bouillons, Consommés, 126
    beef 'base', 127
    canned broth (US), 127
    chicken stock recipe, 127
    cubes, stock & bouillon, 127
    granules, bouillon, 127
    ready-made stocks (UK), 126
    stock jelly/jello, 179
Stone (weight), 189
Storage Time of Parsnips, 95
Stout, 32
Straw Mushrooms, Tinned, 85
Strawberries, 128
Strong Flour [bread flour], 63
Strudel Pastry, 98
Stuffing, 128
Substitutions for
    Baker's chocolate squares, 144
    baking powder, 144, 145
    buttermilk, 148
    carob, 149

Substitutions for, *cont.*
   cornflour [cornstarch, US], 54
   fresh yeast
      in bread dough, 163
      using dried for fresh, 163
      round pans, 251
   self-raising flour, 155
   square pans, 251
   vanilla pods
      using vanilla essence, 162
Suet, 37
Sugar Charts (quick-reference)
   brown sugar, 228
   icing sugar [confectioners', US], 231
   white granulated sugar, 228
Sugar Snap Peas, 78
Sugar, Types of
   brown sugar, 128, 129
      calories of, 228
   caster sugar [superfine, US], 130
   icing sugar [confectioners', US], 129
      calories of, 231
      conversion formulas, 161
      sifted from unsifted, 129, 161
      unsifted to sifted, 129, 162
   molasses sugar, 128
   muscovado sugar, 128
   palm sugar, 130
   sliced sugar, 130
   sugar cubes, 130
   white granulated sugar, 130
      calories of, 218, 228
Sugarpaste Icing [fondant, US], 131
Summer Squash, 126
'Sun-blush' Tomatoes, 135, 136
   directions for making, 162
Sunflower Seeds, 131
superfine. *See Caster Sugar*

Sushi Rice
   conversion formulas, 158
Swede [rutabaga, US], 131
   unpeeled to peeled, 132
Sweet Potatoes, 107
sweetcorn. *See Corn*
sweets [candy, US]. *See Blackpool Rock, Chocolate, etc.*
Tablespoon, 256
taco chips. *See Tortilla Chips*
Tahini (sesame paste), 132
Tamarind, 132
Tapioca, 133
Tapioca Flour, 64
Tarragon, 133
   dried, 133
   fresh, 133
Tea, loose, 133
   amount to brew, 133
Teacup, 248
Teaspoon, 256
Temperatures, 209
   baking temperatures, 214
   conversion formulas, 210
   deep-frying temperatures, 216
   food storage, 212
   outdoor temperatures, 210
   oven temperatures, 211
   reheating instructions, 216
   temperature charts (quick-reference), 209, 210, 211
   to kill bacteria, 213
Thyme, 134
   dried, 134
   fresh, 134
tiger lily buds, dried. *See Golden Needles*
Time
   minute symbol, 256
   second symbol, 256

INDEX *Page 277*

tin sizes, baking. *See Pan Sizes*
Tofu, 23
Tomatillos, 134
Tomatoes
   dried & semi-dried ('sun-blush'),
     135, 136
     directions for making, 162
   fresh, 134, 135
   ketchup, 136
   strained tomatoes
     passata, 136
     tomato puree (US), 137
     tomato sauce (US), 137
   tinned/canned, 136
   tomato pastes
     double-concentrated tomato
       purée, UK, 136
     tomato paste (US), 136
Ton & Tonne, 189
Toor Dal (yellow lentils), 76
Tortillas, 137
   corn tortillas, 137
   flour tortillas, 137
   tortilla chips, 137
Tuna, Tinned/canned, 137
Turmeric
   dried, 138
   fresh, 138
     peeled to unpeeled, 138
Turnips, 138
Udon Noodles, Fresh, 86, 158
US Customary Measurements, 9. *See
also Measurements*
US Measures, 249. *See also
Measurements*
Vanilla Pudding, 58
Vanilla substitutions, 162
Vanilla Wafers, 33
   Vanilla Wafer crumbs, 56
Vege-gel recipe, 181

vegetables. *See Artichokes, etc.*
Vegetables, Preserved Chinese, 108
Vermicelli, Rice (fine rice noodles)
   dried, 87
   how to cook from dried, 157
Volume, 5
   converting to, 14, 16
Waldorf Salad, 175
Walnuts, 139
Water Chestnuts, 139
   fresh, 139
   tinned/canned, 139
Watercress, 139
Wax Beans, 28
Weight, 5
   converting to, 15, 16
Wheat Grains [wheat berries, US],
   140, 141
   dried to cooked, 140, 141
wheatbran. *See Bran*
Wheatgerm, 139
White Mushrooms, 84
White Sugar, 130
Wholemeal Flour [wholewheat flour],
   64
Wild Rice, 116
Wineglass, 257
winter squash. *See Pumpkins &
Winter Squash*
Wood Ears, Dried (fungus), 85
Yeast, 141, 163
   compressed (fresh), 141
   dried, 141
   fresh, 141
   in bread dough
     amount to use, 163
   old, 141
   substitutions for
     in bread dough, 163
     using dried for fresh, 163

Yellow Lentils & Split Peas, 75
   channa dal (split black
     chickpeas), 75
   moong dal (split mung beans), 76
   toor dal (yellow lentils), 76

Yellow Lentils & Split Peas, *cont.*
   using the right one?, 76
   yellow split peas, 76
Yogurt, 142
zucchini. *See Courgettes*